W.E.B. Du Bois

W.E.B. Du Bois

A LIFE IN AMERICAN HISTORY

Charisse Burden-Stelly and Gerald Horne

Black History Lives

 ABC-CLIO®

An Imprint of ABC-CLIO, LLC
Santa Barbara, California • Denver, Colorado

Library of Congress Cataloging-in-Publication Data

Names: Burden-Stelly, Charisse, author. | Horne, Gerald, author.
Title: W.E.B. Du Bois : a life in American history / Charisse Burden-Stelly and Gerald Horne.
Description: First edition. | Santa Barbara, California : ABC-CLIO, an imprint of ABC-CLIO, LLC, [2019] | Series: Black history lives | Includes bibliographical references and index. |
Identifiers: LCCN 2019017435 (print) | LCCN 2019019970 (ebook) | ISBN 9781440864971 (eBook) | ISBN 9781440864964 (print : alk. paper)
Subjects: LCSH: Du Bois, W. E. B. (William Edward Burghardt), 1868-1963. | African Americans—Biography. | African American authors—Biography. | African American intellectuals—Biography. | African American civil rights workers—Biography. | Intellectuals—United States—Biography. | Civil rights workers—United States—Biography. | African Americans—Civil rights—History.
Classification: LCC E185.97.D73 (ebook) | LCC E185.97.D73 B87 2019 (print) | DDC 323.092 [B] —dc23
LC record available at https://lccn.loc.gov/2019017435

ISBN: 978-1-4408-6496-4 (print)
      978-1-4408-6497-1 (ebook)

23 22 21 20 19   1 2 3 4 5

This book is also available as an eBook.

ABC-CLIO
An Imprint of ABC-CLIO, LLC

ABC-CLIO, LLC
147 Castilian Drive
Santa Barbara, California 93117
www.abc-clio.com

This book is printed on acid-free paper ∞

Manufactured in the United States of America

Contents

Series Foreword vii

Preface ix

Chapter 1
A Life Beginning *1*

Chapter 2
A Life of Excellence *19*

Chapter 3
A Life of Protest *35*

Chapter 4
A Life of Creation *51*

Chapter 5
A Life of Pathways *67*

Chapter 6
A Life of Conflict *83*

Chapter 7
A Life in the Talented Tenth *99*

Chapter 8
A Life of Departure *115*

CHAPTER 9
A Life in Wartime *131*

CHAPTER 10
A Life of Radicalism *149*

CHAPTER 11
A Life on Trial *165*

CHAPTER 12
A Life of Redemption *181*

Why W.E.B. Du Bois Matters *195*

Timeline 211

Primary Documents 215

Bibliography 229

Index 243

Series Foreword

The Black History Lives biography series explores and examines the lives of the most iconic figures in African-American history, with supplementary material that highlights the subject's significance in our contemporary world. Volumes in this series offer far more than a simple retelling of a subject's life by providing readers with a greater understanding of the outside events and influences that shaped each subject's world, from familial relationships to political and cultural developments.

Each volume includes chronological chapters that detail events of the subject's life. The final chapter explores the cultural and historical significance of the individual and places their actions and beliefs within an overall historical context. Books in the series highlight important information about the individual through sidebars that connect readers to the larger context of social, political, intellectual, and pop culture in American history; a timeline listing significant events; key primary source excerpts; and a comprehensive bibliography for further research.

Preface

In 2009, Greenwood Press published Gerald Horne's *W.E.B. Du Bois: A Biography* as part of the Greenwood Biographies series. One of the most prolific historians of the twentieth century, Horne produced a rigorous and accessible addition to the trove of Du Bois biographies that includes Francis L. Broderick's *W.E.B. Du Bois: Negro Leader in a Time of Crisis*, Manning Marable's *W.E.B. Du Bois: Black Radical Democrat*, and David Levering Lewis's Pulitzer Prize-winning *W.E.B. Du Bois: A Biography*. In *W.E.B. Du Bois: A Life in American History*, I significantly refocus Horne's 2009 volume to highlight Du Bois's fundamental contributions to Black radical history. This substantial revision helps to elucidate why Du Bois remains one of the most relevant scholar-activists in modern history more than half a century after his transition.

In the narrative itself, I draw on Du Bois's own words and the work of contemporary progressive scholars to develop and expand upon key themes and movements in African-American history. These include share-cropping and debt peonage, the Negro Problem, race riots, the Great Migration, and the Harlem Renaissance. I also specify the unique effects of historical occurrences like World War I, the Great Depression, and anti-communism on African Americans. In addition, I provide detailed discussions about some of Du Bois's most important intellectual and political contributions, including his challenges to ethnological discourse at the turn of the twentieth century, his support of women's rights and equality, and his conceptualization of African Americans as a "nation within a nation." I also situate Du Bois among other important, but often overlooked, Black radicals like Hubert Harrison, Louise Thompson Patterson, and Marvel Cooke. Taken together, these elaborations offer deeper insight into Du Bois's life and times.

Like other biographies in the Black History Lives biography series, I contribute a concluding chapter about Du Bois's contemporary relevance titled "Why W.E.B. Du Bois Matters." In it, I argue that his methodological expansiveness and liberation-centered praxis have withstood the test of time and offer keen insight into some of the most pressing issues we continue to face. Through ideological frameworks including militant liberalism, Pan-Africanism, and Black Marxism, and praxis constituted by anti-imperialism and international peace, Du Bois faced head-on some of the most enduring problems of his—and our—time. His protracted struggle alongside countless comrades against structures of domination including sexism, racism, colonialism, and militarism continue to influence the scholarship and activism of persons committed to social transformation. Likewise, I contend his life's work provided a template for the Black Studies Movement that helped to fundamentally reconstitute higher education in the United States, and his expansive body of work continues to ground curricular and methodological innovations in the discipline.

This new biography offers several more additions. First, twenty sidebars explain and analyze numerous events, organizations, and concepts germane to African-American history, including Black Independence Day, the influence of the Haitian Revolution on the abolition of the trans-Atlantic slave trade in the United States, the Atlanta race riot of 1906, the American Negro Labor Congress, the Peekskill Riot, and apartheid. Second, I include excerpts from and interpretation of five of Du Bois's key writings: "The Conservation of the Races," *The Souls of Black Folk*, "Address of the Niagara Movement, to the Country," *John Brown*, and the "The African Roots of War." There is also an updated chronology that places Du Bois's life in the broader context of American history and an expanded bibliography that lists archives, special collections, and online resources along with new secondary sources.

Though much has been written about W.E.B. Du Bois, there is always more to uncover about a man whose life is in many ways the embodiment of Black history. It is my hope that *W.E.B. Du Bois: A Life in American History* aids in this excavation in distinctive and interesting ways.

Charisse Burden-Stelly

1

A Life Beginning

Nestled in the southwestern corner of Massachusetts in the Southern Berkshires, bordered by Connecticut to the south and New York to the west, Great Barrington—which historically has had a relatively small population of minorities—is not the kind of place where one would expect an African-American leader to be born. But it was there that William Edward Burghardt (W.E.B.) Du Bois was born on Sunday, February 23, 1868. His parents, Alfred and Mary Du Bois, had married just a year earlier in neighboring Housatonic. Du Bois later described the home into which he was born as "quaint, with clapboards running up and down, neatly trimmed," with a "rosy front yard" and "unbelievably delicious strawberries in the rear." It was, he said, a "rather nice little cottage" that was "furnished with some comfort" (Du Bois, *Dusk*, 2007, 91; Du Bois, *Autobio*, 2007, 61; Du Bois, *Darkwater*, 2007, 5).

The anodyne nature of this village that was Great Barrington contrasted sharply with the places Du Bois's ancestors had come from. He, like so many African Americans, had roots that extended deeply into the history of the United States, and into the African Diaspora more broadly.

His mother, Mary Silvina, was born around 1831, and her son spoke of her in his customary rhapsodic words. She was "dark shining bronze," he said, with "smooth skin and lovely eyes; there was a tiny ripple in her black hair, and she had a heavy, kind face." He could have added that she had full lips and riveting eyes (Du Bois, *Autobio*, 2007, 62, 64). Little is known about her background except that she was part of a local farming family. It was in

1

approximately 1867 that she caught sight of Alfred Du Bois in Great Bar-rington. He was from a family of free Negroes, many of whom hailed from Poughkeepsie, New York, and were related to Dr. James Du Bois, an afflu-ent doctor of French Huguenot origins.

Dr. James Du Bois did not join the revolt against British rule in North America, which led to the creation of the United States of America; and when London lost, he decamped to the Bahamas and then developed extensive interests in neighboring Haiti. (Ironically, many Huguenots, who mostly were Protestants, had fled France in the mid-seventeenth century, due in no small part to ongoing conflict with the majority Catholic popula-tion; thus, many of them fled to South Africa, where they made up a sig-nificant percentage of the European minority that imposed apartheid on that land. The struggle against this miserable system was to become one of W.E.B. Du Bois's sacred causes.)

To this day, Haiti occupies an exalted space in the imagination of Black America. From 1791 to 1804, a bloody revolution rocked this Caribbean island nation that eventuated in that rarity of rarities—a successful slave revolt—leading to the creation of an independent republic. The Haitian Revolution had caused Paris to liquidate many of its holdings in the Amer-icas, leading to the Louisiana Purchase by the new government in Wash-ington, DC, and the territorial expansion of the United States. This revolution also concerned slaveholders in the United States, who worried that continued importation of enslaved Africans to the states would, à la Haiti, ultimately tip the numerical balance in favor of these unfree labor-ers, resulting in a replay of what had occurred there. It was in 1808 that decisive steps were taken to curb the slave trade to the United States.

Dr. James Du Bois returned to the United States a few years after the Haitian Revolution. One of his sons, Alexander, who "became a rebel, bit-ter at his lot in life, resentful at being classed as a negro yet implacable in his attitude towards whites," was on his way to becoming a shoemaker but changed course and, instead, became a small businessman in New Haven, Connecticut, the home of that citadel of higher education, Yale University. It was in the Nutmeg State that Alexander Du Bois married Sarah Marsh Lewis, a union that produced a number of children, including W.E.B. Du Bois's father, Alfred Du Bois, who was born in Haiti in 1825. W.E.B. Du Bois's father's birthplace provided Du Bois a direct connection to the tap-root of Pan-Africanism. Alfred Du Bois resided for a while in Haiti, but, like so many others—before and since—he eventually migrated to the United States, where by 1860 he was pursuing various occupations in New York: waiter, barber, cook. He eventually made his way to Massachusetts, where he met, wooed, and married Mary Silvina.

But their union did not last, and unlike other champions of Black equal-ity like Paul Robeson, William Patterson, and Richard B. Moore, Du Bois grew up mostly without the influence of his father. Unsurprisingly, he became uncommonly close to his mother, a relationship that became ever closer when she endured medical setbacks, including a paralytic stroke that disabled the left side of her body and made her very dependent upon him. Forcing him to grow up quickly, this situation compelled W.E.B. Du Bois to become a caretaker at an early age and take a job after school. Simultaneously, Mary Silvina, who had been abandoned by Alfred Du Bois, invested a great deal of emotion and effort in their offspring. She imparted a number of moral lessons to the young Du Bois that he absorbed fitfully, including the perils of imbibing alcoholic beverages (an indulgence that he did not pursue until he was a student in Berlin), smoking (also a habit he subsequently adopted), and the like.

Thus armed, Du Bois—one of the only African Americans in his public school—excelled. He not only pleased his mother with his studiousness, but also created a way to escape from Great Barrington and build a better life for his family. Yet, the road out of Massachusetts was not free of obstacles. As an adult, he was to recall graphically and dramatically a searing incident that occurred when he was merely twelve years old. He and his classmates had decided to purchase cards and exchange them, but, as he recalled with a lingering melancholy, "one girl, a tall newcomer, refused my card—refused it peremptorily with a glance. Then it dawned upon me with a certain suddenness that I was different from the others; or like, mayhap, in heart and life, and longing, but shut out from their world by a vast veil" (Du Bois, *Souls*, 2007, 2).

As he later recalled it, this event was a turning point for him, as it convinced him of the salience of race and racism; the study of race and the fight against racism would come to dominate the rest of his life. Young and fatherless, Black in a world of whites, Du Bois stumbled from time to time, once barely escaping forced detention after pilfering a neighbor's grapes. Like with the young Malcolm Little—who was to become Malcolm X—the authorities concluded that Du Bois (who was to become a leading intellectual) would be better served if he were to learn a trade—a noble pursuit, no doubt, but one that would have deprived the planet of a fearsomely articulated intelligence. It was his high school principal, Frank Hosmer, who rode to his rescue, convincing the judge that a stiff reprimand would be sufficient.

Luckily, Du Bois was able to escape the carceral snares that had entangled, and would continue to entangle, so many African-American youth. He was lucky, but unfortunately, many of his compatriots were not. For it was at this juncture that the promise of Reconstruction was being drenched in a tidal wave of blood, as African Americans were being forcibly deprived of basic citizenship rights, disallowed from voting, and subjected to the vile structures of Jim Crow in schools, employment, and public accommodations. Lynchings were becoming ever more common as the victorious North had tired of conflict with the white South, which sought with vigor and enthusiasm to consign African Americans to what the Black communist Harry Haywood described as a "brutal caste system" (Haywood, 1976, 46).

As the antilynching crusader Ida B. Wells explained, lynching was a tool of white supremacist backlash meant to ensure the economic subjection and disenfranchisement of African Americans. The rule of lynch law stripped Black people of their First Amendment right to assemble, their Second Amendment right to bear arms, their Fourteenth Amendment right to equal protection of the law, and, most significantly, their Fifth Amendment right to due process. She explained that the threat of Black economic independence and political assertion incited thousands of lynchings that undermined and disregarded constitutional and federal law. Further, she held that the refusal of Northern industrial capitalists, the federal government, and public sentiment to condemn this form of white supremacist barbarism gave Southern whites carte blanche to dominate African Americans and to reduce them to slaves and peons (Wells, 1892).

EMANCIPATION DAY/BLACK INDEPENDENCE DAY

Throughout the Anglophone Caribbean, Canada, and other sites in the African Diaspora, Emancipation Day, or Black Independence Day, is celebrated on August 1. It was first celebrated as a holiday in 1893. Emancipation Day commemorates the passing of the Emancipation Act in 1833 that officially ended British participation in the slave trade. The Act also mandated the manumission of enslaved Africans in the West Indies on August 1, 1834, stating: "Be it enacted that all and every one of the persons who on the first day of August one thousand eight hundred and thirty four, shall be holden in slavery within such British colony as aforesaid, shall . . . become and be to all intents and purposes free and discharged from all manner of slavery, and shall be absolutely and forever manumitted."

The Emancipation Act was the culminating event of mounting opposition to West Indian slavery and the monopoly system it maintained. Especially after 1783, British exports primarily consisted of manufactured goods that required payment in raw materials, including sugar; British prohibition on the import of non-British plantation sugar, which benefited slave-owning planters, hindered the development of this trade. Thus, there was a coordinated effort among a variety of interested parties, including sugar refiners, cotton manufacturers, ship owners, and merchants, against slavery and monopoly in the Anglophone Caribbean.

Though slavery was formally abolished, the system of apprenticeship required the formerly enslaved to work without pay for their former master for forty hours a week for an additional four to six years. This practice was abandoned on August 1, 1838.

Given a second chance in his young life, Du Bois did not disappoint. He accepted the challenge that had been originally laid down by his mother and then reinforced by Frank Hosmer. He buckled down and focused intently on his studies. He published his first work at age fifteen in the *New York Globe* in 1883. *The Globe* was a weekly newspaper targeting African-American readers and was edited by Timothy Thomas Fortune (1856–1927), one of the leading intellectuals of his era. For the following two years, Du Bois published twenty-seven different articles in this newspaper, which would become one of the more influential in Black America, establishing himself early on as a force to contend with. Most of the pieces, in retrospect, seem rather mundane, often reflecting the quotidian comings and goings of the small town that was Great Barrington. Occasionally, however, Du Bois's words veered beyond the drearily ordinary. In the September 8, 1883, edition, he informed his readers about his summer trip when he visited New Bedford, Albany, Providence, and other cities. He was "pleased to see the industry and wealth of many of our race," though he was "struck" by the "absence of literary societies, none of which did I see in any of the cities. It seems to me as if this of all things ought not to be neglected" (*New York Globe*, Sept. 8, 1883). This observation portended his staunch support for developing the higher faculties of mind through liberal arts education—though not neglecting industrial training—that, in the coming decades, would characterize his fundamental disagreement with his soon-to-be rival Booker T. Washington.

Even as a teenager, Du Bois strained to raise the intellectual level of African Americans, viewing this as a precondition for progress. Du Bois's predilections were also evident when the intrepid and youthful reporter covered a debate concerning whether Native Americans should be admitted as students to the recently opened Hampton Institute, which had educated Booker T. Washington. The affirmative prevailed, he reported. He went on to contribute 300 carefully argued words urging "colored men of the town" to "prepare themselves" for the coming local and state elections, because within the town, the "colored people . . . hold the balance of power . . . if they will only act in concert they may become a power not to be despised." This article showcases his early interest in political mobilization as a tool of liberation, an interest that was to dominate his subsequent years. Thus, he was pleased to report on the prospect of the "holding of a county convention of the colored Republicans," the political party of the deceased Abraham Lincoln, which was simultaneously the vehicle of those few African Americans who were allowed to cast ballots. Frederick Douglass, a precursor of Du Bois as a political and intellectual force, declared that the Republican Party "[is] the ship, all else is the sea" (*New York Globe*, Sept. 29, 1883).

Similarly striking about Du Bois's early dispatches is the critical role played by an institution that even then had become a leading force in Black

America—the church. By 1877, religious worship had become almost completely separated by race. Independent Black churches, which ascended with the formation of the African Methodist Episcopal Church in 1816 and the National Black Baptist Convention, USA, in 1895, allowed for a modicum of Black independence and self-assertion that transcended religion. These religious institutions provided a public sphere and intellectual commons for Black communities and were often crucibles for the development of political thought and action. The Black church impacted virtually every facet of Black life after the Civil War, providing the template for the formation and administration of secular Black institutions like fraternal organizations and schools, and establishing and disseminating standards of morality (Frazier, 1974). It is not surprising, then, that the African Methodist Episcopal Zion Church was a constant reference point for the young Du Bois (*New York Globe*, Oct. 20, 1883). He was also the recording secretary for the church's Sewing Society, comprising mainly women—perhaps an expression of what was to blossom in the youthful Du Bois as a unique kind of gender egalitarianism (*New York Globe*, Dec. 29, 1883).

Nevertheless, more revealing of the man he was to become was the trip he had discussed in one of his initial articles. In the summer of this pivotal year, 1883, he journeyed to the home of his grandfather, Alexander Du Bois, a man with whom he had the scantest of acquaintance. His grandfather was residing at that point in New Bedford, Massachusetts, a port town that had been an early residence of Frederick Douglass after he had escaped from slavery in Maryland and an abolitionist headquarters that featured a thriving community of Cape Verdeans and others from the centers of Portuguese colonialism. For Du Bois, who would eventually become a globetrotter of some renown, routinely dashing off to Europe, Asia, and Africa, this was the first extended journey of his young life. Along the way he was to absorb experiences that were to shape his adolescent consciousness. For example, in Narragansett Bay, he was moved by a manifestation of what had become a challenger to the July 4 holiday in Black America: August 1, the day when the emancipation of the enslaved in the British Empire was celebrated (*Providence Journal*, Aug. 2, 1883).

Yet as stirring as this episode was, and as indelibly as it marked him, it is evident that most important to his emerging career as a writer and activist was the time spent communing with his grandfather. Du Bois's grandfather, like Du Bois himself, was not tall, but his bearing and carriage emitted an impression of great stature. Given the penury that characterized most African Americans of that era—including the life of Du Bois in Great Barrington—Alexander Du Bois was affluent relative to the times and the community from which he had sprung. His home contained a library and fine wines. As W.E.B. Du Bois stared in awe, Alexander Du Bois entertained New Bedford's finest: "They sat down and talked seriously," he reported

RECONSTRUCTION

In 1961, W.E.B. Du Bois interpreted Reconstruction as the attempt of freedmen, in concert with free Black leaders, to "rescue the South from the accumulated disaster of war." Aided by Northern educators, missionaries, and philanthropists, newly freed Africans doggedly pursued education and helped to establish the first system of free popular education in the South. They engaged in a program of social uplift, establishing hospital, poorhouses, orphanages, jails, and insane asylums. Further, they began to sell their labor in the highest markets when they could, allowing some to accumulate capital and buy land despite competition, lack of protection, and oppression. Moreover, the enfranchisement of Black men helped to reorganize Southern states and restore them to Congress based on the terms set out by the North. Freedmen progressed even though they received neither land nor capital after emancipation; the economic domination of their former masters persisted; and white Northerners and Southerners alike blamed ex-slaves for the theft, graft, and disorder that characterized the end of the Civil War.

It was the successes of freedmen that ultimately led to a compromise between Northern business and former slaveholders to restore the South and to undermine the empowerment of African Americans. The South agreed to high tariffs and war payments in gold in exchange for the disenfranchisement of freedmen and complete control over their labor. The removal of federal troops from the South, the abandonment of Southern voting regulation, and the tacit sanction of Ku Klux Klan violence signaled the end of Reconstruction.

later; "finally my grandfather arose, filled the wine glasses and raised his glass and touched the glass of his friend, murmuring a toast. I had never before seen such a ceremony," he said with wonder. "I had read about it in books, but in Great Barrington both white and Black avoided ceremony. To them it smacked of pretense." Du Bois wrote of that time: "[I] sensed in my grandfather's parlor what manners meant and how people of breeding behaved and were able to express what we in Great Barrington were loath to give act to, or unable. I never forgot that toast" (Du Bois, *Autobio*, 2007, 98).

Alexander Du Bois was to pass away in 1887, but the scene in his home was to stay with his grandson for the rest of his life. His grandfather had become, in a sense, the model on which he was to construct himself: "Always he held his head high, took no insults, made few friends. He was not a 'Negro'; he was a man!" (Du Bois, *Autobio*, 2007, 71). Du Bois's tendency toward rhapsodizing about his grandfather was perhaps intensified by the emotional scars left by his father's absence.

Returning to Great Barrington energized, Du Bois expanded his literary efforts, becoming a correspondent for the *Springfield Republican*, a powerful and influential conduit for his ideas. Though a tender sixteen years of age, he had become a paragon of seriousness, a model student, a budding intellectual. Graduating from high school in June 1884, at the ceremony the highly regarded Du Bois—who had studied Latin and Greek—provided stimulating remarks that hailed the abolitionist Wendell Phillips. Already Du Bois was pointing himself in a direction that would lead to following in the enormous footprints of paragons committed to abolition.

But where was he to continue his studies? In the neighborhood was prestigious Williams College, and in the vicinity was Harvard College, considered widely to be the epitome of higher education in the United States. What was not in doubt was that his studies would not cease with high school; proceeding to university was nonnegotiable. Yet this was easier said than done for one as impecunious as Du Bois. Then there was the weighty matter of his disabled mother to consider—what would happen to her if he departed? Then, with an abrupt sadness akin to a deus ex machina in a tragically well-made play, Mary Silvina died of an apoplectic stroke in March 1885. Then divine providence intervened in the form of Frank Hosmer. He organized an informal committee of local bigwigs, the great and the good of Great Barrington, who pledged to underwrite Du Bois's education at Fisk University. That this school for Negroes in Nashville, Tennessee, was founded by the Congregational church was not coincidental, as it was precisely this denomination in Great Barrington that had contributed the bulk of the funds for his matriculation at Fisk. With the path of his next four years of life set, Du Bois proceeded to a land that only recently had been a battlefield in a gory war that had liberated the enslaved.

Often overshadowed by its larger and more affluent neighbor—Vanderbilt University—Fisk University in Nashville, Tennessee, had been initiated in 1866 by the American Missionary Association. Like its peer historically Black institution of higher education, Howard University, Fisk was named after an officer in the Union or U.S. Army (General Clinton B. Fisk)—in this case one who had commanded Negro troops during the Civil War. Early on it had garnered a global reputation because of the Jubilee Singers, who toured the planet on behalf of the university, raising funds and bringing attention to the institution Du Bois entered as a student in 1885.

The year 1885 was a propitious time in the United States. The promise of Reconstruction had been drenched in tragedy, as federal troops were withdrawn from the South because of enormous pressure from the defeated—though still potent—Confederates, who had sought to secede from the United States and form a separate nation based on African enslavement. Native Americans were being subjected to similar oppression and were steadily being ousted from territory they had once controlled. Labor unions, which had seemed to be on the march, were being driven

into penury. Given such an unforgiving social environment, it was not surprising that as Du Bois was beginning his studies, increasingly insistent
voices were speaking out ever more dramatically against the idea of higher
education for Negroes; proponents of white-only education argued that
educating Negroes was pointless because Negroes were—supposedly—
destined to be "hewers of wood" and "drawers of water."

Undeterred, Du Bois began his studies in September of the fateful year
1885, entering as a sophomore at the tender age of seventeen as his secondary school education in Great Barrington was viewed as providing him
with a decided boost compared to his classmates, who mostly hailed from
the poorest precincts of the South. Quickly acclimating himself to the
peculiar folkways of Nashville, which included a kind of racist segregation
that was not as prevalent in Massachusetts, Du Bois established residence
at a dormitory named—ironically—after David Livingstone, who had
established a reputation as a rapacious adventurer in Africa. Du Bois's
adaptation may have been more arduous than that of his classmates, who
hailed from the comparatively tiny Black middle class and Southern towns
like Memphis, Little Rock, Atlanta, and Chattanooga. The Black middle
class, which included the Black skilled service stratum that dated back to
slavery and the Black petit-bourgeoisie, comprised physicians, clergy,
undertakers, big farmers, entertainers, publishers, teachers, and businessmen. The development of this class can be traced back to antebellum-era
mutual aid societies that laid the foundation for African-American banks,
insurance companies, and professional entities that largely served mar-
ginal and segregated Southern communities. In the early twentieth century, the Black middle class also consisted of those who migrated relatively
early to Northern ghettoes and were able to work as retail merchants,
employment agents, small manufacturers, beauticians, morticians, and
landlords renting to poorer African Americans. Importantly, the formation, sustainability, and ability of the Black middle class to accumulate
wealth were wholly dependent upon Jim Crow segregation.

On the other hand, Du Bois was much more accustomed to dealing
with the white community, who were well represented on the faculty at
Fisk. Hence, it was Du Bois who commented on the irony of a U.S. flag
bedecking the central building on campus, observing acidly, "May the
nation whose colors we fly protect the rights of those we educate!" (*Fisk
Herald*, Nov. 1887). This was not simply unnecessary sarcasm. Lynching
was not unknown in Nashville, and some students felt the need to arm
themselves when they sauntered into town. Though the U.S. Constitution
was amended to guarantee formerly enslaved Africans the right to vote
and equal protection under the law, these high-minded provisos were
rarely applied to Black people in practice. The end of Reconstruction and
the withdrawal of troops from the South indicated that the white elites of

the North and South, recently at each other's respective throats, had reconciled—at the expense of the Negro.

An excellent student, Du Bois rose rapidly in prominence on campus. It was not long before he was editor-in-chief of the university's newspaper, where he was not shy about sharing his often-controversial opinions with readers. For example, he demanded that students raise funds for a gymnasium. By arguing for the university to be funded by African Americans themselves, he figuratively thumbed his nose at the Northern philanthropists who subsidized Fisk. Aware of the unique contribution of the Jubilee Singers, Du Bois repeatedly trumpeted the virtues of music developed by African Americans, notably the spirituals that he characterized as "the strangest, sweetest" in the world. He wanted the "Negro race . . . to build up an American school of music which shall rival the grandest schools of the past" (*Fisk Herald*, Nov. 1887). He was keen to note that "our race, but a quarter of a century removed from slavery, can master the greatest musical compositions" (Munford, 1978).

These words of Du Bois all were uttered in the student newspaper, and it was there that he burnished his growing reputation as an intellectual and thinker. It was in these pages that he expressed admiration for the Black historian George Washington Williams and the activist cum journalist Timothy Thomas Fortune—both of whom came to be role models for him in these ostensibly disparate spheres of history and journalism. Du Bois excelled in both spheres and graduated in June 1888. When he had spoken at his high school graduation, he had hailed abolitionist Wendell Phillips; in Nashville, he chose to speak instead of the Iron Chancellor, Germany's Otto von Bismarck, who was in the process of forging his nation into a powerful force that was to shake the foundations of the world. Incidentally, this topic also served as a harbinger of where Du Bois would travel in order to enhance his intellectual armor in pursuit of his own effort to forge a powerful Black America.

By the fall of 1888 he entered Harvard College in Cambridge, Massachusetts—where many in his hometown had wanted him to study in the first place—as a junior. He received his bachelor's degree in June 1890 and went on—with fellowships—to graduate study. In history his professors were Edward Channing and Albert Bushnell Hart, luminaries in the field; with the encouragement of the latter, in particular, he delivered a paper at the December 1891 meeting of the American Historical Association that focused on the African slave trade. This paper anticipated the theme of his dissertation, which was to be published five years later.

That Du Bois would choose to make this particular topic his priority can be understood in the context of what was occurring as he was obtaining his advanced degrees. It was in 1884—just before he entered Fisk—that the leading European imperial powers had met in Berlin to carve up Africa like a Thanksgiving turkey, dividing among themselves spheres of influence and colonization. That is how Germany wound up controlling the nation that was to become Namibia—larger than Texas and California combined in territory. This marked a new stage in the evolution of colonialism in Africa—a process that had been accelerated by the African slave trade.

In 1886, as Du Bois was settling into Fisk, class warfare erupted in the form of fierce railroad strikes that rocked Missouri, Arkansas, and Kansas. The Knights of Labor were rising, and in June 1886, anarchists were accused of tossing a bomb that killed seven Chicago police officers in an incident known as Haymarket. This incident resulted in the execution of Albert Parsons, the husband of Lucy Parsons, a socialist, labor organizer, and women's rights advocate who helped found the International Workers of the World in 1905 and remained one of the most influential Black radicals of her time (Jones, 2017).

As Du Bois was leaving Harvard, the legislature in Mississippi drafted a new constitution that effectively eliminated African Americans from the voting rolls: a two-dollar poll tax, a literacy test, disqualification from voting for petty crimes, and the ability to recite from memory and interpret arcane provisions of the state's constitution were among the measures adopted. Simultaneously, carnage exploded at the steel plant in Homestead, Pennsylvania, as a fierce strike erupted.

This was occurring as a populist movement of discontented farmers and workers was surging—then ran aground, not least because of an inability to overcome racism within the ranks. Between the Reconstruction era and the turn of the century, farmers and workers organized against merchants, bankers, railroad corporations, and other representatives of the capitalist class to combat low wages, low commodity prices, and high interest rates. They advocated for, *inter alia*, a national bureau of labor, an interstate commerce commission, control over land speculation, a graduated income tax, the founding of agricultural colleges, and an end to convict leasing. Black farmers, sharecroppers, and agricultural laborers in organizations such as the Colored Farmers' Alliance, the Colored Agricultural Wheels, and the Cooperative Workers of America likewise agitated for higher wages, rights protections, a farmer subsidy program, and electoral inclusion. Though white populists were dedicated to progressive reforms that would alleviate their class's debt burden and impoverishment, they had little concern for African Americans suffering the same plight. The former advocated for Jim Crow laws over Black voting rights and supported the increased repression of Black people in the name of preventing friction between the races. This white supremacy, along with increased attacks from the Democratic Party and internal division, accelerated populism's demise (Ali, 2013).

Looked at in this telescoped fashion, Du Bois's return to his home state appears to be a smooth transition from the Deep South—but such was not the case. Massachusetts itself was no paradise for the Negro—it only seemed that way in comparison to Tennessee. Thus, one white Southerner objected to sitting next to Du Bois in a classroom at Harvard, and those who were Jewish or Catholic faced pervasive discrimination, which suggests a full-spectrum bigotry that is shocking by today's standards. Du Bois was rejected by the glee club and generally found it difficult to avoid the snobbery that permeated the core of Harvard: being Black and not wealthy besides, Du Bois was bound to encounter rebuffs of all sorts. Such barriers shed light on the subsequent perception of Du Bois's supposed aloofness. The fact was that it had been burned into his consciousness early on that there were those who sought to shun him because of the color of his skin; being conscious of the prejudices against him helped to generate within himself a certain reticence and shyness. Yet, despite such indignities, Du Bois would not be swayed from his goal of educating himself while obtaining the credentials that would give him credibility in his numerous campaigns on behalf of African Americans.

He was one of a mere handful of African-American students at Harvard; typical of the colleges and universities that abounded in the self-proclaimed "Athens" of the United States (Boston's self-important nickname), Harvard (unlike Fisk) was not founded expressly for African-American students and was not particularly friendly to them. Du Bois had managed to secure a fellowship to continue his education and, perhaps, already feeling the burden of preparation to rescue his compatriots from lynching, racism, and exploitation, he displayed a discipline rare for one of his age. He rose at 7:15 a.m. for breakfast and forty-five minutes later was hard at work, poring over various texts and writing. Lunch arrived at 12:30 p.m., and then there was more work from 1:00 to 4:00 p.m., followed by a trip to the gymnasium for an hour after that. At 5:00 p.m., he would relax and then take dinner from 5:30 to 7:00 p.m., at which time he would read newspapers. Then it was more study—or taking in lectures or social visits—until 10:30 p.m., and then he went to bed. Such rigor allowed him to reap dividends when he received his report card, where he excelled, graduating cum laude on June 25, 1890. As in high school and at Fisk, he was chosen to give a commencement address, and, suggestive of his intellectual evolution, he chose to speak of Jefferson Davis, the leader of the now-defeated Confederate States of America, which had plunged the nation into Civil War in order to preserve slavery (*Fisk Herald*, Nov. 1887). Moving from Wendell Phillips to Otto von Bismarck to Jefferson Davis revealed where Du Bois was going—both intellectually and politically. For initially, it was abolitionism that grabbed his imagination; then he looked abroad and was captivated by the consolidation of a modern German state;

then he came back to the South to take a jaundiced look at the man who had become the symbol of fighting to the death to preserve slavery.

Consequently, though he studied subjects as diverse as geology, chemistry, political economy, and philosophy, he laid a firm foundation for his future campaigns by devoting substantial attention to the prickly topic of how peoples of African descent arrived in this hemisphere in the first place. With this topic in mind, he chose to pursue an advanced degree at Harvard.

Du Bois had other reasons to remain in Cambridge. Beginning at Fisk, he had gained a reputation as a man who was not unattractive to the opposite sex. His appeal did not alter substantially at Harvard, and given that he was a handsome bachelor obviously on the way to fame—if not fortune—it was inevitable that he would become an object of someone's affection. One young woman with whom he became involved was Maud Cuney of Galveston, Texas, daughter of Norris Wright Cuney, one of the most powerful African-American politicians in the nation. Tall, lovely, and vivacious, she studied the piano at the New England Conservatory of Music. Assisting him in his courtship was the inheritance he had received from his grandfather, Alexander Du Bois, who had obviously been impressed when the teenage Du Bois had come to visit him. A mustache was sprouting on Du Bois's face, soon to be supplemented by a pointed beard. Typically well dressed and modest of mien, he cut a dashing figure on the streets of Cambridge and Boston. It was during this time that he made his way to Amherst (where, a century later, his personal papers would be deposited at the University of Massachusetts, Amherst), not far from Great Barrington, where his acute vision settled on the loveliness of the young ladies there, among whom—he was to note—was "Fannie Bailey, hailing from Cambridge," who "was a symphony in purple" (Lewis, 1993).

Yet, he was not sufficiently distracted to ignore his studies. Thus it was that he found himself in December 1891 in Washington, DC, for the annual meeting of the American Historical Association, the capstone of the profession. His remarks on the African slave trade neatly summarized his conclusions, which were far-reaching for the time: "If slave labor was an economic god," said Du Bois, "then the slave trade was its strong right arm; and with Southern planters recognizing this and Northern capital unfettered by conscience it was almost like legislating against economic laws to attempt to abolish the slave trade by statutes" (*Boston Courant*, July 9, 1892). It was such a display of scholarship that led Harvard to award Du Bois a master of arts degree in June 1892.

By 1892, although slavery had officially ended, many African Americans were trapped in a form of debt slavery on plantations in the Deep South. Southern white landowners regulated and controlled Black workers by reducing them to a semiservile class of agrarian laborers. Economic arrangements such as debt peonage, sharecropping, and rent tenancy relied upon relations of exploitation in which Black laborers were supplied with sustenance and supplies at exorbitant interest rates that locked them into long-term indebtedness. African Americans were trapped in this system not least because, instead of earning wages or incomes that would allow them to accumulate savings, they received only the barest provisions to sustain themselves. Du Bois would later write in *The Souls of Black Folk*, "The key-note of the Black Belt is debt . . . in the sense of continued inability of the mass of the population to make income cover expenses. This is the direct heritage of the South from the wasteful economies of the slave *régime*; but it was emphasized and brought to a crisis by the Emancipation of the slaves" (Du Bois, *Souls*, 2007, 94).

Du Bois was in a unique category of African Americans who had been able to pursue higher education; however, he was not content with this formidable accomplishment. He applied for and received a fellowship from the Slater Fund, which was underwritten by philanthropists including Rutherford B. Hayes, who as U.S. president had effectively terminated Reconstruction a few years earlier. The Slater Fund made possible two years of graduate study—mostly in history and economics—at the University of Berlin. This opportunity was bittersweet as Du Bois would have to not only leave Maud Cuney behind, but also leave all that was familiar for the uncharted territory of Germany.

Du Bois was also uncharted territory for Germany. The "Iron Chancellor's" effort to consolidate his nation and place it in a position to be a challenger to Britain and France for domination of the wealthiest continent had attracted Du Bois's attention early on. He informed his classmates at Fisk that the rise of Germany held acute lessons relevant to "the rise of the Negro people" (Du Bois, "Enforcement," 1892, 163–174). Unfortunately, what seemed to inflame the ire of Berlin was the fact that the territory controlled by Paris and London in Africa was much more extensive than that of Germany, a reality that the seizure of Namibia had not assuaged. Hence, in strolling the broad boulevards of Berlin, Du Bois could easily have been mistaken as a prize from Germany's newly minted African empire rather than the diligent student he actually was.

In July 1892, the youthful Du Bois boarded a ship headed for Rotterdam and then Dusseldorf—the first German city in which he set foot. The Iron Chancellor had grand plans for this bustling, crowded metropolis, which even then was renowned for its Ruhr-fueled industry. One advantage that Du Bois held over the typical U.S. visitor was his flawless mastery of the German language (his dedication to learning German shows the extent of his fascination with Germany itself and the lessons Black America could glean from its rise).

In the fall of 1892, Du Bois ambled into a classroom at the University of Berlin, founded in 1809. Despite its relative youth—dwarfed in this regard by Oxford, Harvard, and Charles University in Prague—the University of Berlin had attracted eminent faculty, including the philosopher Georg Hegel (whose ideas deeply influenced Du Bois), the historian Leopold von Ranke (whose attempt to promote a scientific view of history also influenced Du Bois), and the sociologist Max Weber (whom Du Bois was to challenge eventually for his title as the most influential scholar in sociology).

Convinced that he was well on his way to attaining the credentials and knowledge that would allow him to help lift his people—only recently removed from enslavement—to ever greater heights, Du Bois buckled down to the rigors of graduate study in Berlin. Renting a room from a local family, Du Bois retained the rigorous discipline that had served him so well at Harvard. Despite his fluency in German, the youthful Du Bois, who maintained a lifelong sensitivity to slights—racist and otherwise—could often be spotted sitting or walking alone. In February 1893, on his twenty-fifth birthday, he was characteristically alone and reflecting on the next period in his life with the vision and utter seriousness that was to become his hallmark. He pledged that the great heights he would attain would not merely be for himself but, more importantly, would be of profound importance for Black America. "These are my plans," he cried, "to make a name in [social] science, to make a name in literature and thus to raise my race." It would be an error to mistake as megalomania Du Bois's equation of his own rise with that of a much-beleaguered Black America. For a people who had been deprived systematically of education—at one point it had been a crime to allow a slave to learn to read and write—desperately needed intellectual candlepower. Sadly, there were very few in Du Bois's position to obtain higher education, and he knew this fact all too well (*Fisk Herald*, Sept. 1893).

Thus inspired, Du Bois felt it his duty to apply himself with iron regularity to his education. He became a devotee of a German culture he had come to appreciate, as embodied by the works of writers such as Johann Wolfgang von Goethe and Heinrich Heine; he imbibed a form of German Romanticism that was to be espied—by some analysts—in his coming fascination with Pan-Africanism.

As the academic year came to a close in the late spring of 1893, Du Bois found it necessary to traverse the continent—or as much as his limited funds would allow. In visiting Switzerland, Hungary, and Austria, he had the opportunity to obtain a panoramic view of the persecution of various minorities, particularly those who were Jewish. Learning more about how discrimination affected the lives of Jews in Europe helped him to contextualize what was befalling Black America and helped him recognize that

---

ABOLITION OF THE SLAVE TRADE AND THE HAITIAN REVOLUTION

In 1807, with the support of President Thomas Jefferson, the U.S. Congress passed the Act Prohibiting Importation of Slaves. The Act took effect in 1808 and formalized the illegality of the trans-Atlantic slave trade in the United States.

The Haitian Revolution (1791–1804) was in many ways a catalyst for this legislation. Its political, economic, and social threat to the global slave system incited protracted slave trade debates between 1804 and 1807 that led to the formal end of U.S. participation. The insurrection of enslaved Africans in what was then called Hispaniola or Saint Domingue stoked fear in U.S. slaveholding states in which the enslaved constituted the numerical majority, not least because their property, livelihood, and very lives were at stake. That Haitian revolutionaries had killed many of the Europeans—particularly the French— on the island as one method of preventing counterrevolution was particularly menacing to U.S. slaveholders.

These anxieties were exacerbated by slave uprisings from Virginia to Louisiana from the 1790s onward—believed to be inspired in so small part by the "Black Jacobins"—and by the spike in British-led abolition activities as a result of the Haitian Revolution. The white slaveholding elite, including Jefferson and James Madison, were suspicious that Great Britain would manipulate Africans in their former colony to take up arms against the United States. For state and federal governments, then, prohibiting the importation of slaves was a potential means of quelling internal Black revolution resulting from endogenous Africans' own volition, orchestrated by the Haitian military, or instigated by the British.

---

the plight of his people was not wholly peculiar but shared commonalities with that of others. He also found time to visit Venice, and in Italy he got as far south as Naples where he witnessed the kind of regional discrimination that had led to the acerbic aphorism that "Africa starts south of Rome." Throughout Europe, Du Bois often was mistaken for a "Gypsy" or a Roma or a Jew; his experiences gave him a unique vantage point from which to comprehend Europe.

Perhaps inspired by his European peregrinations and struck by the abject poverty of those in rural areas of Europe—and the obvious parallels with Black America—Du Bois launched a major study that was translated as "The Large and Small-Scale System of Agriculture in the Southern United States, 1840–1890," shards of which were to inform a good deal of his subsequent research back in the United States. He also found time to study statistics—in some ways, the heart of social science—and the Protestant Reformation, an apt topic of study in the land of Martin Luther.

In the midst of travels and study, Du Bois would have been purblind if he had ignored what amounted to the strongest socialist movement then extant. The strength of German socialism dated back to the publication of the *Communist Manifesto* of 1848, the circulation of the principles in Karl Marx's *Das Kapital* starting in 1867, and the merging of the "Lasallean" and "Eisenacher" factions into a unified socialist party in 1875. By 1890, it had become the strongest party in Germany, overthrowing Otto von Bismarck and overturning the Anti-Socialist Law. Even though the prospect of war threatened the spread of socialism at the dawn of the twentieth century, the German socialist party led the international working-class movement by gaining a stronghold on political power. As such, in 1892 it was the most advanced party, and, according to Friedrich Engels, it was German socialism that represented the proletarian revolution (Engels, 1892).

Karl Marx himself had studied at the University of Berlin and, like Du Bois, had been inspired to deepen both his activism and his research by what he saw in Germany. Du Bois began attending socialist meetings in his neighborhood and took notice of their spectacular electoral rise and the wafer-thin distinctions that separated one faction in this fractious movement from another.

Perhaps those who funded his education had gotten wind of this radical turn, for the Slater Fund arrived at the decision to terminate financial support. This meant that Du Bois failed to earn a University of Berlin doctorate. And so, after spending two action-packed and stimulating years in Berlin, Du Bois reluctantly retreated to Harvard, his second choice, to obtain his doctorate.

2

A Life of Excellence

After two years in Europe, Du Bois returned to the United States by boat, across the choppy waters of the North Atlantic. The plight of African Americans that had existed when he had left for Europe had yet to change: African Americans continued to endure lynching and disfranchisement as the promise of Reconstruction continued to be suffocated. The now twenty-six-year-old scholar traveled in steerage along with prospective European migrants who upon arrival in New York would immediately be deemed of a higher status than Du Bois, whose roots in the United States ran deep. Yet despite this obvious handicap, it was not long before he possessed one advantage that few have shared before or since: although he had failed to obtain a doctorate from the University of Berlin, he was able to "settle" for the same degree from Harvard, a credential that also placed him in the educational stratosphere of the entire nation.

He also was ready to enter more directly into the fray and seek to stem the tide that was capsizing his people. He applied to teach at several colleges designated for African Americans. After the Civil War, a number of these institutions had arisen—including his alma mater Fisk—as the United States endured an apartheid-like educational system that even a prospective Harvard doctorate had difficulty penetrating. The first acceptance came from Wilberforce University in Ohio, appropriately named after the famed British abolitionist (William Wilberforce) who had done so much to ban slavery. By late 1894, Du Bois was ensconced in the faculty there; he taught Greek,

Latin, English, German, and history—a crushing load of courses that hardly left time for the research and writing he craved.

On the outskirts of Dayton, this area had thrust itself into the consciousness of African Americans as the home of Paul Laurence Dunbar, who, by the time of Du Bois's arrival, was in the process of establishing himself as a talented poet of no small notoriety. Wilberforce was also quite close to nearby Yellow Springs, the home of Antioch College, which was to become a lodestar for student activism in years to come. But in 1894, Du Bois had good reason to feel that he had descended from the lofty altitude signaled by Cambridge and Berlin to the depths of academia, as Wilberforce's sparse and spare facilities—particularly in what was of crucial importance to the scholar: the library—hardly met the standards to which he had grown accustomed. From the concrete canyons of major metropolises, Du Bois now found himself in the midst of cornfields as far as the eye could see. Having cultivated a finely manicured beard (which was to complement his increasingly balding pate)—and often sporting a deftly carved cane and elegant gloves, Du Bois was instantly identifiable on a campus replete with students often a generation removed from enslavement.

His dapper appearance could not mask his seemingly inexhaustible ability to work, leading some to believe that he must have survived without sleep. For within months of his arrival, Du Bois had finished his masterful Harvard dissertation, "The Suppression of the African Slave Trade to the United States of America, 1638–1870," a landmark in the field of history. It was in June 1895 that his Harvard professors placed their imprimatur on this exemplar of historical excavation, conferring upon him the title for which he was to be known for the rest of his life—Dr. Du Bois.

His Harvard instructors maneuvered to ensure that his scholarship was published—a rarity for doctoral dissertations, which are routinely consigned to obscurity on dusty library shelves. Instead, the significance and profundity of Du Bois's work was ratified when it appeared in book form as the first monograph in the famed series known as Harvard Historical Studies.

More than a century after it was first pored over by eager readers—and unlike many of its late nineteenth-century peers—Du Bois's book continues to withstand the test of time. Constructed from primary documents (parliamentary and colonial records, federal and state legislation, census figures, court cases, and journalistic accounts), "The Suppression of the African Slave Trade to the United States of America, 1638–1870" was a reflection of the gathering consensus that had taken hold at Berlin, Johns Hopkins, Harvard, and like-minded institutions that history should be built, to the extent possible, from such eyewitness accounts. Given such firsthand verification, it was hard to dispute Du Bois's conclusion that indicted the United States—its nationals and authorities—for its promiscuous participation in the African slave trade, even after it was thought to have been banned in 1808. This odious commerce, Du Bois had concluded, received a de facto sanction from Washington, not least because of the weighty influence of slaveholders in government; moreover, the immense market for enslaved Africans that then existed in Cuba and Brazil was much too profitable for U.S. slave dealers to ignore. This conclusion—bold for the times—has been verified by today's scholarship, unavoidably grounded in assertions made by Du Bois decades earlier (e.g., Horne, 2007).

Du Bois's masterpiece served as a precursor for the work of the Trinidadian scholar, Cyril Lionel Robert (C.L.R.) James, in that Du Bois's work connects the epochal Haitian Revolution to France's hurried sale of the Louisiana Territory to the United States (James, 1989). Du Bois also knew that it was the turmoil in Haiti that convinced slave traders in the United States that the better part of wisdom would be to avoid importing more enslaved Africans—thus risking the dire prospect of "Africanization" or creating a racial ratio disadvantageous to the enslavers. He also recognized the significance of slavery for the U.S. economy, then on a glide path to becoming the planet's weightiest; this observation anticipates the implication of the scholarship of yet another Trinidadian scholar, Eric Williams (1944).

Decades later, Du Bois was to subject his first book to withering—and, perhaps, unfair—criticism, lamenting his inattention to Marx (economics) and Freud (psychoanalysis) in explicating the horrors of enslavement (Du Bois, *The Suppression*, 1896). Nevertheless, the fact that this book continues to be consulted and quoted suggests its ongoing relevancy.

Even as Du Bois was putting the finishing touches on this manuscript, the very modern idea that now governs academia—"publish or perish"—was not altogether absent from his world. He had good reason to believe that if he was able to garner attention as a published scholar, his chance of being rescued from the relative backwater of Wilberforce would be greatly improved.

But Du Bois did not envision for himself a life solely as a scholar cloistered in the ivory tower; consequently, early on, he found time to comment on pressing matters of public import—the death of human rights leader Frederick Douglass was just such an event. Born enslaved in Maryland, Douglass was able to escape bondage for a new life in Massachusetts and New York, where he penned works about his life so riveting that they continue to be read. He then became the leading antislavery campaigner of his era, which brought him on more than one occasion to tumultuous and rapturous crowds in Europe. On February 20, 1895, Douglass died— strikingly, just as his putative successor, Du Bois, was establishing himself as the leading tribune of Black America. A memorial service for Douglass was held at Wilberforce on March 9, and Du Bois, the youngest faculty member, addressed those assembled. In praising Douglass for his stead-fastness and vision, he accidentally and serendipitously—or not—sketched the role he was to play in the coming century (Du Bois, "Douglass," 1964).

Though only twenty-seven years of age and weighted down with a burdensome teaching load, Du Bois was still able to draw attention to himself—as he did with well-received remarks about Douglass—from oth-ers who were renowned, such as the elderly and graying seventy-six-year-old Alexander Crummell, who had come to Wilberforce in the spring of 1895 to address students and faculty. An Episcopal cleric, a her-alded intellectual, and a man who had toiled in Liberia (the West African state settled by "free" Negroes from the United States), Crummell also foreshadowed a brand of Pan-Africanism that Du Bois was later to embody.

Modern Pan-Africanism—the ideas, activities, and movements preemi-nently concerned with the commonality of purpose among, and the social, political, and economic emancipation of, African peoples on the continent and dispersed throughout the world—became a centerpiece of Black

---

JIM CROW

Jim Crow refers to race and color segregation and subordination based on the doctrine of "separate but equal" established in the 1896 Supreme Court decision *Plessy v. Ferguson*. Through de jure and de facto policy and practice, it entrenched what Du Bois called the "color line." Jim Crow was a system of purposeful, continuous, and organized discrimination that circumscribed the advancement, equality, and access of African Americans to ensure the polit-ical, economic, and social predominance of the white population.

For African Americans, Jim Crow made prejudice and injustice the rule and equality and justice the exception. In the South as well as the North, segrega-tion extended to every aspect of society, including transportation, housing, education, and employment. Not long after its founding, the NAACP con-tended that Jim Crow shackled African Americans to slavery, pushed them physically into peonage, kept them mentally ignorant, politically disenfran-chised them, and subjected them to enduring insult.

In the 1930s, Du Bois began to advocate voluntary separation as the only antidote to this all-encompassing color discrimination. He argued that, along with protest against Jim Crow, there must be positive and united action against Black suffering through self-assertion, self-respect, and self-segregation. To continue to rely on a change in white attitudes for Black progress would be race suicide. This system of white domination, enforced inferiority, and sys-temic exclusion, upheld by courts, customs, public opinion, and racial vio-lence, was sanctioned by law until separate was ruled inherently unequal in *Brown v. Board of Education of Topeka Kansas* in 1954.

political thought starting in the late nineteenth century. Thinkers including Martin Delaney, Edward Blyden, and Joseph Ephraim Casely Hayford struggled against the enslavement, colonization, and denigration of African people throughout the world by devising strategies that ranged from self-government to repatriation. Starting in 1900, Du Bois began to participate in, lead, and organize Pan-African Congresses in which African descendants met, planned, and built networks; passed resolutions condemning colonialism, imperialism, white supremacy, and European domination; aired their grievances to an international audience; and agitated for mutual progress (Adi & Sherwood, 2003).

Much like he had emulated his grandfather, from that point forward, Du Bois chose to walk in the large footprints of Alexander Crummell (Du Bois, *Souls*, 2007). In line with Crummell, for example, Du Bois embraced ethnological discourse to challenge "scientific" arguments about Black inferiority. By the end of the nineteenth century, ethnology—the comparative study of the development and culture of social man that prefigured cultural anthropology—had become one of the most significant social scientific fields of study. Ethnologists linked the transcendence of "nature" and "savagery" to a drive toward democracy and discernible contributions to civilization. Apropos of the times, Crummell and Du Bois understood race as a naturally occurring law of development; but unlike racist ethnologists like Herbert Spencer and Lewis Henry Morgan, their approaches centered on cultural, moral, and ethical development—not natural selection or pseudoscientific measures like craniometry—in theories of racial progress (Crummell, 1889).

For these Negro leaders, race was a spirit, an idea, and an ideal that produced psychic and cultural differentiations constituted by, inter alia, common blood, history, habits of thought, and conscious striving toward a particular conception of life. Each race, they believed, possessed a different articulation of civilization that contributed to the progress of humanity as a whole. Likewise, they insisted that while race had cultural, historical, and sociological significance, it had little explanatory value in terms of biology. Like his mentor Crummell, Du Bois represented the idealist wing of ethnology; their emphasis on the development of mind was a direct critique of not only somatic approaches to ethnology, but also of materialism, whose main proponent at the time was Booker T. Washington, a founder of Tuskegee, which continues to be a beacon of higher education in Alabama. Materialism linked racial progress to practical labor, entrepreneurship, economic prosperity, and property ownership, along with more abstract principles like thrift, delayed gratification, and prudence. Idealists, on the other hand, proffered improvement in conduct and conscience, alongside imagination and inventiveness, as the keys to full equality. They linked self-help not to brute toil, accumulation, and commercialism but to racial integrity, collective identity, and cultural reform.

In Du Bois's canonical text, *The Souls of Black Folk*, he rhapsodizes about his fortuitous encounter with Crummell and intimates how it shaped his own accelerating consciousness. "Tall, frail and black he stood," says Du Bois, "with simple dignity and an unmistakable air of good breeding." Theretofore, Du Bois's life had been shaped by his high school principal in Great Barrington and his professors at Harvard and Berlin, but now he had the rare opportunity to meet face-to-face an African-American man who had also devoted his life to "racial uplift."

At this time, racial uplift was the leading social and political force in Black life. For Du Bois's contemporary Nannie Helen Borroughs, a prominent educator, orator, and civil rights activist, racial uplift was essential to Black progress because "the race that fails to do all within its powers to help itself will never rise. . . . God does not do for us what we can do for ourselves" (Johnson, 2000, 131). Crummell, Burroughs, Du Bois, and other racial uplift proponents held that, through a combination of self-help, moral reform, cultural development, and mutual aid, African Americans could radically improve their living conditions, ensure group survival, and combat racism. Black bourgeois women and men promoted racial self-help through philanthropic, welfare, educational, and mutual aid activities, while the Black masses were instructed to pool their meager resources, save their earnings, sacrifice for the good of the community, and patronize and support Black-owned businesses. Moreover, it was the responsibility of the Black educated class to model and enforce the values, ethics, and morality without which racial uplift would be impossible.

Douglass's death and Crummell's arrival on campus were twin shocks to the young Du Bois, reminding him at once that time was short, and the need for successors to giants who were passing away or in their dotage was great. While Du Bois was bogged down in a blizzard of classes, others were stepping forward to fill the vacuum left by the passing of Douglass. At the Cotton States International Exposition on September 18, 1895, Washington—who was to become Du Bois's antipodal foil for years to come—shook the South and the nation. Washington in his "Atlanta Compromise" offered to accept the Jim Crow regime, which mandated racist segregation and severe restrictions on the right to vote, in return for the white South accepting minor steps forward in Black progress in the realms of business and agriculture. "Cast down your buckets where you are," Washington advised, "by making friends in every manly way of the people of all races by whom we are surrounded." In exchange, said Washington, Euro-Americans must cast down their buckets "among those people who have, without strikes and labor wars, tilled your fields, cleared your forests, [built] your railroads and cities." At a time when obstreperous trade unions and angry farmers were stirring the streams of discontent, powerful elites were bound to lend an ear to the comforting idea that African Americans would not contribute to this overall disarray. Unlike Douglass, Washington was not a spellbinding orator, but his words were no less riveting to those who were listening. "In all things that are purely social we can be as separate as the fingers," he said with a display of his digits, "yet one as the hand in all things essential to mutual progress" (Aptheker, 1973, 39; Lewis, 1993, 175).

In later years, Du Bois was to confront Washington, though initially he seemed as taken by the words of the Wizard of Tuskegee as any. "Let me heartily congratulate you upon your phenomenal success at Atlanta—it was a word fitly spoken," Du Bois enthused. "Here might be the basis of a real settlement between whites and blacks in the South, if the South opened to the Negroes, the doors of economic opportunity and the Negroes cooperated with the white South in political sympathy" (Du Bois, *The Philadelphia*, 1973, 16). Perhaps Du Bois was inundated with classes and lectures; perhaps he did not pay careful attention to the demobilizing import of the Wizard's words; perhaps he was shading toward opportunism—whatever the case, he did not emerge initially with full-throated opposition to Washington.

Meanwhile, Wilberforce had its diversions, including the friendships of Paul Laurence Dunbar and the military man Charles Young, both emblems of the "Talented Tenth" of Negroes that Du Bois was to hail subsequently. There was another friendship that the attractive young bachelor developed during that time. Often besieged by dinner invitations and social engagements from those who viewed him as a handsome betrothal catch, Du Bois ultimately retreated from this snare when he met Nina Gomer. She was his student whose family resided far away, in Cedar Rapids, Iowa. Wilberforce was not their only commonality. Like Du Bois, she was an African American who had roots in the Francophone world—Alsace in her case. They were married on May 12, 1896, in her hometown. Though they remained married for decades, their relationship was star-crossed, and it is fair to say that he did not find true marital bliss until his second marriage—when he was an octogenarian—to the writer and activist Shirley Graham.

With a Harvard doctorate in hand by 1895 and a marriage a scant year later, Du Bois had attained two notable landmarks. Yet he was still trapped at Wilberforce teaching a crushing load of classes. He also found it difficult to escape the swamp of petty politics that too often was the norm in college life—politics that were exacerbated by the debilitating Jim Crow that inherently generated frustrations and anger with hardly an outlet.

But rescue from this dilemma came in the form of a letter from the University of Pennsylvania in Philadelphia, an Ivy League institution of some repute, that offered him a position—not as a professor (Jim Crow veritably forbade this) but as an investigator to conduct a study of African

Americans in this major metropolis. Philadelphia in 1896 had the largest, and perhaps most influential, African-American population in the nation. Philadelphia had spawned one of the more significant religious denominations among African Americans: the African Methodist Episcopal faith. It was also home to the Society of Friends—or the Quakers—who had helped to generate one of the strongest abolitionist movements in the nation during the antebellum era and later produced Bayard Rustin, a communist-turned-anticommunist, pacifist, chief theoretician of the civil rights movement, and top aide to Dr. Martin Luther King Jr.

But, like other U.S. cities, Philadelphia had been unable to escape the pestilence of racism, as bloodily racist attacks on African Americans had become as much a part of the city's landscape as the sprawling oasis of greenery that was Fairmount Park. Part of the problem in the City of Brotherly Love—as was the case nationally—was that those African Americans who could vote were aligned with the party of business elites, the Republican Party, while the white working class was aligned traditionally with the Democratic Party. Because African Americans were also overwhelmingly working class, this meant that the working class was torn asunder on a political axis, which generated enormous tension and frequent confrontations between Black and white workers. This was the fractious climate into which Du Bois and his newly betrothed were thrust.

The nation was not doing much better than Philadelphia itself, as the challenge of the Populist movement (discussed in the previous chapter) was continuing to shake the stability of the nation. Then there was the rising influence of the Progressive movement, of which it was said would steal the clothes—and programs—of the Populists whenever the latter went swimming. The Progressive movement was shaped by the perception that all of the unrest at the end of the nineteenth century, brought about by class conflict, was causing a profound social crisis. Thus, it attempted to construct a "common good" and "public interest" that superseded corporate greed and sectarian class interests by focusing on individual opportunity and betterment within existing power and property relations. Progressives—largely middle-class women, labor activists and liberal politicians—believed that healthy and clean homes, safe and responsible communities, and productive and efficient workplaces would help to ensure a united citizenry and a humane industrial society. As such, the Progressive movement promoted citizenship, democratic politics, universal education, and basic social services. It also supported modest reforms to manage the excesses of inequality that impeded individual advancement, stifled economic opportunity, and threatened democratic institutions. Because Progressives believed in abstract social good over class interests, they eschewed militant labor organizing and redistributive government intervention on behalf of the working class. Instead, they advocated industrial expansion, economic growth, socially responsible capitalism, and voluntary mutual aid to alleviate poverty and ensure prosperity (Stormquist, 2006).

The class and race tensions across the United States that the Progressive movement both addressed and evaded were creating momentum for change akin to a gigantic snowball hurtling down a steep mountain. As political conflict escalated, there were those who were interested in accumulating more information about Black Philadelphia, whose votes could tip the balance in close elections—hence the invitation to Du Bois to organize a study of this sector. There were about 40,000 African Americans living in Philadelphia's crowded, densely populated neighborhoods that served as a virtual incubator for all manner of maladies. They were overwhelmingly poverty stricken, and life—in the words of the philosopher Thomas Hobbes, referring to his native England—was "nasty, brutish and short."

Thus it was that the dapper Dr. Du Bois, attired quite fashionably as was his wont, found himself canvassing Black Philadelphia for data to use in his pioneering sociological study, *The Philadelphia Negro*. His friend, the historian Herbert Aptheker, calculated that Du Bois expended 835 hours in interviews involving 2,500 households during a ninety-day period of intensive research commencing in August 1896. All told, this research involved talking with approximately 10,000 men, women, and children (Harlan, 1972, 218). Piling fact upon fact and statistic upon statistic, Du Bois mounted a devastating indictment of the carking conditions Black Philadelphia was accorded, which was all the more devastating because of its scientific veneer. *The Philadelphia Negro*, along with his first book on the African slave trade, not only established him as the premier scholar in Black America but also served as bookends of an era, rigorously documenting the perilous journey African Americans had made from slavery to freedom.

Du Bois's epochal study of Philadelphia in some ways mimicked a similar study conducted decades earlier by Friedrich Engels, which examined the working class in Manchester. Unlike Engels, who, as an affluent businessman and close comrade of Karl Marx, was only moonlighting as a social critic, Du Bois actually lived among those who were the target of his research. Thus situated, Du Bois was able to produce an exhaustive examination of every aspect of Black life: history, demography, family, migrations, education, occupations, health, organized life (especially in the churches), prisons, pauperism, alcoholism, housing, amusements, class differentiations, voting, and political activity. Du Bois's study even goes as far as including a word to concerned whites about their responsibility for the dire situation he describes so meticulously and their role in negatively shaping contact across the color line.

The concept of the color line explicated European domination of persons originating from Africa, Asia, and the Americas and described the relation of the "darker to the lighter races of men" as the foundational antagonism of the century. By 1900, Du Bois had thoroughly developed his influential proclamation, "The problem of the twentieth century is the problem of the color line," in two papers, the first before the American Negro Academy in "The Present Outlook for the Dark Races of Mankind" and the second at the first Pan-African Conference in "Address to the Nations of the World." For Du Bois, the conflation of color and inferiority was a direct result of the enslavement of African peoples and the reduction of the African continent to a space of savagery and backwardness suited only for pillage. He likewise argued that the color line was born out of white supremacy, colonialism, imperialism, and the superexploitation of the world's racialized working classes.

It was becoming increasingly difficult to ignore the intellectual firepower that Du Bois was unleashing in defense of Black America. Meanwhile, back in Philadelphia, Du Bois, who had reached his twenty-ninth birthday in 1897, also experienced the joy of the birth of his firstborn on October 2, a son named Burghardt. This added responsibility did not lessen his anxiety at the thought that his temporary academic appointment at the University of Pennsylvania was expiring within a few months of this exhilarating birth. Though he was producing scholarship of an extraordinary character at a relatively young age, Du Bois was confronted with the distinct possibility of unemployment, adding a peculiar poignancy to his explications in *The Philadelphia Negro* concerning the toxicity of joblessness. Seeking to preempt this unsavory possibility, Du Bois thrust himself further into the national spotlight by publishing in the celebrated *Atlantic Monthly*, which had a justifiable reputation as a beacon of intellectualism. It was here that he introduced his now famous line, "the Negro is a sort of seventh son, born with a veil, and gifted with second-sight," and began to develop the idea of "double-consciousness" that he subsequently expanded upon in his soon-to-be-published classic, *The Souls of Black Folk*. Du Bois grappled with the inexorable anxiety that flowed from the enslavement and abuse of those then known as U.S. Negroes, coupled with the reality that there appeared to be no possibility of returning to the African homeland. It was here, too, that Du Bois raised searching and disturbing questions about Black America's primary gatekeeper, Booker T. Washington, a radical move for the time since the Wizard of Tuskegee then had the power to advance (or retard) the career of a scholar then contemplating the possibility of unemployment. Yes, Du Bois said, the industrial training then sanctified at Tuskegee was welcome, but, he continued, in an implicit rebuke of Washington's "Atlanta Compromise," "the power of the ballot was [needed] in sheer self-defense." Taking a more comprehensive view of the Negro's plight than that suggested by Washington, Du Bois added portentously that "work, culture, liberty—all these we need, not singly but together, gained through the unifying idea of Race" (Du Bois, 1897, 195).

Du Bois's words were an early signal that the delicately cast compromise brokered by Washington would not be greeted with unanimous glee. Also percolating in Du Bois's ever-active consciousness was another notion that would soon emerge and roil the waters of Black America. For it was in *The Philadelphia Negro* that Du Bois adumbrated the idea of the "Talented Tenth," the purported "best" among African Americans—those like Du Bois himself—who would lead the masses to the Promised Land. This thesis—as much as anything else that he wrote or did—contributed to the ultimately misleading idea that Du Bois was an "elitist," somehow disconnected from those for whom he purported to speak. Later, of course, Du Bois was to revise this controversial notion to the point that the "Talented Tenth" came to resemble a self-sacrificing political vanguard. In any case, Du Bois added ballast to this conception by pleading for a scientific study of the realities of the "Negro Problem."

As early as 1895, Du Bois contended that the "Negro Problem" was, at its core, a modern problem of white ignorance, prejudice, and evasion. In other words, what whites had named the "Negro Problem" was actually a nexus of social problems, rooted in the dehumanization of African Americans, that was concealed by "the chaos of opinion, allegation, and prejudice" rather than clarified with fact and systematic study. This problem of "humanity and national morality," Du Bois opined, could only be resolved through "careful statistical analysis, historical research, and scientific investigation." Such an approach would dispel the myth that the "Negro Problem" was born out of the fact that African Americans were ignorant, lazy, immoral, and lawless and thus unfit for citizenship. Careful inquiry would also reveal that, in the final analysis, the "Negro Problem" was a moral question that was no fault of African Americans but was rather a function of the "unreasoning and unreasonable prejudice of this nation, which persists in rating the ignorant and vicious white man above the intelligent and striving Colored man, under any and all circumstances" (Du Bois Papers, "The Afro-American," ca. 1895).

Though Du Bois's call to study the "Negro Problem" has been much reviled and discussed, scholarly neglect of African Americans often meant that those who were thought to speak on their behalf were frequently flying blind, wholly unaware of the nuances and crevices of Negro life that would make for reasonable policy prescriptions on their behalf (Du Bois, *The Philadelphia*, 1973, 16). Thus, even his jab at the "Atlanta Compromise," with all the danger for his career that it suggested, could not obscure Du Bois's increasing prominence. Ironically, it was Atlanta University itself—a historically Black school in the Wilberforce tradition, albeit with a higher profile in basic research—that offered him a post that he quickly accepted, moving to the "City Too Busy to Hate" by 1897.

Hard by the serpentine Chattahoochee River, Atlanta housed a sprawling complex of Negro colleges, including the schools that came to be known as Morehouse and Spelman. A bulwark of the erstwhile Confederate States of America, Georgia had been devastated during the Civil War, emerging afterward with bruised feelings—notably among the Euro-American elite—toward the United States, feelings that were inevitably visited upon a long-suffering African-American population. Atlanta was a citadel of Jim Crow and a frequent site of lynchings—and worse. It was not the kind of place that Du Bois would find congenial, but at this juncture he did not have many options, despite his sterling doctorate from Harvard. Du Bois quickly plunged into a maelstrom of beaver-like busyness that included teaching, speaking engagements, polishing manuscripts, writings for popular publications—and more. It was here that Du Bois was to spend twelve long and transformative years of triumph and travail that were so engaging that it was to this city that Du Bois later returned for another decade of residence, beginning in 1934.

Atlanta University, being situated in a major metropolis, had more allure and charm than that possessed by Wilberforce. Du Bois taught courses in economics, history, and sociology, among others, while also finding time to play competitive tennis. The sight of Du Bois rushing to whack a small ball across a wide net humanized him in the eyes of his students, many of whom were intimidated by his classroom presence, which was deeply influenced by the martinets who had instructed him in Berlin.

Du Bois felt, however, that his lasting contribution would be in the realm of research, and in 1897 he initiated a renowned series of studies on such disparate matters involving African Americans as poverty rates, wages, churches, business enterprise, and the like. These studies involved the dispensing of numerous questionnaires to collect data necessary to illuminate the plight of African Americans; Du Bois was a pioneer in collecting and scrutinizing mounds of data, from which he was able to draw conclusions and construct the narratives of his studies. Du Bois's multidisciplinarity, rigorous research, and community orientation would provide the model for Black Studies—an insurgent discipline that would change the landscape of higher education six decades later (Warren, 2011).

By dint of tireless labor and a steady stream of publications, even before a new century dawned and an old one concluded, Du Bois was becoming better known widely as a model of scholarly rectitude—and, possibly, an antipode and alternative to the model provided by Washington. For example, in March 1899, Du Bois delivered a series of lectures at Hampton Institute in Virginia, Washington's alma mater. "It is doubtful," said one well-informed commentator, "if any visiting lecturer has ever more successfully won the admiration and swayed the thoughts of the students here" (Du Bois, "The Study," 1898).

At roughly that same moment—that is, by 1898—the United States had embarked on a new departure, waging war against the tottering Spanish Empire and emerging triumphant with domination over Cuba, Puerto Rico, and the Philippines. During this same era, the United States had collaborated in dislodging indigenous rule in Hawaii, and, in the process, had become a budding imperialist power—though still far distant from Britain, the leader in this realm. Bringing under the U.S. flag many more millions of "non-Europeans" created strains within the United States, which Du Bois was among the first to notice. On the one hand, many white Southern politicos resented the notion that their beloved nation was being "overrun" by these "non-Europeans." On the other hand, there were those—particularly among the Northern elite—who were happy to see their nation accumulate more markets for export goods and more cheap labor to be exploited.

All the while, Du Bois continued to labor tirelessly. By 1898 the Bureau of Labor Statistics of the U.S. government had begun publishing some of Du Bois's special studies that focused on African Americans, particularly in the South. Yet amid the blizzard of memoranda and conference papers, lectures and pamphlets, books, and detailed letters, Du Bois endured a staggering blow that was to pierce his psyche. It was in April 1899 that the ghoulish lynching of Sam Hose—an African-American farmer from the area surrounding Atlanta—occurred. Hose got into a bruising fracas with a white counterpart, which led to the latter being shot and killed. In retaliation, a white lynch mob brutally tortured, immolated, and killed Hose. As was often the case with these ritual executions, the mob of thousands of Euro-Americans who had witnessed this outrage and/or killed him distributed Hose's various body parts as souvenirs. Du Bois was depressed and stunned by this macabre exercise and promptly marched to the office of the editor of the local paper, Joel Chandler Harris—soon to garner fame as a popular writer notorious for vicious stereotypes of African Americans—to deliver a protest for publication. As he walked in distress to his appointed designation, Du Bois little knew that like ham hocks in the window of a butcher shop, Hose's mangled knuckles were on display in a store window—when he espied this ghastly sight, Du Bois could hardly contain himself and wept uncontrollably.

It was beginning to dawn on him that scholarly productivity—no matter how enlightening or rational or exquisite—was simply not enough to confront the mammoth magnitude of prejudice and hate that African Americans had to confront. Hose's lynching occurred as another monumental event occurred—the brutal coup that dislodged African-American officeholders in Wilmington, North Carolina, which also led to those that voted for them fleeing far and wide. As if that were not enough, it was during this same period of angst and pain that his son passed away. He had come down with diphtheria, a common illness of an unhealthy era, and died on May 24, 1899. As his son was wailing in agony, Du Bois frantically had sought to reach one of the few African-American physicians in segregated Atlanta who would be willing to treat his rapidly diminishing loved one. Of course, white doctors would not deign to attend to an infant not of their racial group. Infant mortality among African Americans was endemic during this era, which Du Bois well knew, but—unsurprisingly—the shock of this tragedy being visited upon his own family was almost too much to bear. In his much-honored book, *The Souls of Black Folk*, he reserves pride of place for reflections on this catastrophic heartbreak. "A perfect life was his," he moaned, "all joy and love, with tears to make it brighter—sweet as a summer's day beside the Housatonic. The world loved him; the women kissed his curls, the men looked gravely into his wonderful eyes, and the children hovered and fluttered about him" (*Southern Workman*, 28, Apr. 1899, 149–151). Burying one's child is thought to be a tragic calamity that indelibly marks the parent; certainly this was true in Du Bois's case. More than this, this misfortune also left a deep imprint on his marriage, and though he and Nina Gomer remained married for decades, there was a certain distance between them after their son's death—a distance that was often punctuated by frequent periods of separation between them.

Du Bois had witnessed Jim Crow up close as a teenager in Nashville, and now its poison had permeated the fabric of his being with the horrific Hose lynching and the death of his firstborn. Such experiences were moving him perceptibly from the tranquil groves of the academy to the rough-and-tumble world of activism. This transition would inexorably involve a bruising confrontation with the strategy and tactics of Booker T. Washington, yet, ironically, his stellar academic credentials led to Tuskegee offering him a post for the 1900–1901 academic year. That is how he found himself in February 1900 at Washington's campus—at the Wizard's invitation—in what amounted to a job interview. Amid the buildings mostly constructed by the labor of students and bearing the names of the titans of Northern capital—Phelps, Huntington, Parker—was a larger community where Jim Crow reigned.

Simultaneously, Du Bois was being considered for a high-level post as an administrator of the public schools of Washington, DC, the capital city of the rising power that was the United States. Although Washington, DC was racially segregated, it was not segregated to the extent of Atlanta or Tuskegee, and thus it held some attraction for the Du Boises. Moreover, though it had yet to assume the title it garnered in the 1960s—"Chocolate City"—Washington, DC contained a sizeable African-American population (a real attraction for a social scientist of Du Bois's bent) and numerous amply stocked libraries and archives, notably the library at Howard University (the self-proclaimed "capstone" of Negro education) and the Library of Congress, not to mention what was to become the U.S. National Archives.

As it turned out, offers were tendered neither from Tuskegee nor Washington, DC, and the disappointed Du Bois had good reason to believe that Booker T. Washington was behind it all. A simmering conflict between these two men was now metastasizing into a boiling and rancorous dispute, the ramifications of which were to shape Black America for decades to come.

Licking his wounds, Du Bois returned to what had become his second home, Western Europe. It was a propitious moment to do so. In 1896 Ethiopia resisted Italy's attempts at colonization and, therefore, became a beacon of hope and pride for Black America. A few years later, war erupted in South Africa between the British Empire and the "Boers," or the descendants of the mostly Dutch migrants who had begun migrating to the Cape of Good Hope in the mid-seventeenth century; if nothing else, Africans had reason to think that white racial solidarity might be fraying. Then in 1905, Japan defeated Russia in a war that seemed to suggest that the rapaciousness of white supremacy had hit a formidable stumbling block. In the middle of this vortex of change, Du Bois crossed the Atlantic once more, this time to England and France.

From July 23 to 25 of this fateful year, 1900, he attended the first Pan-African Conference in London as Chairman of the Committee on the Address, and later that summer, he decamped to France, where he served as an organizer of the American Negro Exhibit, which was part of the U.S. building at the World's Fair in Paris. Both stops were important but, as it turned out, it was London that echoed through the ages for it was here where the radical idea was formalized that peoples of African descent should unite based on their commonality of concern, that is, opposition to labor exploitation and support for decolonization. This idea, though intended for African people wherever they might be, was led by those of the diaspora, such as Du Bois, the Trinidadian barrister Henry Sylvester Williams, the prominent African-American educator Anna Julia Cooper, and Benito Sylvain of Haiti, who exuded this reinvigorated Pan-Africanism as he had served as a top aide to Ethiopia's emperor.

Hence, at Westminster Town Hall in southwest London and on leafy Chancery Lane, Du Bois presented profound words that continue to resonate to this very day. In the opening paragraph of this manifesto addressed "To the Nations of the World" appear the tossed-down gauntlet: "[T]he problem of the twentieth century is the problem of the colour line, the question as to how far differences of race, which show themselves chiefly in the colour of the skin and the texture of the hair, are going to be made, hereafter, the basis of denying to over half the world the right of sharing to their utmost ability the opportunities and privileges of modern civilization." Du Bois urged that peoples of African descent "take courage, strive ceaselessly, and fight bravely, [so that] they may prove to the world their incontestable right to be counted among the great brotherhood of mankind" (Du Bois, *Souls*, 2007, 99–102).

This crucial gathering did not emerge from out of the blue, for African-American interest in Africa had not flagged over the centuries. This was reflected in the names of religious denominations (e.g., the African Methodist Episcopal faith or the Abyssinian Baptist Church in Harlem) or the continued interest in Ethiopia or the efforts by African-American missionaries in Africa. Thus, it was not terribly surprising when this July 1900 meeting proved to be such a rousing success, including the formation a permanent organization—the Pan-African Association—with Du Bois as the Vice President of the U.S. branch.

The ambitions of this trailblazing meeting were rather modest: there was no full-throated demand of immediate independence of the African and West Indian colonies, for example. Yet it was undeniable that this London confab was a shot over the bow at the colonizers and that a turning point had been reached that signaled the imminent demise of colonialism, which had denuded Africa in particular of wealth, just as the slave trade had been responsible for uprooting millions of Africans and depositing them in the Americas as slave laborers.

Thus, what came to be known as the First Pan-African Conference was an auspicious opening of what was to become a critically important century. That Dr. Du Bois was present at the creation of this new departure was an indication that this man, who had emblazoned his name in the annals of academia, was now entertaining broader goals. That these ambitions would bring him into conflict with Booker T. Washington was easily foreseeable.

3

A Life of Protest

Du Bois's tenure at Atlanta University occurred as the nation in which he resided witnessed an ossifying of Jim Crow. It was in 1896 that the U.S. Supreme Court in the profoundly significant case, *Plessy v. Ferguson*, placed its imprimatur on the system of "separate but equal" (which amounted to separate and unequal); this racist system often descended to the level of absurdity, for example, "separate but equal" graveyards, "separate but equal" Bibles to swear witnesses in courtrooms, or mandates that workers of various ancestries were forbidden to peer out of the same windows in factories. This totalizing—actually totalitarian—regime seemed so pervasive and formidable that, inevitably, a number of African Americans decided that the better part of wisdom was to find a way to make peace with Jim Crow by rationalizing deprivation of the vote and lynching and all the rest. Foremost among these advocates was Booker T. Washington, who seemingly had taken the measure of Du Bois—whom he probably accurately envisioned as a potentially dangerous rival—by inviting him for a job interview (or, more likely, an inspection) in February 1900.

While the nascent Progressives were not above pilfering the policy clothes of Populists, the latter were swimming toward the mainstream. Washington similarly seemed to adopt as his own some of the ideas and data generated by Du Bois. Thus, in 1901, Washington founded the National Business League—an organization of actual and would-be entrepreneurs—which became the apex of the Tuskegee notion that building enterprises and generating prosperity was the surest way to confront

Jim Crow. Yet in assessing the promise and prospects of this still negligible class of businessmen, Washington had to rely upon studies conducted by Du Bois.

Still, despite this reliance, Washington—like many of the white businessmen of the North upon whom he depended—was deeply suspicious of African-American intellectuals like Du Bois, fearful of their critique of accommodation to Jim Crow and the way a rejection of the separate-but-equal doctrine could influence Negroes at large. Washington's benefactors in the North were suspicious of Du Bois's ideas about unions and his developing socialist ideology, which—they thought—could portend expropriation of their wealth and enterprises. On the other hand, there were some among Washington's coterie who decided that co-opting Du Bois might be the wiser course. Thus, in 1902, Du Bois received an invitation to leave Atlanta for Tuskegee with a promise of a substantial increase in salary. Among those counseling that he do so were New Yorkers including the financier Jacob Schiff; the president of the Long Island Railroad, William Baldwin Jr.; and other captains of industry such as Robert C. Ogden, J. G. Phelps Stokes, and George Foster Peabody.

Understandably, Du Bois proceeded cautiously in mounting full-fledged opposition to the powerful Washington. After all, Du Bois was a young man with a family and, given his trenchantly articulated viewpoints, uncertain job prospects. He had reason to think that the Tuskegee Wizard had not only blocked a possible job in Washington, DC, but had also "facilitated" his failed visit to Alabama in February 1900. Washington was not a man to trifle with, in other words. This much Du Bois knew. Thus, a scant year after his earlier journey to rejection in Tuskegee, February 1901 found Du Bois again in Alabama, this time for a conference in which Washington's cautious ideas served as the centerpiece. An impressed Du Bois took to the pages of the widely circulated *Harper's Weekly* to sing the praises of this gathering, brushing aside misgivings (Du Bois, "Results," 1901, 641). Du Bois even expressed interest in spending personal and intimate time with Washington, though apparently this wish was not fulfilled. For his part, in his lavishly praised autobiography, Washington recalled fondly the time before Du Bois's later visit to Alabama: "[T]here came to me what I might describe as almost the greatest surprise of my life," he said brightly. "Some good ladies in Boston arranged a public meeting in the interests of Tuskegee," which said Washington with his usual class-tinged brio, "was attended by large numbers of the best people of Boston, of both races." Washington addressed the assembled, along with Paul Laurence Dunbar, and, the Wizard added pointedly, "Dr. W.E.B. Du Bois read an original sketch" (Washington, 1986, 270).

Washington, born a slave in 1856 on a Virginia farm, was a mere twelve years older than Du Bois—but his experiences in bondage and growing up in the harshness of the South gave him a perspective that differed substantially from that of his academically trained counterpart. By dint of tireless labor and shrewdness, Washington had built an empire headquartered at Tuskegee, but he also had a far-reaching influence on the Baptist church—the largest of the Black denominations whose parishioners extended throughout Black America. His allies were potentates of the leading Black fraternal orders. He controlled the editorial policies of nearly all of the Black weekly newspapers through subsidies and, in a few cases, through outright ownership. Through his close ties to the presidencies of Theodore Roosevelt and William Howard Taft, he controlled lucrative patronage posts, a power that was wielded deftly to reward his backers—and punish those not so blessed. Crossing Washington was a must to avoid.

What Du Bois coined the "Tuskegee Machine" was the confluence of Washington's relationships with white philanthropists, politicians, and scholars; his monopoly on the Black press, and thereby his disproportionate sway on public opinion; and the concentration of influence at Tuskegee Institute through the efforts of Washington and his secretary, Emmett Scott. The Tuskegee Machine allowed Washington to control the funding of Black institutions, appointments to prestigious posts, and the careers of those who opposed him. His funding came largely from white Northern capitalists and employers who wanted to shape the Southern Black masses into profitable laborers who could crush the demands of white workers and unions and help to curb the spread of socialism. Funders also had a vested interest in suppressing the Black intelligentsia and keeping them out of positions of power. Hence, Washington's public philosophy was useful to their aims, and they poured astronomical sums of money into the Tuskegee Machine to achieve their ends (Du Bois, *Autobio*, 2007).

Du Bois presumably did not know—but well could have suspected—that the crafty Washington was, typically, a double-dealer. That is, though piously disclaiming any interest in voting rights for African Americans, he covertly worked behind the scenes to fund lawyers to challenge suffrage restrictions in Alabama and Louisiana. He also battled racist discrimination that stained railway cars in Tennessee and elsewhere (Lewis, 1993). If Du Bois suspected this kind of progressive activity, there would be little reason for him to challenge this deviousness—not to mention that confronting Washington seemed to be a sure route to ostracism, isolation, and, possibly, financial disaster. Thus, Du Bois was upset with Washington's *public* posture, which seemed to portend a great leap backward for Black America.

Besides his prodigious labor and the desire to avoid running afoul of the influential Washington, there were other reasons for Du Bois to avoid ensnaring tensions: A few years after the death of his son, he and his wife were blessed to give birth to a daughter, Nina Yolande. Moreover, Du Bois was developing friendships—with the Atlanta educator John Hope, in the first place—that tended to occupy more of his time. Yet, as things turned out, his talks with the insightful Hope served as a sounding board for his increasingly distressed opinions of Washington's initiatives. Thus, it would be an error to assume that Du Bois's diplomatic effort to avoid alienating the powerful Washington was akin to a surrender to Tuskegee's agenda. Du Bois continued to call for more analytical studies of Black America on the premise that knowledge was a useful precondition for racial progress; by publishing a detailed study of one typical Georgia county that contained more than a modicum of African Americans, Du Bois was engaged in a kind of proto-political warfare (Du Bois, "The Negro," 1901). Besides, even Washington—a man to be feared—could hardly object to gathering data.

In line with his effort to convey basic data to the nation, Du Bois penned a comprehensive examination of the economic realities of the dual education system in the former slave South, which doomed African-American youth to inferior education and diminished life opportunities. Du Bois painstakingly showed the awful inadequacies of a separate-but-equal education and demonstrated that much of the money to support this obscenity came directly from African Americans themselves. Thus, in his view, financial support from the U.S. government for education was necessary. Simultaneously, he produced two nearly book-length studies on the inferior housing Negroes had to endure (Du Bois, "The Home," 1901). Immersing himself in the grim realities of Black America, Du Bois produced an analysis of the impact of the economic downturn that gripped the nation at the turn of the century and how the downturn had devastated African-American lives (Du Bois, "The Savings," 1901).

Du Bois was a pioneer in exposing the grimy underbelly of the convict lease system, which led to mass arrests of African-American men in particular, after which they were turned over to plantations, large corporations, and small business owners for brutal labor. The "crime" for which these men (and women) were most often convicted was vagrancy: the inability to prove that they were employed at a given moment. They could also be conscripted into the pernicious system of unfree labor for other petty offenses like riding a train without a ticket, speaking too loudly, engaging in sexual or intimate relations with white women, or switching employers without permission. If the indigent African Americans could not pay the steep fines and fees assessed, their sentence of hard labor was often extended indefinitely. Many died of disease, accident, gross abuse, and even homicide. The purpose of the convict lease system was ultimately to force newly freed Blacks to comply with white ruling class labor demands, to curb African-American freedom and free will, and to accelerate Black disenfranchisement. In a prescient comment, Du Bois concluded that by referring to "that sort of social protest and revolt which we call crime," we elide the wider point that "we must look for remedy in the same reform of these wrong social conditions, and not in intimidation, savagery, or the legalized slavery of men" (Du Bois, "The Spawn," 1901).

As a relentless social science investigator, Du Bois was privy to information about the condition of African Americans that made him indisposed to accept Washington's roseate acceptance of Jim Crow. Thus, it was easy to see why Du Bois may have concluded that Washington was too clever by a half and had to be confronted. Washington's public opposition to the antiracist struggle, irrespective of his progressive subterfuges on behalf of positive causes, were too demobilizing and damaging, particularly in the midst of the unfortunately predictable waves of lynching. As such, in mid-1901, Du Bois wrote a review of Washington's highly praised autobiography in a widely circulated journal. It was a "partial history of the steps which made him a group leader," Du Bois sniffed, that exposed "but glimpses of the real struggle which he has had for leadership." Yes, conceded Du Bois, it was true that Washington had not invented that which had brought him fame (and scorn from a growing number of African-American activists), in other words, industrial education or training Blacks for proletarian posts (bricklaying, carpentry, mechanics, etc.). The problems were, among other things, that these occupations were rapidly disappearing because of automation or fiercely racist competition, and that this training at Tuskegee was accompanied by a disdain for the liberal arts, the study of foreign languages, and rigorous social science research that had propelled Du Bois. Du Bois also argued that the autobiography glossed over how much Washington compromised his ideals in order to secure the support of white elites. What Washington did, charged Du Bois, was to "put life, unlimited energy and perfect faith into this programme" and thereby converted the program into virtual dogma. Washington had triumphed, Du Bois said accusingly, because he had accepted Jim Crow in the South and "by singular insight he intuitively grasped the spirit of the age that was dominating the North," in other words, the "spirit of commercialism." In contemplating the Wizard's philosophy, Du Bois was aghast: "it is as though Nature must needs make men a little narrow to give them force." Du Bois went further, saying, "[Washington] pictures as the height of absurdity a black boy studying a French grammar in the midst of weeds and dirt. One wonders how Socrates or St. Francis of Assisi would receive this!" (Du Bois, "The Evolution," 1901).

After crossing the Rubicon and confronting Washington publicly, Du Bois kept up a steady drumfire of opposition against the Wizard. While the fabled Tuskegee Machine was counseling—at least publicly—meek acceptance of the vulgarity of racist segregation, Du Bois led a delegation of African Americans to protest the notion that the public library in Atlanta should be confined to whites only (Du Bois, "The Opening," 1902).

While Washington was telling African Americans to keep their heads down and labor tirelessly and silently, Du Bois, with rising temper, averred that his people "never will abate one jot or tittle from his determination to attain in this land perfect equality before the law with his fellow citizens" (Du Bois, "Hopeful," 1902).

Meanwhile, as Du Bois was raising an ever more insistent voice against accommodation to Jim Crow, Washington officially disagreed. John Hope, the antilynching crusader Ida B. Wells-Barnett, Du Bois, and a growing coterie, who Du Bois considered to be the Talented Tenth, were appalled by Washington's attitude, and they were increasingly unafraid to say so. Among this increasingly disgruntled group was the famed attorney and novelist Charles Waddell Chesnutt. "I take a firm stand for manhood suffrage, and the enforcement of the constitutional amendments. I stake no stock whatever," he groused to Du Bois, "in these disenfranchisement constitutions" (Aptheker, 1973). These intellectuals perceived accurately that Washington had another agenda, namely to demonize his opponents with slighting words, which was not only anti-intellectual (and quite dangerous for the besieged community of African Americans, who needed thoughtful strategies to escape from their plight) but was also dangerous in the mounting climate of the violent and powerful Ku Klux Klan and other proponents of Jim Crow. In the argot of the era, Du Bois and his comrades were deemed to be "uppity," and such an explosive charge in the then-prevailing climate could lead directly to fatalities, as the history of lynching amply demonstrated.

Yet Du Bois and his allies would not retreat. Soon, their dispute was to be characterized as a death-match between the Tuskegee Machine and the Talented Tenth. This was true—but it was more than this. For from the bad old days of slavery to the exhilaration of its abolition, and beyond, there had been a fundamental ideological split among African Americans that inflamed the Du Bois–Washington confrontation.

Prior to emancipation in the United States, there were those like Frederick Douglass, who counseled confrontation of the slave system, and Martin Delaney, another justly celebrated abolitionist, who looked abroad for aid to and solidarity with the enslaved. During the "nadir" of African-American history, there were those like Amy Jacques Garvey who saw demands on the U.S. government as futile and a return to Africa as the best solution for African descendants, while radicals including African Blood Brotherhood cofounder Grace Campbell demanded the U.S. state redistribute wealth and resources to the benefit of Black people. The Congress of Racial Equality's James Farmer and the Nation of Islam's Malcolm X debated the merits of integration versus separation, respectively, in 1962—an ideological split that also distinguished "Queen Mother" of the Civil Rights Movement Septima Clarke from the Black nationalist and

---

Ku Klux Klan

The Ku Klux Klan (KKK) was formed in December 1865 in Pulaski, Tennessee, by General Nathan Bedford Forrest and a group of former confederates. This secret society originated to maintain the white supremacy it believed was ordained by God. Also known as the "invisible empire," the KKK sought to prevent the purported "contamination" of white blood, practice "pure" Americanism, save what was called Anglo-Saxon civilization, and secure the alleged chastity of white womanhood. Likewise, it took action to defend "racial law" against the Freedmen's Bureau and its "Carpetbagger" and "Scalawag" supporters who, the Klan claimed, humiliated and debased the South by empowering and enfranchising "lust-crazed" African Americans. These white-robed vigilantes purported to be a holy, chivalric, manly, and patriotic organization that operated without prejudice, injustice, or malice. In reality, throughout the Southern states, the KKK attempted to preserve white domination through lynchings, torture, sexual assault, and other acts of terrorism against Black men and women.

Though Forrest attempted to disband the KKK in December 1869, and the 1871 anti-Klan Third Force Act resulted in its assumed weakening, the organization was resuscitated by William Joseph Simmons at a meeting of thirty-four men convened near Atlanta, Georgia, on October 26, 1915. There, the Knights of the Ku Klux Klan—inspired by D. W. Griffith's infamous film *The Birth of a Nation*—was founded. Members pledged allegiance to the "ABC" of the fraternal order—America First, Benevolence, Clannishness—and also promised to uphold the legacy and deeds of the Reconstruction-era KKK. It has existed with varying degrees of popularity since its rebirth.

---

former communist "Queen Mother" Audley Moore. Today, there are those like Senator Maxine Waters who work for change within the U.S. political system, and others like Black Radical Congress co-founder Rose Brewer who advocate a combination of grassroots activism and Black internationalism to implement change.

It was during the uncertain post-Reconstruction years that Du Bois published his classic and perhaps best-known book, *The Souls of Black Folk*, comprising a series of essays that included a devastating critique of one Booker T. Washington. A mere 265 pages, this book—one of the classics in the English language—emerged from its Chicago publisher in 1903 and catapulted Du Bois to center stage in Black America. Over the decades, it has sold hundreds of thousands of copies. Several of its chapters had been published earlier—in somewhat altered form—in magazines; however, the essay on Booker T. Washington, which was considered radical and bold at the time, was largely new, and it was momentous in that it publicized the fundamental differences that separated the two men. These differences led to the development of the Niagara Movement in 1905 and then, in 1909, its successor, the National Association for the Advancement of Colored People (NAACP). The influence of *The Souls of Black Folk* ricocheted not only throughout Black America but also the Pan-African world. Casely Hayford, a West African lawyer and author who was then making his mark in the nation that was to be called Ghana, told Du Bois of the "pleasure" he had derived from his book (Aptheker, 1973, 76).

As is apparent in the book, Du Bois had obvious affection for his people. He clearly believed that they had a special and ennobling mission to perform for humankind, as their oppressed condition was encased in their great and dramatic artistry. The book radiates with what could easily be characterized as a Black nationalist consciousness, which prefigures this trend's efflorescence in the movement of the Jamaica-born Marcus Garvey (who, ironically, famously crossed swords with Du Bois shortly after Washington's death in 1915). The book also reflects a keen awareness of Du Bois's realization that African Americans were tied inexorably to darker peoples worldwide—which, too, was a response to his nation's most recent imperialist turn, as evidenced by the seizure of Hawaii and the ouster of Spain from Puerto Rico, Cuba, and the Philippines.

Each essay makes a significant contribution to understanding the racial, political, economic, cultural, and affective conditions of African Americans at the time. One essay gives a touching assessment of Alexander Crummell, a man who had served as a role model for Du Bois. Another provides a painfully explicit treatment of the death of his firstborn son, Burghardt. At a time when those of African origin allegedly lacked humanity, the very title of this remarkable book forcefully rejected such a notion. This distillation of the humanity that characterized African Americans—a radical thought for the time—continues to give the book vitality, even as the idea of their inhumanity has dissipated (or taken on different valences). Du Bois accomplishes this exacting task by citing Negro spirituals—of the kind that the Fisk Jubilee Singers had made famous—throughout. Du Bois's unique ability to evoke the awful present while peering over the horizon to detect the shape of the future is no better glimpsed than in the signature line of the volume: "[T]he problem of the Twentieth Century," he intoned portentously at the dawn of this new century, "is the problem of the color line," a weighty point that he had enunciated previously. It was Du Bois who remarked that "the relation of the darker to the lighter races of men in Asia and Africa, in America and the islands of the sea" was the crux of decades to unfold (Du Bois, *Souls*, 1903, 35, 49, 59). Yet in framing this question, Du Bois presupposed that it was a problem that was hardly insoluble (if it were, it would hardly be worth a remark), and thus, he anticipated the anticolonial wave that was to envelope the planet by the time of his death.

That is not all. Again, Du Bois posed a question in this notable volume that continues to resonate: "How does it feel to be a problem?" With these few words, he captured the vexing dilemma of African Americans, who could not be seen in their humanity or even as distinct individuals but, instead, as little more than exemplars of a "problem people." He did not stop there. It was in this book that Du Bois articulated yet another theme that was to illuminate the Black condition while igniting a debate that rages to this day. For it was here that Du Bois remarked that the African American "ever feels his two-ness," that is, being "an American, a Negro; two souls, two thoughts, two unreconciled strivings." In other words, the African American has "two warring ideals in one dark body, whose dogged strength alone keeps it from being torn asunder." Heretofore, dissenting and radical African-American thinkers had—like Martin Delany or Henry Highland Garnet—counseled expatriation or separation as the preferred road for the Negro. Those like Douglass had advised that complete assimilation was the way out of the awfulness of racism. Du Bois sliced the Gordian knot—or, perhaps more precisely, untied it—by acknowledging that there was a recurring tension between the two viewpoints that was unavoidable. *Souls of Black Folk* has, in short, proven to be a book for the ages.

Despite the wealth of ideas in the book, what riveted the attention of many readers of that time was Du Bois's frank airing of his differences with Booker T. Washington, a man whose power to retaliate was both fearsome and predictable. Du Bois's challenge was not merely articulated on his own behalf; he purported to speak for the Talented Tenth who railed against the Tuskegee Wizard's disparagement of intellectual accomplishment and political engagement. Du Bois's book caused a debate to erupt in Black America that was to result in a more formal and organizational challenge to Tuskegee's hegemony. Du Bois had been a man of words and study, but with the publication of this book, he was to be propelled more overtly into the arena of activism. Soon his name was to equal that of Booker T. Washington in fame and high regard.

Buoyed by this newfound recognition, which included more requests for public speaking and literary contributions, which in turn brought larger and larger audiences (often predominantly of Euro-Americans, interestingly enough), he chose not to dilute his message to make it go down easier. Instead, he sharpened his sword, affirming that racism in the United States was a form—albeit an especially virulent form—of elitism and class oppression. This, too, was a radical breakthrough of sorts, marking a great leap forward from the thinking of Douglass, Crummell, and, certainly, Washington. This bombshell was delivered in Manhattan at the Twentieth Century Club, many of whose members were both outraged and frightened by the explosion of labor militancy, anarchism, and socialism

PLESSY V. FERGUSON

In *Plessy v. Ferguson*, the U.S. Supreme Court ruled on May 18, 1896, that in mandating "equal but separate accommodations for the white and colored races," the state of Louisiana had not violated the civil rights of the "octoroon" petitioner Homer Plessy. Similar to the strategy employed half a century later during the modern civil rights movement, Plessy had been voluntarily arrested in New Orleans in 1892 as part of a coordinated challenge by African-American elites to upend segregation.

Louisiana District Court Judge John Howard Ferguson upheld the Jim Crow law. Plessy's lawyer, Albion Winegar Tourgée, argued Jim Crow laws denied Negroes due process under the Fourteenth Amendment because the prevalence of "race mixing" in Louisiana made the determination of race both arbitrary and virtually impossible. He also contended racial segregation violated the Thirteenth Amendment by upholding the foundational features of slavery.

The Supreme Court ruled the social distinction of the "races" was natural and did not infringe upon Negroes' political rights. It also ruled that states had the "universally recognized power" to separate the "races"; that because the Louisiana Law mandated separate *and* equal facilities, there was no imposition of inferiority on the "colored race," namely African Americans; and that because each "race" was forbidden from using the other's cars and facilities, each "race" was treated equally under the law. With only Justice John Marshall Harlan dissenting, the ruling in *Plessy v. Ferguson* made segregation legal across the nation until it was overturned by in *Brown v. Board of Education* in 1954.

that Du Bois's words about class seemed to portend. In recent years, Populists had rocked the countryside while labor militants in the Knights of Labor had been busily organizing factories, and anarchists were enmeshed in the "propaganda of the deed," which did not exclude targeted assassinations of the rich and the powerful. Socialists were on the march on both sides of the Atlantic, and the Industrial Workers of the World (whose greatest strength was in the mines and timberlands of the far West and the vessels that delivered both exports and imports) had had a spurt of growth as well. Du Bois, who had witnessed many of these trends while in Europe, seemed to be suggesting that the plight of African Americans was not far distant from the situation faced by those targeted by the radical left and that an alliance of more than convenience was in order. He would continue with such a position in the coming decades as he, in collaboration with radicals like Shirley Graham, James E. Jackson, and Doxey Wilkerson, moved decidedly leftward.

Du Bois's perception was fueled by associations he had developed, among which was his tie to S. M. Sexton of the United Mine Workers (UMW). It was early in 1903 that Sexton informed Du Bois that his union had "always welcomed the Negro" into its ranks. "Many Negroes hold responsible offices both in local and state organizations" of the UMW, he said (Aptheker, 1973, 50). Of course, it was in the very nature of their labor that miners—enmeshed in what may have been the most hazardous occupation of all—exuded solidarity; in the bleakness and darkness underground with sooty faces all around, obliterating distinctiveness, and a necessity to rely upon one's fellow worker in order to leave the mine alive, miners had come to exemplify a class solidarity across racial lines that contrasted sharply with the policies of other unions. Nevertheless, the members of the Twentieth Century Club had to realize that failing to ease the burden pressing down on the Negro was likely to bring such an alliance closer to fruition. (Du Bois's weighty words were reported widely; see *Boston Transcript*, Feb. 21, 1904; *San Antonio Gazette*, Apr. 17, 1904; *Des Moines Register Leader*, Oct. 19, 1904; *Savannah News*, Oct. 19, 1904; *Denver News*, Oct. 19, 1904; *Chicago Tribune*, Dec. 16, 1904.) Du Bois did not reassure these elites when he announced shortly thereafter, "I have many socialistic beliefs," not to mention "sympathy with the movement" itself (Aptheker, 1973, 82).

Of course, the high and mighty could attempt to ignore Du Bois and give even more support to the Tuskegee Machine. Thus, Du Bois sought to block this option by escalating his assault on Booker T. Washington, informing a reporter from the journalistic empire of William Randolph Hearst that "we refuse to kiss the hands that smite us"—unlike the Alabamian. He went on to say that "the way for black [people] today to make these rights the heritage of their children is to struggle for them unceasingly, and [if] they fail, die trying" (*World Today*, Apr. 1904, 521–523). But Du Bois chose to assail not just the puppet but also the puppeteer. For he pursued the then-audacious maneuver of denouncing the Jim Crow titans of the U.S. Senate, including "Pitchfork" Ben Tillman of South Carolina and James Vardaman of Mississippi, the two leading voices of not only Negro disenfranchisement but overall defenestration (Du Bois, *The Problem*, 1905, 1324–1325). Today, it is difficult to imagine how courageous it was to criticize these men who were not above launching lynch mobs.

Undoubtedly, Du Bois's example caused others to enter the fray. Foremost among these was William Monroe Trotter, a fellow Harvard man who continued to reside in Boston, where he toiled as a gutsy, plucky writer whose frequent flayings of the Tuskegee Machine rivaled those of Du Bois. At a now-renowned event in Boston, Trotter received word that Washington was coming to town to address members of his National Negro Business League who were gathering at the African Methodist Episcopal Zion church on Columbus Avenue. It was a hot summer day in 1903—July 30 to be exact—when Trotter and his hearty band erupted and seemingly rushed the podium to confront Washington physically. Pandemonium reigned, along with shouting and cries of anguish. Punches were thrown. Reportedly, a police officer who had rushed to the scene was stabbed. Washington could only gape in amazement as some of Trotter's comrades bellowed in his direction, "We don't like you"—a sentiment that they then were acting out in dramatic fashion (*Boston Globe*, July 31, 1903; see also Stewart, 1977, 50–51).

The Trotter-led demarche was symptomatic of a growing militancy in Black America, a refusal to accept supinely the veil of oppression. The convulsion in Boston was a rejection of Washington—his surreptitious activism notwithstanding—and his call to build enterprises, a directive that made no sense considering that, as Ida B. Wells had clearly exposed in her courageous journalism, Negro entrepreneurs were a prime target of lynch mobs, as their very existence violated the basic precepts of white supremacy. As difficult as the struggle might have been, there was no escape from the battle for basic rights, particularly voting rights.

Yet just as Du Bois had sought to reconcile the contrasting philosophies of Douglass and Delany by writing eloquently about "double-consciousness"—the ability to think of oneself as both "American" and "African"—Du Bois continued to think (at least for a while) that he could bridge the choppy waters that separated Trotter from Washington. In addressing the influential donor George Peabody, for example, he criticized Trotter's "lack of judgment" and noted that he possessed "less and less faith in Mr. Washington," who was "leading the way backward" (Aptheker, 1973, 67–68). Du Bois also continued to seek an entente between Trotter and Washington, including planning for a confab to that end to be held in Manhattan at Carnegie Hall in early 1904. It was an opportunity for a "heart to heart talk with Mr. Washington," Du Bois said hopefully, though he must have known that the Wizard would not have found the agenda appealing given that first on this list was "full political rights on the same term as other Americans"—though it was followed by a concession to the Tuskegee Machine: a call for "industrial education for the masses." Yet Du Bois made it clear that the Atlanta Compromise was not the guiding light he had in mind for this gathering. "The general watch word must be," he concluded, "not to put further dependence on the help of the whites but to organize for self-help, encouraging 'manliness without defiance, conciliation without servility'" (Aptheker, 1973, 53; see also Aptheker, 1949, 345–351).

Agreeing that "we ought to have as far as possible, all shades of opinion represented," Washington seemed to meet Du Bois halfway; however, he also said that "our people are in the South [and] we should be very sure that there is a large element in the conference who actually know Southern conditions by experience" and "to [not] depend too much on mere theory and untried schemes of Northern colored people"—a direct jab at Du Bois's

Talented Tenth (Aptheker, 1973, 53–54). Ritualistic bowing to the necessity of Negro unity in a hostile environment ultimately could not bridge the increasingly wide chasm that separated Trotter from Washington, and the Carnegie Hall gathering predictably failed to lead to an entente between the warring factions.

This was so in no small part because, perhaps, even more than Trotter, it was Du Bois who was growing more distant from Washington. While Du Bois was sympathetic to unions, Washington thought they were little more than folly. Washington was disdainful toward women's suffrage; Du Bois decidedly was not. Washington tended toward xenophobia and nativism, a position Du Bois did not share. While Du Bois spent most of his life in cosmopolitan sites such as Philadelphia, Atlanta, and New York, Washington resided in rural Alabama. There was a fundamental difference in these men's respective ideologies that simply making nice with each other could not overcome. It was inevitable that their paths would diverge. Yet, more than the individual differences that separated these two men, their respective paths represented alternative modes of handling Jim Crow—resistance versus accommodation. This difference took organizational form when Du Bois helped to initiate the Niagara Movement and then the NAACP.

Meanwhile, the opposition that had congealed to block the ascendancy of Washington's ideology had broadened into a full-scale challenge that would transform Black America and the nation as a whole. On January 13, 1905, a meeting was held at William Trotter's office in Boston. The capital of the Bay State was an appropriate venue for this important confab for although Boston was a citadel of abolitionism, it was not above enforcing Jim Crow measures. Hence, at this meeting a decision was made to seek a meeting with President Theodore Roosevelt with the aim of compelling him to command his attorney general to uphold the Fifteenth Amendment (mandating the right to vote for the formerly enslaved) in cases that reached the U.S. Supreme Court. Second, this group demanded that the White House enforce the Interstate Commerce Clause of the Constitution with regard to curbing Jim Crow on trains in particular. Finally, Du Bois's comrades wanted the Roosevelt regime to encourage national aid to education in the neediest states.

These three demands—the right to vote, curbing Jim Crow, and education—were not only to become the hallmark of the Niagara Movement that Du Bois was to spearhead that same year, but were also to be the epicenter of the civil rights earthquake that erupted in the 1950s. Still, Roosevelt chose not to meet with Du Bois and his crew, not least because he was decidedly favorable to the Tuskegee Machine (Aptheker, 1973, 92–93).

Yet in some ways, the opposition from the White House was not the most impregnable roadblock encountered by Du Bois and his fellow dissidents. The fact was that the Tuskegee Machine had a virtual stranglehold on the many newspapers that catered to African Americans, and ever since the first of this genre, *Freedom's Journal*, had come into existence in 1827, these organs had been essential in shaping consciousness and attitudes among this oft-besieged community. Thus, Du Bois complained bitterly that "in order to forestall criticism of certain persons [Washington's] money has been freely furnished [to] a set of Negro newspapers in the principal cities," and the continuously lengthening list of Black newspapers included the prime organs in New York City, Chicago, Boston, Washington, and Indianapolis, among other metropolises. And this filthy lucre came directly from Tuskegee. These funds, carped Du Bois, had come in part as a "direct bonus, part in advertising & all of it has been given on condition that these papers print certain matters & refrain from other matters. This movement has been going on now for 3 or 4 years." Du Bois groused in March 1905, "[This situation is now] notorious among well-informed Negroes & a subject of frequent comment" (Aptheker, 1973, 96; see also Meier, 1953).

This was no minor matter, as Washington's veritable control of the newspapers—the major means of communication in an era before radio and mass profusion of telephones—gave him almost untold influence, which made it exceedingly difficult for anyone, including Du Bois, to carve out an alternative agenda to Washington's. Thus, by confronting Tuskegee, Du Bois had placed himself in a vulnerable and sensitive position. Washington had a record of crushing opponents with little hint of mercy. Moreover, Washington had powerful winds at his back, something that Du Bois well knew. As Du Bois put it, "he has the support of the nation, he has the political patronage of the [Roosevelt] administration, he has apparently unlimited cash, he has the ear of the white press" (Aptheker, 1973, 98–102).

As was his wont, Du Bois not only chose to challenge Washington's undue influence on the press but, in addition, chose to construct an alternative. As a college student he had served as the editor of the *Fisk Herald*, and had long expressed an interest in building his own journal to intervene forcefully in the battle of ideas. This opportunity arose in the midst of his jousting with Washington when he accepted the opportunity to serve as editor of *Moon: Illustrated Weekly*, a journal that was published on Saturdays at a printing shop on Memphis's famed Beale Street. He was still teaching at Atlanta University, still conducting groundbreaking research, still challenging Washington, and yet, he found the time to take on another pressing responsibility. *Moon* had the distinction of being the first illustrated weekly in Black America and attracted a slew of advertisers, including real estate companies, dentists, insurance companies, and the like. But then as now, launching a new publication was more than a notion, and this journal that began with such promise in 1905 was defunct within a year. Undaunted, Du Bois quickly proceeded to launch a brand-new publication, *The Horizon: A Journal of the Color Line*, which he owned and edited, though it was printed in Washington, DC.

Both of these publications prefigured his trailblazing editorship of the *Crisis*, which lasted for more than two decades, beginning in 1910. All of these journals displayed his lifelong concerns: a dedicated interest in Africa and a concerted sympathy for the poor and working classes. Clashing with the Tuskegee Machine had led Du Bois to the realization that scholarship was simply not enough to undermine the towering edifice that was Jim Crow, which is why, during the summer of 1905, Du Bois and his comrades found themselves in Canada, where they forged an agenda that meant nothing less than a major course correction for Black America.

4

A Life of Creation

Why would African Americans who were interested in blazing a new trail for Black America in the early years of the twentieth century choose to meet in Canada?

The northern neighbor of the United States had long been a sanctuary for African Americans escaping enslavement; the British Empire, of which Canada had been a prime part, had abolished human bondage well before the United States, and even before that hallowed time, this huge colony had evinced a decided sympathy for abolitionism. More than half a century before Du Bois's arrival in Ontario, Frederick Douglass had arrived in Seneca Falls, New York—about a hundred miles away on Lake Ontario—to demand equality for women. As Douglass and his compatriots arrived in upstate New York, enslaved Africans in the United States were escaping bondage by the thousands by following the "North Star" to freedom in Canada. When John Brown carried out his powerful antislavery raid in 1859 at Harpers Ferry, Virginia, the basic planning for this epochal event had taken place in Canada. Certainly, those who were worried about the reach of the Tuskegee Machine's snooping would feel more comfortable meeting in a jurisdiction where the government was not thought to be an ally of Booker T. Washington. Indeed, during the War of 1812, Canadians—contrary to the way this war was perceived south of the border—harbored the disturbing impression that the United States wanted to seize their homeland. Over the years, Canadians had developed a healthy skepticism of the beneficence of the United States, an ethos shared by many African

Americans; thus, this huge, sprawling nation was a logical choice for a meeting of Black America's leading dissidents. Ironically, these race rebels had wanted to meet in Buffalo, New York, but—predictably—a surge of Jim Crow had compelled them to seek refuge across the border.

Thus it was that twenty-nine men and one teenage boy arrived on July 10, 1905, at the charming and venerable Erie Beach Hotel in Ontario, Canada's richest and most populous province. Their clarion cry had been endorsed by fifty-nine men—subsequently, the dearth of women in what came to be called the Niagara Movement would become a source of contention—from sixteen states and the District of Columbia. The mission they chose to accept was no less than the bold reinvention of the politics of Black America. To that end they devised a structure that included a Press and Public Opinion Committee with the preeminent among them, Du Bois and Trotter, in the leadership, suggestive of the desire to confront the overwhelming control exerted over newspapers by the Tuskegee Machine. Du Bois was also elected as the chief administrative officer of this group and selected to draft the primary document that emerged from their urgent huddling.

Their now-celebrated "Declaration of Principles" bore the indelible imprint of Du Bois's thinking, with its anguished lamentation of what had befallen African Americans and its bitter denunciation of Jim Crow. Likewise, its interest in class-based organizations such as trade unions, although hopeful, was still clear-eyed about the reluctance among many union leaders to embrace the darkest among us.

As things turned out, the founding of the Niagara Movement occurred at a fortuitous moment. While acknowledging that "the color line belts the world," Du Bois remarked that Japan's defeat of Czarist Russia in a bloody war in 1905 signified the beginning of the end of "white supremacy" (Du Bois, *The Color Line*, 1906, 20). This was a startling assertion in light of contemporaneous developments in Du Bois's own backyard. For as Du Bois was drafting his prescient words about white supremacy, one of the worst pogroms against African Americans that had occurred up to that point broke out in Atlanta in September 1906.

By the 1880s, Atlanta had become the hub of an ever-growing economy, with its population soaring from 89,000 in 1890 to 150,000 in 1910. Rapid change and growth are often unsettling; competition for employment is frequently heightened in such circumstances, and reactions against alleged "foreign" elements fuel xenophobia and fear. It was in this context that Tom Watson—who had been catapulted into prominence as a Populist, fighting the malefactors of great wealth—devolved into a race-baiting reactionary, eager to castigate African Americans. When in 1906 local newspapers reported inflammatorily that white women had been assaulted by Black men, a racist and murderous riot took place. Thousands of whites fell upon and viciously beat every African American they could lay hands on. Blacks were ejected from trolley cars and chased, and the sidewalks were soon bathed in blood. Strikingly, a number of African Americans had armed themselves and were able to beat back the howling mobs—but others were not so lucky, falling victim to bloodlust. Among the former, however, was Du Bois, who, in a moment of tension, grabbed a shotgun in order to protect his family. Nonetheless, at most two whites died as a result of this riotous episode, whereas an estimated forty Negroes were killed (Bauerlein, 2001; Mixon, 2005).

Interpretations of the Atlanta Race Riot—and of race-based conflagrations more broadly—differed depending on which side of the color line one fell. Irrespective of the actual cause of violence, whites tended to argue that, because the virtue and purity of their women was at stake, human nature demanded swift and immediate action against any purported or actual assault. The instinct of revenge in white men, they held, was both justifiable and necessary to ensure the safety and security of *both* races; such vengeance reminded Blacks that whites had the advantage in numbers and equipment and a monopoly on force. This imbalance of power demanded the cooperation and discipline of Black leadership to maintain orderly and amicable race relations. By contrast, African Americans understood that white violence was overwhelmingly a product of the defamation, slander, and systematic oppression of Black people. Politicians, police, and ordinary citizens alike continually stirred up fear and hatred against this despised group, unjustly criminalized them, and punished them for defending themselves. For African Americans, then, race riots were a product of white lawlessness and dishonesty, an unfair criminal justice system, structural inequality, disenfranchisement, and the unwillingness and inability of the federal government to enforce laws meant to protect its Black citizens (Graves & Du Bois, 1906).

The riot was a sobering reminder of what Du Bois and the Niagara Movement were up against. As if that were not enough, in that same year—1906—in Brownsville, Texas, a gun battle involving Negro soldiers occurred. This was on the border with Mexico; tensions with this southern neighbor were waxing as a revolution was brewing that would transform this nation and the borderlands generally. In response to this outbreak of violence, all the Negro men of these segregated units were ordered discharged—dishonorably—by President Roosevelt. Ultimately, this harsh decision was reversed, but there is little doubt that this incident soured Du Bois further on Roosevelt and his party, the Republicans, for which those few Negroes who could vote had cast their ballots (Du Bois, *The President*, 1906, 552–553).

These events helped fuel an escalation of Du Bois's ongoing radicalization. In his own journal, *Horizon*, he declared himself a "Socialist-of-the-Path," that is, he endorsed government ownership of railroads, coal mines, and certain factories. As he saw it then, in the "socialistic trend . . . lies the one great hope of the Negro American." He was not in accord with the Socialists on all matters; yet, he added tellingly, "in trend and ideal they are the salt of this present earth" (*Horizon*, Feb. 1907). Shortly thereafter, Du Bois joined the Socialist Party (SP) itself in 1911. That same year, he argued that the SP must develop a position on the race problems and look beyond "European civilization for its program, lest African Americans view them with the same contempt and suspicions as they viewed other whites" (Du Bois, "Socialism Is Too Narrow," 1911). In 1913, a year after he had left the SP, but a year before he joined the editorial board of its journal *New Review*, he likewise observed, "The Negro problem . . . is the great test of the American Socialist," not least because they continued to exclude nonwhites. Despite these critiques, and though his party affiliations varied thereafter, his socialist viewpoints remained with him to his death (Du Bois, "The Economic Aspects," 1910, 488–493).

On the other hand, Du Bois's disaffection with the hegemonic GOP was reflected in a series of what he termed "heart-to-heart talks with the Negro American voter." The first offering in this series noted tartly that "aside from special consideration of race, the policy of the Democratic Party is the best policy for this nation." He chose to elide this party's horrible racism, which included an ongoing alliance in the Deep South with the terrorists known as the Ku Klux Klan, because the Democratic Party was more favorable to the cause of organized labor (and organized labor's cause "is the cause of black laborers") and because the party was seen as more hostile to both monopolies and imperialism, as manifested most dramatically in Cuba and the Philippines (Du Bois, "The Economic," 1910). Thus, Du Bois announced boldly in 1908 that the "Democratic Party deserves a trial at the hands of the Negro" and that "the best thing that can happen in the next election will be a big black [William Jennings] Bryan vote." Bryan was a silver-tongued Nebraskan whose stem-winding perorations had long captured the imagination of the nation (*Horizon*, July 1908). When Bryan was defeated at the hands of Republican William Howard Taft, Du Bois noted acidly that "we did not happen to have the power in the last election of deciding who should be President but we will have the power in certain future elections" (*Horizon*, Sept. 1908).

Du Bois's newfound affection for the Democrats—which was to blossom decisively with the rise of Theodore Roosevelt's kin, Franklin—can be interpreted as a rejection of the GOP, which, he thought, had "forfeited its claim to the Negro vote" (*Horizon*, Nov.–Dec. 1908). This was a growing sentiment among African Americans, propelled in large part by Roosevelt's blatant kowtowing to racist sentiment in order to reassure the doubting that he was not as close to the Negro people as his relationship with Booker T. Washington may have indicated. Neither did Roosevelt's ejection of Negro soldiers from service after the Brownsville episode help his case (*Horizon*, Aug. 1908).

It was in such an unforgiving atmosphere that the Niagara Movement chose to meet again, this time on August 15, 1906, at a site pregnant with meaning—Harper's Ferry. It was here in 1859 that the heroic John Brown had sought to spark a massive slave uprising but, instead, helped to foment a Civil War that had the same effect: abolition. Du Bois did not disappoint, as the Blue Ridge mountains that had resonated with cries of emancipation decades earlier now rang with his call for enforcement of the U.S. Constitution, specifically the Fourteenth Amendment proviso for reduction in the congressional representation of states where African Americans were deprived of the vote. Yet Du Bois did not stop there. He went on to make demands that have yet to lose relevance: "We claim for ourselves," he said, "every single right that belongs to a freeborn American political, civil and social; and until we get these rights we will never cease to protest and to assail the ears of America. The battle we wage is not for ourselves alone but for all true Americans. It is a fight for ideals, lest this, our common fatherland, false to its founding, become in truth the land of the thief and the home of the Slave—a byword and a hissing among the nations for its sounding pretensions and pitiful accomplishments" (*Horizon*, Nov.–Dec. 1908).

Though claiming equality today seems to be the most commonplace of common sense, in 1906 this was far from the case. Negroes could be lynched—brutally murdered—for simply hinting that they were equal: this was the quotidian application of the doctrine of white supremacy. White supremacy in the context of the United States can be understood as a "racial identity politics," born out of the cross-class alliance among European settlers dating back at least to the "apocalyptic" developments of the seventeenth century, and predicated upon settler colonialism, emerging capitalism, the violent expropriation of indigenous land, ever-increasing enslaved African labor, and the looting of all groups beyond the pale of whiteness (Horne, 2017).

Consider, for example, that as Du Bois was heroically raising his voice in opposition to Jim Crow, the Reverend T. Nelson Baker—who was also African American—was chiding Negro youth for refusing to adhere to segregated arrangements in Nashville, a town that Du Bois knew all too well. Baker suggested that Jim Crow resulted not from the diktat of white supremacy but, instead, from the supposed "defects" of African Americans themselves. He berated what he saw as the "chronic state of whining and pouting" among these youth and argued that the "degradation of Negro women"—they were routinely subjected to sexual harassment by white men—was driven by the women's supposed "perverted aesthetical taste" for these men (Du Bois, *The Address*, 1906).

Reverend Baker was expressing the prevailing nonsense about the presumed "bestiality" of the Negro, and, therefore, Du Bois's rising in opposition to his diatribe should be seen as courageous, as it was at that juncture. It was "sad," said Du Bois, that the Reverend Baker would speak so disparagingly of his own people; this "vicious and wanton attack which you have made on educated Negro womanhood—the nasty slur on the chastity of that class of Negro women to which my wife belongs and the young women whom I teach every day [belong]—is the most cowardly and shameless thing I have recently read." Du Bois did not flinch in stoutly "expressing to [Baker] my indignation and my righteous contempt for a man who thus publicly maligns that very class of women to which his own wife and mother belong" (*Congregationalist*, Apr. 7, 1906, 508).

Du Bois held a similar perception of the mixed-race William Hannibal Thomas after the publication of his controversial book, *The American Negro: What He Was, What He Is, and What He Might Become: A Critical and Practical Discussion*, in 1901. That the text was even condemned by Booker T. Washington speaks to its gross vituperation against African Americans. Thomas argued that African Americans should never have gained voting rights, that they were idle and had a strong aversion to manual labor, that they lacked the mental capacity to maintain the essential skills acquired during slavery, and that they generally lacked knowledge, honor, refinement, and honesty. While whites overwhelmingly praised the work and accepted its conclusions, Du Bois upbraided the author and his assertions. Thomas, Du Bois chided, had been rejected by his own race before whites accepted him and was maladjusted, disgruntled, and disreputable. Likewise, his book was vindictive, exaggerated, and a "sinister" rationalization of centuries of white maltreatment of Black people (Du Bois Papers, Du Bois to A. G. Thurman, Feb. 25, 1908; Du Bois to Arna Bontemps, Jan. 12, 1953; Du Bois, *The Storm*, 1901, 262–264).

It was not only the Reverend Baker and William Hannibal Thomas who were compelled to endure Du Bois's testy rebukes. Joining him in being castigated was the noted Boston attorney Samuel May Jr., son of the staunch abolitionist Reverend Samuel J. May. After May Jr. expressed support for Jim Crow, Du Bois reprimanded him. He argued that "segregation of any set of human beings, be they black, white or of any color or race is a bad thing, since human contact is the thing that makes for civilization and human contact is a thing for which all of us are striving today" (Aptheker, 1973, 117).

Baker, Thomas, and May should not necessarily be viewed as outliers; in many ways, they represented the mainstream of what passed for "respectable" opinion. It was the radicalism of Du Bois and the Niagara Movement that seemed to be beyond the pale. Thus, David Wallace, a civil rights activist who was about to move from the relatively mild racial climate of

Chicago to the decidedly more chilly atmosphere in Chattanooga, Tennessee, reminded Du Bois that "there are many who dare not, for good reasons, speak or contribute openly ... to a cause which, I am sure, lies close to really all Negroes' and many white men's hearts." Thus, reluctantly, Wallace concluded that he might "later find it possible to be associated with you openly but for the present my resignation is final." However, he added, "you shall have a secret comrade in me" (Aptheker, 1973, 138).

With all due respect to Wallace, what the Niagara Movement needed was men and women bold enough to stand openly by Du Bois's side. Nevertheless, the anger and fury in Du Bois's words in his retort to Baker and, above all, in his declaration on behalf of the Niagara Movement marked a watershed in the evolution of the politics of Black America. It marked the beginning of the end of the accommodation to Jim Crow represented by the Tuskegee Machine and the rise of a fierce militancy that eventuated in the founding of the NAACP in 1909.

Now with organizational heft behind him in the form of Niagara, Du Bois attacked the Tuskegee Wizard. Taking to the pages of the *Moon*, which he had helped to initiate, he excoriated the regression Negroes had been forced to take under Washington's less-than-inspiring leadership. Disenfranchisement had spread like mushrooms after a brisk spring rain, as had separate—and inferior—train cars for Blacks people (Aptheker, 1973, 142).

This was the grim reality that greeted the beleaguered members of the Niagara Movement as they gathered in Oberlin, Ohio, in August 1908. The GOP was rapidly deserting the Negro, while the Democrats—albeit having more union support—were not above dalliances with the Ku Klux Klan. The leafy and bucolic Midwestern college town of Oberlin was known for its antiracism, having admitted Negro students even before the Civil War erupted, and it continued to boast of its abolitionist credentials. Yet Oberlin in its uniqueness stood starkly as something of an admonition to the nation as a whole, where such progressive sentiments were hardly evident. In the early twentieth century, liberal antiracism of the Oberlin variety advocated education, moral improvement, and cultural development alongside modest political and economic reform as the means to racial equality and full citizenship for African Americans. Moving away from biological determinism that construed Black people as naturally inferior, liberal antiracists acknowledged that this group—despite pervasive ignorance, immorality, and criminality—possessed an "inherent capacity" toward improvement. Liberal antiracists also acknowledged that inequality and poor social and economic conditions were a product of racism, not the innate inability of African Americans. Liberal antiracism promoted the gradual inclusion of African Americans into the polity through a set of

Atlanta Race Riot of 1906

From September 22 to September 25, 1906, at least one hundred people, predominantly African Americans, were killed in Atlanta, Georgia, after a mob of mostly young white men attacked Black citizens. The failure of the law and "public sentiment" to protect the "virtue and good reputation" of white women ostensibly propelled impassioned white men to seek "swift and terrible" revenge against the entire Negro race for the purported crimes of a few.

An alternative interpretation was that the riot was caused by gubernatorial candidates Hoke Smith and Clark Howell intentionally stirring up racial hatred against African Americans in Atlanta for political gain. This was exacerbated by police harassment and excessive arrests of the Black population, often predicated upon trivial charges; disenfranchisement that precluded peaceful defense of life and property; and lack of investment in the Southern public-school system that resulted in entrenched ignorance, illiteracy, and barbarism.

Yet another explanation sees lynching as a sacrament of the veritable religious intensity of white supremacy.

Thus, targeted by the law and the lawless alike, Black Atlantans began to arm themselves against the mob to prevent further violence and to protect their families and property, while authorities immediately moved to disarm them. Though a score of whites were arrested, most continued to amass weapons to use against the beleaguered population until finally the state militia was called in to restore order.

---

community-based reforms and democratic uplift that would eventually ameliorate the "Negro problem."

The meeting in Oberlin had been preceded by the Niagara Movement's meeting in Boston, Trotter's hometown and site of his disruption of Booker T. Washington's conference, which had catapulted these dissidents into organizing an alternative movement (*Moon*, Mar. 2, 1906). Du Bois was general secretary of this organization, which carried the hopes of so many under increasingly adverse conditions. Traveling southward, Du Bois spoke before an energized crowd of 500 cheering Negroes at the Shiloh Baptist Church in Washington, DC, whose pastor, the Reverend J. M. Waldron, was a fellow member of the Niagara Movement. "It is high time to take steps to show our power," Du Bois bellowed, but the hopefulness of Oberlin and Boston could not obscure the grim realities that had set upon Black people (*Daily Republican*, Aug. 29, 1907).

In short, despite the yeoman efforts of Du Bois and his fellow strugglers, the path to freedom led steeply uphill. Increasingly, the mainstream press was pitting Du Bois against Washington—to the detriment of the former. One journalist claimed that it was Du Bois who was "ashamed" of being a Negro because he demanded a swift end to racist discrimination (presumably, the unashamed welcomed racism). A restrained Du Bois could only respond that he found it "very extraordinary that you should regard the man who stands up for his rights as being ashamed of himself" (*Washington Post*, Oct. 1, 1907). His life in Atlanta easily confirmed this reality, if there was any doubt. Jim Crow reigned supreme, which meant that the city's commodious library was barred to him. The mass transit system had severe Jim Crow restrictions, which he and his spouse, Nina, would not deign to patronize. They were also excluded from the better retail stores, which did not leave either in an ideal mood. Then there were the general indignities to which they were subjected, such as having to be careful about which water fountain from which to take a cold drink on a hot day or what park bench upon which to rest after a taxing stroll.

Subjected to such casual cruelties, Du Bois, a proud man, was understandably resentful and, like many Negroes, was quick to discern slights from whites who seemed oblivious to the blows to which he was subjected on a routine basis. Thus, he developed a reputation for possessing a cold reserve that, fundamentally—to the extent it existed—was a reflection of the circumstances in which he found himself as a Black man who had to be quite careful in expressing himself or displaying any visible emotion, lest it engender an extremely adverse reaction.

Of course, there were compensations. One was the easy relationship he developed with Mary White Ovington, a reformer and socialist. Born three years before Du Bois, as the Civil War lurched to a close, she became a social worker of note with sterling expertise. She was strikingly beautiful, with blond hair and penetratingly blue eyes. Du Bois came to rely upon her because of her deep understanding of urban poverty—based upon experience in both New York City and London—and her even deeper recognition of the need for far-reaching change in the United States and the world. Ultimately, she was to become essential in helping Du Bois launch the NAACP. Yet Jim Crow cast a shadow over this friendship, too, for he was unable to set foot in the lobbies of the hotels in which she resided when she visited Atlanta; such restrictions placed an undue strain upon their relationship.

But the strain was insufficient to bar her participation in a momentous gathering, for it was on May 31, 1909, that Du Bois hosted in New York City the modestly titled "National Negro Conference" (sometimes referred to as the "National Committee on the Negro"), which marked the founding of the long-awaited NAACP. In addition to Du Bois, also present at the creation of this momentous organization were Ovington, Oswald Garrison Villard (a lineal descendant of the famed abolitionist, William Lloyd Garrison), and William English Walling (like many of the participants, a man of socialist beliefs). It was Walling's chilling and expansive account of the anti-Negro riots that rocked Springfield, Illinois—the city that propelled Abraham Lincoln—that was the proximate cause of this august meeting.

It seemed that the terribly tumultuous events that some had thought were only indigenous to the Deep South (e.g., Du Bois's own Atlanta) were spreading northward at a dangerous pace, removing any idea that there might be a sanctuary or haven for an increasingly besieged population. For it was in this otherwise drab and unprepossessing Midwestern town that white mobs rampaged through the streets for weeks, setting fire to Black businesses, beating up Black people whenever they found them, and demanding that two Black inmates—both accused of crimes against whites—be handed over to them by the county sheriff. It took 5,000 federal troops to restore calm and order. It was all a familiar story. Again, the press was complicit, for it was on August 14, 1908, that the *Illinois State Register* had reported in hysterical terms the alleged rape of a white woman by a Black man; it was "one of the greatest outrages that ever happened in Springfield," it was reported with fury barely abated. It was a "premeditated assault," and "no effort should be spared to find the black viper." Weeks later, the woman in question, Mabel Hallam, would confess to having fabricated the entire story.

As this catastrophe was unfolding, also concluding was the first genocide of the new century, as imperial Germany intentionally devastated the Herero and Nama peoples of the southwest African nation that is now Namibia in a brutal battle over land and resources, in a prophetic but little-noticed rehearsal of what was to befall Europe a few decades later. As this awful genocide was ending, on the other side of the world in Australia, Jack Johnson, an African American boxer, stirred fury when he decisively defeated—and pummeled—a white opponent. Johnson's victory was a setback not accepted supinely in the United States and elsewhere. The upset spurred a search for a "White Hope" who could beat Johnson and put him in his place. In such a fetid and fervent atmosphere, Du Bois—and those who joined him in New York City in 1909—knew that they had to build an organization to confront the barbarity that seemed to be encircling the globe. They had arrived at this realization not least because, as Du Bois declared remarkably, "Negro slavery exists on a large scale in the United States today" (*Kansas City Star*, Feb. 7, 1908). He was referring to the pervasive debt peonage that had entrapped too many Negroes in a system whereby they grew crops for a landlord but somehow never escaped debt, and a convict-lease system based upon casual mass arrests of Negro men particularly, who were then hired out to employers with none-too-tender mercies.

Thus, the need was crying and urgent when Du Bois arrived in New York City for this important meeting. He was pleased with his handiwork. The "net result" of this epochal gathering, he announced, was "the vision of future cooperation, not simply as in the past, between giver and beggar—the older ideal of charity—but a new alliance between experienced social workers and reformers in touch on the one hand with scientific philanthropy and on the other with the great struggling mass of laborers of all kinds, whose condition and needs know no color line" (*Cincinnati Times-Star*, Dec. 5, 1910). As Du Bois then saw it, African Americans were "girding themselves to fight in the van of progress," not only for themselves but also for "the emancipation of women, universal peace, democratic government, the socialization of wealth and human brotherhood" (Du Bois, "The National Committee," 1909, 407–409). This democratically capacious and profoundly altruistic vision of the struggle of African Americans, which was established and first articulated by Du Bois, was to be the keynote of their human rights crusade for the rest of the century. Thus, Du Bois also was well aware that racism was a crosscut saw that did not slice in only one direction and that the battle for equality on behalf of African Americans was not for themselves alone. In a short reflection, purposefully entitled, "The Souls of White Folk," he recorded that because of racism, these "souls" were "daily shriveling and dying [in] the fierce flame of the new fanaticism." He went on to ask, "Whither has gone America's proud moral leadership of the world?" (*New York Times*, Dec. 12, 1909)

Not least because of the depth and pervasiveness of this kind of white racial chauvinism that then existed, which Du Bois knew so well, perhaps it should come as no great surprise that there was initial controversy as to whether Du Bois himself should play a leading role in the nascent NAACP, even though he was its guiding spirit and the best-known Negro in the organization of this important body. Part of this was reflected in Du Bois's star-crossed relationship with Oswald Garrison Villard. Born four years after Du Bois, the son of Henry Villard, a railroad magnate, founding president of the behemoth General Electric and owner of the influential *New York Post*, the younger Villard was not a man to be trifled with—an idea he, above all, took quite seriously. It was fortunate that he took a clear interest in the plight of the Negro, for in 1897, he took control of the *Post*, whose influence stretched beyond the already powerful sway of Manhattan. He also owned the weighty journal of ideas, *The Nation*, and his philanthropies had included generous donations to Booker T. Washington—a source of some friction with Du Bois, even before their contretemps over the direction of the NAACP.

The proximate cause of their latest controversy was the unusual fact that both had been working on biographies of the heroic John Brown, the white man who gave his life in 1859 in a failed attempt to foment an insurrection among the enslaved. Unfortunately for Villard, he was beat to the chase by Du Bois, whose justly praised volume was published in 1909, a year before that of his competitor. Du Bois considered this book one of his favorites, and it did not help things when Villard—in a move of questionable ethical dimensions—chose to review his colleague's biography in a sharply ungenerous and ungracious manner. Villard adamantly denied that the review in question was "written with the intent of giving an unfair drubbing to a supposedly rival book of mine," as he proceeded to turn the tables and charge Du Bois with perpetuating an "injustice" with his allegation. "I do not think there can be too many books about the John Brown period," said Villard with perspicacity, though his statement evaded the point about the dubious nature of his own review of Du Bois's work (Du Bois, "The Souls of White Folk," 1910, 339–342).

For Du Bois had poured heart and soul into his rehabilitation of Brown, a man then widely viewed as a calloused madman, a wild-eyed zealot, and a bloodthirsty fiend. By Du Bois's own admission, this biography of vindication was more of an interpretation than an attempt to dredge up new revelations via immersion in primary sources. Yet, more than a justification of Brown's militant abolitionism, this book also marked an evolution for Du Bois in the way it commingled scholarship with advocacy. In this, it differed from his earlier work, particularly his first book on the African slave trade.

The conflict between Villard and Du Bois settled down to the extent that it was possible, as Du Bois chose to leave Atlanta University and join the staff of the newly born NAACP as its leading African-American operative. With that, the ongoing challenge to the Tuskegee Machine that had been percolating for years reached a decisive and transformative stage.

"Of course," said Walling to Du Bois in mid-June 1910, "we shall be able to pay you what is right and proper during the first year—$2,500, plus your expenses—and shall fully hope to employ you in after years, perhaps even at an increasing salary"; the Socialist leader conceded that the "main sacrifice will be yours, in leaving a position which you have filled with such credit, and probably with such satisfaction to yourself, for so many years" (Aptheker, 1973, 158–159). This was true. This was an immense sacrifice for Du Bois, for he would leave not only his family behind in Atlanta to migrate to a bustling and crowded Manhattan but also his scholarship—his other love—in order to plunge headfirst on behalf of a despised minority into the rough-and-tumble politics of a hostile atmosphere.

What was to follow proved to be of monumental significance for both Du Bois and Black America. For it was not preordained that this fledgling grouping would take flight—not to mention becoming a battering ram against Jim Crow in a process that lasted decades. As for Du Bois, the longest sustained piece of work by him was his editorship of the *Crisis*, organ of the NAACP; this magazine appeared each month under his editorship from its first number, dated November 1910, through June 1934, when he and the organization he had helped to found, came to a parting of the ways.

In the earlier volumes, nearly the entire journal was written by him; later, departments of the magazine appeared by him—signed and unsigned—as did particular essays often signed by him. This journal had a dramatically profound impact on Black America, solidifying militant opposition to the accommodation of Tuskegee and blazing an alternative path. Yet its impact soared far beyond the realm of politics. In the first issue, November 1910— years before the "Harlem Renaissance" was proclaimed as a turning point in the arts—attention was called to the fact that "New York is becoming an art center for colored people," with such performers as Bert Williams, Cole and Johnson (comprising Bob Cole, J. Rosamond Johnson, and James Weldon Johnson), and Will Marion Cook and the Clef Club Orchestra of 130 musicians under James Reese Europe. The first issue of the journal ended with the listing of eleven relevant books: one on Cuba, eight on Africa, and two biographies—one of John Brown by Villard and one of the latter's lineal ancestor, William Lloyd Garrison by Lindsay Swift. The inclusion of these biographies reflected Du Bois's political acuity in stroking carefully a man with whom he had only recently been in conflict.

Just as the success of the NAACP was not a certainty, the triumph of the *Crisis* was not predetermined either. This Du Bois knew more than most, given his experiences with the *Moon* and the *Horizon*. Even before Du Bois's deflating experiences with journalism, there had been the rise—and fall—of *Freedom's Journal*, and the varied experiences of Frederick Douglass in this field, none of which survived (unlike the *Crisis*). Suggestive of the extraordinary nature of this journal is that, even today, it would be neither easy nor simple to launch a magazine of ideas with a progressive and antiracist message. That in the foreboding and forbidding days of 1910 a journal could be launched with 5,000 initial subscribers at the rate of one dollar per year—or ten cents a copy for a sixteen-page edition—remains a wonder.

Officially, Du Bois was director of publicity and research at the infant organization, lodged at 20 Vesey Street in the crowded confines of lower Manhattan. Unofficially, there was a considerable amount of wrangling in the upper reaches of the group not only about Du Bois's role but also about what the organization would become. Contrary to what the NAACP is today, at the beginning there was substantial backing for the idea that it should be primarily a white group dedicated to Black uplift, and this viewpoint contrasted with what was emerging as the consensus view: an interracial group dedicated to a protracted struggle for equality. Undoubtedly, Walling, a millionaire, and Ovington, a social worker, were the progenitors of the NAACP—yet, it is also true that Du Bois quickly became the public face of the group and his labor, as much as anything else, helped to guarantee its extraordinary longevity. Yet also present at the creation of what became the NAACP was an all-star team of African Americans, including

Ida B. Wells-Barnett, the justly celebrated antilynching crusader; Mary Church Terrell, the multilingual descendant of one of Black America's most affluent families; and a sprinkling of suffragettes, including Fanny Garrison Villard, Inez Milholland Boissevain, and Isabel Eaton. Their collective triumph in defeating the vision that called for a less ambitious, less racially diverse grouping was signaled in its very name: in highlighting the advancement of "Colored People"—as opposed to the Negro or the Afro-American—the point was adumbrated that the agenda would be expansive, encompassing the darkest among us, wherever they might be. This expansive vision was also reflected in the group's organ, which was formally entitled *The Crisis: A Record of the Darker Races*.

Indicative of the ambitiousness of what the NAACP intended was the selection of their first president. Born in 1845, Moorfield Storey had served as secretary to the legendary abolitionist Senator Charles Sumner and was thereafter one of the leading attorneys in the nation and had been a president of the American Bar Association. More telling about his political tendencies was his service as president of the Anti-Imperialist League. He brought his anti-imperialist beliefs to the NAACP until his untimely death in 1929. The relationship between the courtly Storey and the hardworking Du Bois was to be exceedingly important for Black America during the tenure of their relationship, which lasted from 1910 to 1929.

For it was during that important period that the NAACP journal edited by Du Bois took the nation by storm. Black businesses flocked to take out advertisements, providing another revenue stream beyond the subsidy from the group's board of directors. Businesses who bought advertising were followed rapidly by a good deal of the nation's major historically Black colleges and universities, including Fisk, Howard, Shaw, Virginia Union, and Wilberforce (conspicuously, Tuskegee and Washington's alma mater, Hampton, were not among these distinguished advertisers). By bringing these eminences on board, Du Bois had succeeded in co-opting them, giving them a stake in the journal's—and the organization's—success. By April 1912, circulation skyrocketed to 22,500. By way of comparison, Jesse Max Barber, founder and editor of the *Voice of the Negro*, established in 1904 in Atlanta—before being forced to evacuate to Chicago because of the pogrom there—told Du Bois directly that the largest number of copies ever printed by his publication was 17,000 in that same year, 1912 (Aptheker, 1973, 169–170).

In 1912 both the nation as a whole and Black America as a part of this whole were reaching a momentous fork in the road; it was a timely moment for hungry eyes to be poring over the luster of Du Bois's prose. For by the time of this bump in circulation, a revolution had erupted on the nation's southern border, as Mexico was undergoing the first radical transformation of the century. This radicalism infected numerous Mexican Americans and then spilled over to those African Americans with whom they shared numerous neighborhoods along the 2,000-mile border stretching from Texas to San Diego. Moreover, Black America remained upset by what had befallen Negro soldiers in Brownsville, and young men from some of those same regiments were now duty-bound to patrol a border where revolutionary violence had become endemic. In addition, other nations had begun to fish in these troubled waters, as Japan and Germany began to cultivate allies in the borderlands, thereby further jeopardizing U.S. national security.

Especially after the publication of the "Zimmerman Telegram" on March 1, 1917, rumors that German agents were plotting "Negro uprisings" in the South and accusations that Southern Blacks were susceptible to Mexican and Japanese manipulation caused the U.S. government much anxiety. The Bureau of Investigation of the Department of Justice spent considerable time and resources attempting to substantiate conspiracies to manipulate Black loyalty, particularly scrutinizing Black migration to the North, Black newspapers (like the *Chicago Defender*) encouraging this migration, and reports that African Americans were being urged to migrate to Mexico. Du Bois quickly dismissed claims of African-American "pro-Germanism," and African-American disloyalty more broadly, as attempts by white Southerners to curtail recent African-American economic advances, to stop the formation of Black army regiments, and to forcibly prevent Black labor migration to the North. Nonetheless, newspapers like the *New York Tribune* and the *New York News*, as well as letters written by "worried citizens" to the president, the U.S. government, and the Secret Service, continued to insist that Germans were inciting African Americans to organize against the U.S. government, and the white population more broadly, with claims that if Germany was victorious over the United States, Negroes would enjoy equal rights, full citizenship, and special privileges (Ellis, 1984).

As things evolved, it was becoming ever clearer that Jim Crow was jeopardizing U.S. national security, not least because the indignities of entrenched segregation could cause Mexican Americans and African Americans to lend a willing ear to real and imagined foes of the United States. It was Du Bois's genius that he was the first Negro leader to not only acknowledge this sensitive conjuncture but, more than that, to take advantage of it to the detriment of Jim Crow and the benefit of Black America.

5

A Life of Pathways

Du Bois's leadership of the NAACP indicated that Black America was embarking on a new path. Booker T. Washington had not disappeared, but he did not have behind him a membership organization comprising the Negro masses, and though he had bribed and browbeaten a good deal of the Negro press, he also did not have under his administration an organ of opinion that was growing by leaps and bounds.

Yet by 1912, Du Bois might have acknowledged more directly why the Tuskegee Machine might have chosen to accommodate the powerful, for it was evident then that this small planet was entering a time of bloodlust and violence that was of particular consequence for Black America, which tended to get pneumonia when the nation as a whole was enduring a head cold. For it was not just the Mexican Revolution that had exploded—the Great War that was about to burst forth in Europe in 1914 would require a meaningful complement of Negro soldiers, who were to suffer mightily before this conflict ended. This suffering was not unrelated to increased African-American agitation during the war, due in no small part to the fact that Black military service had not resulted in a concomitant increase in freedom, rights, or equality. The government and the white citizenry treated African-American demands for better treatment in the military and in society generally with hostility and considered such activism disruptive, opportunistic, and taking advantage of the war to place the interests of the race above national security. In the context of war, documenting and protesting lynching, encouraging African Americans to leave the

South, condemning the racist treatment of Black troops, and engaging in any activity that would cause white resentment was considered disloyal and unpatriotic, bordering on subversive. As such, African Americans who were the victims of white supremacist violence, assault, and terror were seen to be at fault because they stirred up race tension and put their grievances above the war effort.

All was not gloom and doom, however, for moving from the comparative parochialism of Georgia to the relatively cosmopolitan New York was liberating for Du Bois. Jim Crow was less intense in Manhattan than Atlanta, and besides, coincidentally, Du Bois was part of a great migration from South to North that was to transform the nation. Starting in 1890, over one million African Americans migrated north, with more than 500,000 moving between 1916 and 1918. They converged with hundreds of thousands of African descendants from the Caribbean, resulting in increases in Black populations between 10 and 300 percent in many Northern cities. Most ended up in industrial and cosmopolitan cities alongside groups of immigrants from southern and eastern Europe and Asia. This seismic demographic shift produced an urban landscape in which Black workers and Black culture became central to American society and its ascent to the position of capitalist superpower and global hegemon.

For it was at this precise moment that Harlem—the multiblock neighborhood of northern Manhattan that encompassed a great university (Columbia) and a very good college (City College of New York) and was speckled with tenement buildings and underpinned by a rumbling subway system—began to receive thousands of migrants of African descent from the former slave South and the Caribbean basin. The island of Manhattan is only twelve miles long, and Harlem is a relatively small part of that, but its size was (and still is) belied by the magnitude of this neighborhood's contribution to the politics and culture of the nation. But what was occurring in Manhattan was occurring simultaneously in Philadelphia; in Chicago as Negroes departed Mississippi; and in Boston as Negroes departed the Carolinas. The migrations to these cities were occurring for similar reasons. Racist terror pushed Negroes northward. The boll weevil devastated agricultural crops. Northern factories began to ramp up production in anticipation of supplying a European market that was gearing for war, which necessitated more workers. Such workers could not be sufficiently supplied by immigration insofar as the impending conflict reduced the number of immigrants.

As Negroes escaped the Deep South, they obtained the right to vote and participate more freely in organizations like Du Bois's NAACP. This provided jet propulsion to his efforts and shook up politics nationally. Du Bois also took advantage of his migration northward by plunging more directly into the operations of the Socialist Party (SP). Yet Du Bois remained flummoxed by the party's unwillingness—or inability—to tackle racism forthrightly. He took his concern directly to an audience of 1,000 socialists—almost all white—on January 20, 1912 (*Socialist Call*, Jan. 21, 1912). The SP was of the opinion that the socialist utopia would resolve the prickly matter of racism that was inextricably tied to the innards of capitalism. Thus, this august organization tended to disdain the difficult day-to-day battles against intractable problems like lynching. This was all well and good in theory, but it was a hard proposition to sell to African Americans seeking to avoid gory and ferocious lynch mobs. Rather than wait for utopia, they might decide to heed the siren songs emanating from Tokyo and Berlin to the effect that this nation's rulers were simply too beastly for redemption.

Du Bois insisted that disenfranchisement of African Americans was not simply a matter for them alone—whose resolution had to await the establishment of socialism—but that this deprivation vitiated democracy as a whole. The disenfranchisement of African Americans virtually guaranteed the rule of Dixiecrats and demagogues, and made next to impossible the rise of any to their left, socialists least of all (*New York Times*, Nov. 3, 1912). He thus reminded his fellow party members that it was incumbent upon them to turn their attention to the plight of Negroes (*New Review*, Feb. 1, 1913). He was pleased to observe in the *Crisis* in December 1911 that the SP was "the only party which openly recognizes Negro manhood"; thus, he queried, "is it not time for black voters [to] carefully consider the claims of this party?" Likewise, he continued, one in five workers in the nation were African American, and, he added prophetically, "the Negro Problem then is the great test of the American Socialist," a test that this party failed generally (*New Review*, Feb. 1, 1913). On the other hand, all of Du Bois's engagements with the socialists were not as problematic, for he shared membership in the party with both Walling and Ovington, and their shared ideology improved their own collective functioning within the NAACP.

Despite the SP's intrinsic weaknesses, Du Bois clung to the socialists like a life raft in a storm-tossed sea, for the alternatives were so unpromising—a bitter reality that was manifest in the pivotal election year of 1912. For as revolution brewed in Mexico and war loomed in Europe, presidential candidates at home were disappointing for African Americans, to say the least. They included the elephantine incumbent William Howard Taft of the GOP, whose party had for years now seemed embarrassed and discomfited by the support of Negroes. Then there was Theodore Roosevelt, running on a third-party ticket, who, despite his bluster against entrenched monopolies, exposed disdain for the Negro when he cruelly mistreated the soldiers of Brownsville. And finally, the Democrat was Woodrow Wilson, a native of Virginia, though he had been yanked into prominence as president of his alma mater, Princeton University. The latter became a launching pad for his election as governor of New Jersey who did nothing to dislodge Old Nassau's distaste for admitting Negro students and seemed to be more a man of the Old South than of the more enlightened precincts of central Jersey (Wolgemuth, 1959). In August 1912, Du Bois informed readers of the *Crisis* that if he could assure the presidency to the socialist Eugene Victor Debs, he would do so, for of all the candidates, "he alone, by word and deed, stands squarely on a platform of human rights regardless of race or class (*Crisis*, Dec. 1910).

Wilson emerged triumphant—the first Southerner since Zachary Taylor and the first Democrat since Grover Cleveland to enter the White House— which only meant that Du Bois and the NAACP had to work that much harder to destroy Jim Crow. Though a member of the Socialist Party, Du Bois knew that given the construction of the Electoral College and the winner-take-all nature of U.S. elections, his choice could not prevail. Thus, he advised a vote for Wilson, hoping and praying that the working-class base of his Democratic Party would somehow come to its senses and pursue a path of concord with a mostly working-class African-American community. Not for the first or last time, this fervent wish proved unavailing. Yet so strongly did Du Bois hold to this belief at this time that he chose this precise moment to resign from the Socialist Party. This resignation did not spell the end of his attempt to entice these radicals to pay much more attention to those most likely to respond to their entreaties. "There is a group of ten million persons in the United States toward whom Socialists would better turn serious attention," he said, referring to African Americans in what was becoming a mantra. "The Negro Problem then," he repeated as if it were a magic incantation, "is the great test of the American Socialist" (*New Review*, Feb. 1, 1913). Of course, Du Bois's political dalliances with the left were not limited to him alone. In one of the first editions of the *Crisis* he edited, it was reported that in Guthrie, Oklahoma, representatives of various Negro organizations denounced the GOP leadership and urged the "Negroes of the state to support the entire Socialist ticket" and called for the enfranchisement of women (*Crisis*, Dec. 1910; see Kellogg, 1967).

Thus, the "Negro Problem" was also a "great test" for Du Bois himself that he rarely failed to pass. This was reflected in his first novel, *The Quest of the Silver Fleece*, which was published in the immediate aftermath of the founding of the NAACP (Du Bois, *The Quest*, 1911). It was an attempt to provide a realistic portrayal of the impact of cotton, racism, and peonage in the nation in the early twentieth century, as Upton Sinclair and Frank Norris had done about the same time with meat and wheat. The novel's realism derives in part from the fact that it is a fictionalization of the sociological study of sharecroppers Du Bois—with the help of Monroe Work,

Richard R. Wright, and other researchers—conducted in Lowndes County Alabama from 1906 to 1907 on behalf of the U.S. Department of Labor. Given his meticulous scrutiny of land ownership, labor relations between landlords and tenants, political and sexual mores, and other controversial topics, the Department of Labor first stonewalled the report's publication, then ultimately destroyed the only copy of it given that it "touched on political matters" (Lewis, 2009, 235–237). The Negro characters—particularly the women—are strong, and the whites are drawn in varying form, that is, the hesitant liberal, the evil Bourbon, the courageous and dedicated white opponent of racism (also a woman and perhaps inspired by Mary White Ovington). The lasting significance of this work is that it portends the arrival of the Harlem Renaissance, a remarkable flowering of literature and the arts among African Americans that was to erupt more than a decade later.

Nevertheless, Du Bois had come to recognize that placing all his eggs in the basket of the United States itself, when it came to the destruction of Jim Crow, may not have been a fool's errand—but it was not far from it. Having spent considerable time in Europe and being aware of the direct challenge provided by Japan in particular—whose defeat of Russia in 1905 he had hailed as a signpost in the global struggle against white supremacy, Jim Crow's blood relative—he knew that extending his political tentacles abroad was eminently desirable. Making this goal even more appealing was the fact that the Tuskegee Machine had an international component of its own. In 1910 Washington himself was in London, where he opined that the plight of the Negro was well on its way to being resolved. John Milholland, a NAACP founder, happened to be in London at that time and immediately informed Du Bois that The Tuskegee Wizard's wild distortion had to be refuted—which Du Bois promptly did.

Meanwhile, Du Bois became aware of an important gathering that was to occur in London in July 1911. He coordinated the U.S. delegation of this First Universal Race Congress and took the opportunity to interact with the novelist and futurist H. G. Wells; Sir Roger Casement, a crusader against colonialism in the Congo; and a leading politician, J. Ramsay MacDonald. Though this London confab presented a rare opportunity to advance the global struggle against Jim Crow, Du Bois was reluctant to abandon his battle station in Manhattan. "We are just getting into working shape the NAACP," he said. "It has been far more successful than we dreamed but not successful enough to stand at the moment my prolonged absence" (Aptheker, 1973, 173–175).

Nevertheless, one constant in Du Bois's seemingly contradictory political career was his engagement with the international community. He knew that the plagues and vicissitudes visited upon African Americans—white supremacy, massacres, and the like—were not unique to North

America; hence, bonding and building alliances with others abroad similarly situated was crucial. Moreover, he also knew that the balance of forces globally (Was white supremacy on the upswing or a downslide? Was the United States growing or diminishing in influence?) was, ultimately, a critical factor in determining the destiny of African Americans, and this could best be gauged beyond these shores. Thus, Du Bois crossed the choppy waters of the Atlantic once more to commune with a thousand delegates, representing what was loosely termed "fifty races," who had gathered in the Fishmongers' Hall. "When fifty races look each other in the eye, face to face," he enthused, "there arises a new conception of humanity and its problems" (Lewis, 1993, 441).

This gathering in London ratified Du Bois's faith in global alliances, which he was to pursue to his dying days. Yet this farsighted viewpoint was not shared universally within the leading circles of the NAACP, the organization for which he toiled. More to the point, Oswald Garrison Villard, a leading member of the organization's board, continued to dog his every move, seemingly uncomfortable with the idea that Du Bois—as an African American—would be seen as preeminent in an organization dedicated to Negro advance. Du Bois was not comforted by the well-known reality that Villard's wife, whose roots in the Deep South ran deep, contradicted her spouse's abolitionist heritage by refusing to have Negro—or Jewish—guests at their home. Villard himself tended toward imperiousness, and the ever-sensitive Du Bois, keenly attuned to the poisonous nature of Jim Crow, found it easy to interpret this attitude quite negatively.

As so often happens, Du Bois's absence from the office due to his lengthy sojourn in London allowed these tensions to fester and boil over. Referring bluntly to the "passage of words between us in the board meeting," Du Bois acknowledged Villard's assertion that "you do not think further co-operation between us in the work of the association is possible." Du Bois begged to differ but made it clear in words that contradicted the essence of Jim Crow that "I count myself not as your subordinate but as a fellow officer," adding pointedly, "I decline to receive orders from anyone but the board" (Aptheker, 1973, 181).

Villard did not cease in his attempt to rein in Du Bois, clip his wings, and place him under tighter control. "Mr. Villard has been frank from the beginning," Du Bois contended. "He opposed my coming to the position in the first place and has systematically opposed every step I have taken since. He has told me plainly," he cried, "that he should not rest until I and the 'Crisis' were 'absolutely' under his control or entirely outside the organization." As Du Bois saw things in words that echo through the ages, "Mr. Villard is not democratic. He is used to advising colored men and giving them orders and he simply cannot bring himself to work with one as an equal." For Du Bois, the NAACP had reached a critical juncture, for "in most organizations of this kind the problem has frankly been given up as insoluble and usually an entire force of one race or another is hired. It has been my dream to make this organization an exception," he insisted, "and I have tried desperately and have failed." This was premature pessimism, but more timely was his assertion that "if in this Association white and black folk cannot work together as equals; if this Association is unable to treat its black officials with the same lease of power as white, can we fight a successful battle against race prejudice in the world?" (Aptheker, 1973, 188–191).

Joel Spingarn, a Jewish American, replaced Villard as chairman of the NAACP board in January 1914, though the latter remained a member of the board, and Du Bois's relationship with this literary scholar and his brother, a noted attorney, was much closer than that with Villard. Yet Spingarn, too, reproached Du Bois for what he perceived as his less than comradely attitude to cooperation with others on the board; but the editor of the *Crisis* said without hesitation, "[Yes,] my temperament is a difficult one to endure. In my peculiar education and experiences it would be miraculous if I came through normal and unwarped" (Aptheker, 1973, 203–207). Du Bois may have been overly self-effacing here. It was true that he already had developed a reputation for being standoffish, though this was more a product of shyness and a reticence born in being an African American who often found himself among Euro-Americans who were less than diplomatic. For example, Villard thought the journal Du Bois edited should have spent more time highlighting the crimes of Negroes, as opposed to documenting the massive crimes targeting Negroes.

Between 1890 and 1940, crime statistics exploded in importance as a means of describing and understanding the "Negro Problem" and its relation to criminality. In the midst of the publication of the first census data in 1890, the Great Migration, increasing urbanization, and rapid industrialization, the specter of the Black criminal shaped public and intellectual debates about myriad issues, including access to resources, citizenship, and the efficacy of education. Blacks who migrated northward came to be understood as threats to the progress and safety of cities like Chicago, Philadelphia, and New York City through the one-sided reporting of crime, to the detriment of Black people, and the racially biased use of crime statistics. Racial inferiority, pathology, and criminality became sutured to Blackness, rationalizing prejudice, discrimination, and racial violence in the North and the South alike. At the same time, Du Bois and other Black sociologists, social workers, and activists worked tirelessly to dispel the racist myth that criminality was unique to and endemic in African Americans. They adamantly pointed out the differential standards used to measure Black and white crime, the gross mistreatment of African Americans by police and in the criminal justice system, and the lack of police protection in Black communities. They argued that Black crime was a direct result of poor living and social conditions, and that welfare programs afforded to new immigrants should likewise be extended to African Americans to curb crime. Nonetheless, African Americans continued to be stigmatized as the paradigmatic criminals, while white immigrants received aid from welfare agencies, community investment, and public resources to prevent crime (Muhammad, 2010, 1–14).

The heart of the dispute between Du Bois and factions of the NAACP board, in sum, was the *Crisis* and its unvarnished reporting of lynchings, colonialism, and the ugliness of white supremacy; this warts-and-all portrait was made all the more problematic—in the eyes of some—due to its being engineered by an African American. Du Bois had threatened to resign, which would have been disastrous for a fledgling organization struggling to establish its credibility in the face of the stiff challenge provided by the Tuskegee Machine. The reality was that the nation as a whole was ill prepared for Du Bois's scalding and scolding reporting. This included the NAACP board, who were deemed to be among the angels.

Looking back at this stimulating journal, one is still struck by the militancy of it, particularly when contrasted with its peers—before and since. The very first issue, published in November 1910, sets the tone with graphic reports on Black men who, in self-defense, killed their bosses and were now facing death. In December 1910, Du Bois reports on physical resistance by Negroes in Oklahoma to efforts to disenfranchise them. In November 1911, he again notes that in recent weeks, there were reports of fourteen Negro men being killed in the South, but that ten white men were killed by Negroes in the South during this same time frame. This idea of militant self-defense was a repetitive one and was unsettling to the fiercest advocates of Jim Crow. This prescient approach—which prefigured the ideas of Malcolm X and the Black Panther Party, which were thought to be unique when they emerged decades later—reached a crescendo in the May 1913 when he penned a startling editorial, "The Vigilance Committee: A Call to Arms," in which he observed casually, though explicitly, that "there is scarcely a community in the United States where a group of colored people live that has not its vigilance committee." In an italicized paragraph, Du Bois unequivocally states that *the object of the National Association for the Advancement of Colored People is to offer a central headquarters and a collective force to ensure the greater effectiveness and permanence of such committees.* Few things could be more unnerving to the perpetrators of racist violence than the idea that intended victims would fight back ferociously.

In May 1911, he declaimed at length on the paradox that racism often took the form of special attacks against African Americans precisely because they had attained some element of economic independence, the condition that they had been told would eliminate racism! This was the cruel dilemma that the Tuskegee Machine, which was premised on the notion of economic independence for Negroes, could not or would not confront (Du Bois, "Violations," 1911, 32).

Du Bois was not simply a cloistered member of the literati, churning out intriguing articles and reviews. He had become a chief organizer of the NAACP, often touring the nation and speaking before appreciative audiences bedazzled by his erudition. Thus, it was in July 1913 that he completed a lengthy lecture tour, covering 7,000 miles and bringing him before audiences aggregating 18,000 people. Those he addressed were overwhelmingly African American, and he "thanked God" that he had "the privilege of working for them" (*Crisis*, July 1913).

With fits and starts, the NAACP gradually took off to assume its still preeminent position in Black America. At the wheel was Du Bois as this historic process was launched. Yet, seemingly, this mighty task was insufficient to assuage Du Bois's apparently insatiable appetite for labor. For in between editing what had become a leading journal and speaking before adoring audiences, Du Bois also found time to pursue a punishing schedule of writing, publishing his still enlightening book *The Negro*. This book is a pioneering effort at depicting within one volume the entire scope of Africa's past (a Herculean task, surely), but Du Bois does not stop there. He goes on to contextualize the position of African-derived peoples in the United States, Latin America, and the West Indies as he demonstrates the relationship between the exploitation of Africa and the rise of capitalism and imperialism in Europe and the United States. Rather modestly, Du Bois points to limitations of his previous research, his own linguistic limitations, especially in terms of African languages (a number of which have descended into desuetude since *The Negro* first emerged in 1915) and the brevity of the effort, as precluding the possibility of his being a definitive treatment of the capacious topic. Still, he expresses hope that his effort would "enable the general reader to know as men a sixth or more of the human race" (Du Bois, *The Negro*, 1915).

Increasingly, Du Bois was coming to see that the beleaguered plight of Africans and African Americans alike was not merely a matter that afflicted them alone. Instead, as World War I erupted in 1914, he had arrived at the weighty conclusion that Europeans' and Euro-Americans' squabbles over the spoils and carcass of a weakened Africa was a major source of war—with the snatching and dragging of Africans to North America being early evidence of this extremely stressed situation. Weeks after the guns had sounded in Sarajevo, Du Bois appeared before an attentive audience of 900 in New Hampshire. The weather was cold and inclement, but Du Bois's penetrating words burned hot. He insisted that "the present [war] is caused by the jealousy among leading European nations over colonial aggrandizement." Compared to France and Great Britain, who had garnered the lion's share of colonies, most notably in Africa, Germany had arrived tardily at the colonial feasting table, and the onset of war was, among other things, an attempt to rearrange the status quo. Yet amid the often-deafening roar of the present, Du Bois had the perspicacity to peer over the horizon and around the corner to espy China's awakening, which had been signaled by the overthrow of royalty there a few years earlier: China's rise would be "irresistible," he prophesied (*Manchester Leader*, Nov. 16, 1914).

Subsequently, Du Bois expanded upon his controversial thesis in one of his more influential writings, "The African Roots of War," published in May 1915. "In a very real sense," writes Du Bois, Africa was the prime cause of the war. The battering of this continent was highly profitable—to some. The title of this article says it all and also points to decolonization and the uplift of Africa as a route to erode the lineaments of war. There, too, he spoke hopefully of the "awakening leaders" of China, India, and Egypt. He suggested that African Americans had a pivotal role to play in this profound historical process (Du Bois, "The African Roots," 1915, 707–714). In Du Bois's estimation, descendants of enslaved Africans in the Caribbean also had an essential task to perform. For in the midst of preparing for publication his influential article on the roots of war, he seized the opportunity to visit Jamaica for the first time, where he bumped into a young man whose name came to be linked with his controversially— Marcus Mosiah Garvey—who was tarrying in his native Jamaica before migrating to the United States. At a dinner in honor of Du Bois, the mayor of Kingston, and the U.S. Consul, Du Bois again spoke of the interconnections of the struggles of colored peoples of the world and the central role of Africans in the Western Hemisphere in the movement that had come to be known as Pan-Africanism (*Jamaica Times*, May 8, 1915).

Du Bois's journey to the Caribbean seemed to reawaken his awareness of the importance of this region, which included his own familial beginnings. For from 1905 to 1941, the United States maintained a customs receivership over Haiti, followed by the direct intervention by the U.S. military. It was in July 1915, shortly after Du Bois's return from Haiti's neighbor Jamaica, that U.S. Marines stood by as the congress in Port-au-Prince approved a Washington-selected president for this beset nation. Figuratively—if not literally—at gunpoint, this man, appointed by President Wilson, signed a treaty under which U.S. citizens appointed by Washington controlled the nation's finances, police, public works, and the like. After the dissolving of the Haitian congress by the U.S. military, a new constitution allowing foreign landownership was "approved." Interestingly, this constitution was drafted by Wilson's assistant secretary of the navy, Franklin Delano Roosevelt.

U.S. INVASION OF HAITI, JULY 1915

In July 1915 the U.S. government sent marines to Port-au-Prince, Haiti, inaugurating an occupation that lasted until 1934. Plans for "intervention"—growing out of concerns about the destruction of foreigners' property given the pervasive political turmoil on the island—were bruited virtually from the day Haitian independence was proclaimed in 1804. Through occupation, the United States protected foreign banking and property interests by propping up a corrupt government and suspending the constitution and the legislature.

The U.S. government implemented a program of forced labor called corvée that coerced Haitians to construct air strips and other facilities for very little pay under the surveillance of armed soldiers. Occupying forces also instituted a curfew, censored the press, and controlled every aspect of Haitian society. Given that the Haitian government—under duress—had signed a treaty, it was powerless to stop these impositions, the worst of which were "bandit-suppression" campaigns, violent suppression of peasant resistance, and racially motivated attacks on Haitians.

This export of Jim Crow terrorism to the island drew the ire of Black Americans, including James Weldon Johnson and the NAACP. In 1915 Du Bois demanded the Wilson administration prove to Haitians and African Americans alike that it had "no designs on the political independence of the island and no desire to exploit it ruthlessly for the sake of selfish business interests here." These protests did little to quell the brutality and economic exploitation unleashed in Haiti for the next two decades.

Thus, shortly after returning from Jamaica, Du Bois took his objections to Washington's Caribbean policy directly to President Wilson: "The United States has throughout the world a reputation for studied unfairness toward black folk," he charged. "The political party whose nominee you are is historically the party of Negro slavery." Changing course on Haiti, Du Bois suggested, would go a long way toward assuaging the widespread concern in the Pan-African world about U.S. policy (Aptheker, 1973, 211–213). The president chose not to respond.

Though he was to be accused of inconsistency and ideological reversals, Du Bois was interested in global issues throughout his long life, and he continued throughout his lengthy career to connect global concerns with the concerns of his homeland. He was among the first to acknowledge early on that as long as Africans abroad were being pulverized, African Americans could hardly escape battering. There was a global correlation of forces that virtually dictated that, for example, a nonviolent civil rights protest could erupt after World War II, whereas it might have been drenched in a tidal wave of blood and gore after World War I. So, despite President Wilson turning a blind eye and a deaf ear to his insistent pleas,

Du Bois did not flinch from pressing his global concerns on the White House, even as the scene at home showed little sign of improving. For as Du Bois was raising his eloquent voice against U.S. intervention in Haiti, he was also objecting strenuously to the simultaneous intervention in neighboring Mexico as it was enmeshed in the first great revolution of the twentieth century—an intervention made even more problematic by the dispatching south of the border of Negro troops in search of Pancho Villa, the celebrated revolutionary (Horne, 2005).

Perhaps Woodrow Wilson—an unreconstructed segregationist— decided to ignore Du Bois's entreaties due to the NAACP's constant prodding of Wilson on so many different fronts. Not least due to the ministrations of NAACP lawyers, the U.S. Supreme Court ruled unconstitutional Oklahoma's preferential registration of white voters—the first opinion to nullify a state law under the Fifteenth Amendment. Then the NAACP prevailed in a case from Louisville, which—at least on paper— guaranteed the right to buy decent housing. With Du Bois, an intellectual turned propagandist at the helm of a monthly magazine that was growing by leaps and bounds, the NAACP seemed to be reaching a new stage in its lengthy battle with the Tuskegee Machine.

This perception took on a sad reality when, on November 14, 1915, Booker T. Washington passed away. He had taken ill in New York City and, with his typical bullheadedness, rebuffed the counsel of his physicians and took a train to Tuskegee. But his body was wracked by all manner of maladies, seemingly induced by an especially virulent sexually transmitted disease, and the train ride to Alabama turned out to be his final journey. At his final resting place in Alabama, there then arose an imposing statue of the Wizard of Tuskegee seemingly lifting a veil of ignorance from a bent Negro beneath him. Critics charged that Washington and the policies he fought for had actually *placed* a veil of ignorance over African Americans. Du Bois, who had been catapulted into the public arena not least due to his challenge to Washington, was balanced in his analysis of his frequent sparring partner. Yes, he was "the greatest Negro leader since Frederick Douglass and the most distinguished man, white or black" to come from the Deep South since the conclusion of the Civil War. And, yes, the educational institution he constructed at Tuskegee and his desire to build businesses were both admirable. Yet, Du Bois could not avoid the conclusion that Washington erred grievously in downplaying disenfranchisement and his public approach of acquiescing to the most egregious aspects of white supremacy. Du Bois could have added that Washington's program had little purchase for an African-American community in the midst of a great migration from South to North that would transform this community for all time. More than this, Washington's program, such as it was, seemed to accept the status quo rather than challenge it (*Crisis*, Dec. 1915; Du Bois's words on Washington were reproduced and circulated widely—see *Chicago Evening Post*, Dec. 13, 1915; *Sioux City Journal*, Dec. 7, 1915).

Washington's acceptance of the status quo had been adamantly rejected by Du Bois and the NAACP, and with Washington's passing, the opportunity was created for the rise of the "New Negro" and the "Harlem Renaissance," both of which embodied a militancy that the Tuskegee Machine abjured. This confrontational style was exemplified when Du Bois and the NAACP decided to protest *The Birth of a Nation*, a production from the then-infant motion picture industry. Based upon Thomas Dixon's novel *The Clansman*, and directed by Hollywood's first wunderkind, D. W. Griffith, this film was a caustic history lesson meant to glorify the "lost cause" of the Confederacy, which had plunged the nation into the Civil War, leading to over 600,000 deaths—equivalent to over 5 million on a per-capita basis if calculated on today's population. The movie was intended to inflame, with its scenes of a dainty white woman committing suicide rather than submit to the bestial passions of an African-American man pursuing her (actually a white actor in blackface acted in this scene, as the filmmakers chose not to hire Negro performers). Reconstruction following the Civil War, which Du Bois was to portray in one of his more celebrated works as an era of democratic promise, here was presented as an era of rampant corruption and venality.

The film raked in huge profits and was shown—and praised—in Wilson's White House. Sensing immediately the power of this new medium that was cinema, Du Bois leaped into action. On May 30, 1915, 2,000 protesters packed an energetic meeting held at Boston's Faneuil Hall that sharply criticized this cinematic assault. Du Bois gave the main address, in which he contrasted the film, its content, and its spirit with what actually occurred during Reconstruction (*Boston Traveller*, May 31, 1915). *The Birth of a Nation* emerged at a time when lynching was skyrocketing, residential segregation was ossifying, and Jim Crow showed no signs of dissipating. The results were predictable: it was not unusual for white patrons of this cinematic provocation to launch attacks upon Negroes upon departing movie houses. Simultaneously, civil libertarians fretted that protesters might violate the free speech rights of moviemakers if they could prevail upon the authorities to shut down this outrage. Not for the last time, civil libertarians and civil rights advocates disagreed: in his justly praised autobiography, *Dusk of Dawn*, Du Bois observed that coincidentally enough, the "number of mob murders so increased that nearly one hundred Negroes were lynched during 1915 and a score of whites, a larger number than had occurred for more than a decade." It was "dangerous to limit expression," Du Bois opined. "Yet without some limitations civilization could not endure." It was a "miserable dilemma," he concluded—but one whose brunt he did not shirk (Du Bois, 1983, 340). The upside of this controversy centered on a racist extravaganza that propelled more positive developments, for this film inspired the NAACP to become more involved in Hollywood, seeking to intercept noxious scripts, spur the hiring of Negro performers, and, ultimately, galvanize a new generation of Negro filmmakers.

For Du Bois, his festering irritation with Hollywood was merging with his growing disapproval of the current occupant of the White House. He was coming to regret his past support for Wilson, but the U.S. political scene did not offer an array of pleasant alternatives. There was "little to choose," he lamented, between "these two great parties," referring to Wilson's Democrats and the Republicans (*Crisis*, Oct. 1916).

Du Bois had long been a fierce advocate of women's suffrage as a means of changing the political scene. He understood that racial and sexual exploitation were mutually constitutive; as such, he opposed the position of many of his male contemporaries, like the dean of Howard University Kelly Miller, who considered women to be the weaker sex. In a 1915 *Crisis* editorial, Du Bois equated such statements to pejoratives about the "darker races" and "lower classes." He held that difference did not mean inferiority or weakness, and that true democracy could not be achieved until women had the right to vote. While he has been criticized for his "masculinism," detractors have nonetheless acknowledged his vehement opposition to patriarchy and misogyny. While Du Bois was a proponent of women's equality generally, he was particularly committed to the uplift and inclusion of his "darker sisters." His 1912 pledge to defend them from the insults and aggression of white and Black men alike was part of a long tradition of advocating for Black women's equality. In 1913 he noted that Black women were the archetypes of economic independence, personal liberty, and spiritual poise, and as such, they were the purveyors of ideals, strength, and opportunities for womanhood. As well, he proffered that it was Black women's "revolutionary ideals" that would have the most influence on the thoughts and actions of U.S. society (Du Bois, "Woman Suffrage," 1915; "I Am Resolved," 1912; "The Woman in Black," 1913).

Hence, it was at this juncture that the journal he edited, *Crisis*, took a page from that movement's playbook by advocating a "Negro Party [along] the lines of the recently formed Woman's Party." Barring that, Du Bois felt that African Americans, like picky diners at a Chinese restaurant, should select discriminately from an array of possible options, including candidates from the two major parties, the Socialists, and, possibly, their own political organ. As for the presidential candidates, Du Bois suggested that his constituency should vote for the Socialist—or stay home. These were unappetizing selections because the labor-backed Socialists were reluctant to confront racism directly, envisioning the proclamation of the socialist commonwealth as the only way out for the Negro—in the meantime, presumably suffering was the only available option—while the two major parties were either in league with the Ku Klux Klan (Democrats) or so wedded to Big Business (the GOP) that they could hardly ally effectively with a mostly working-class Negro community (*Crisis*, Nov. 1916).

Still, Du Bois seemed most disappointed with the Socialists, whom he seemed to think should be in the vanguard of the antiracist struggle; instead, they seemed to be perpetually lagging in this all-important realm. Their passivity toward fighting racism, he thought, cast the gravest doubt upon their sincerity and vitiated the possibility of their ever-mounting effective action (Du Bois, "The Problem," 1917–1918, 5–9).

Given his staunch opposition to President Wilson, friends and enemies alike were stunned when Du Bois lent support to what was probably the most controversial decision of Wilson's presidency—the decision to enter World War I on April 2, 1917. Du Bois's decision to support Wilson was even more surprising given his intimate knowledge of Germany— particularly its language and culture—and the presumed immunity to the anti-Berlin hysteria that it provided, hysteria that was then coursing throughout the land. To be sure, Du Bois then thought that positive developments could emerge from this conflict, not least because the major powers—notably the United States, Britain, and France—were so heavily dependent on troops of African descent. It was in that spirit that he appeared on a platform with Lajpat L. Rai, the great anticolonial crusader from British India (*Crisis*, Nov. 1916). The two friends addressed a session on the plight of the colonized and the oppressed shortly after Wilson's fateful decision. Sponsored by the Intercollegiate Socialist Society and held in Bellport, Long Island, it was there that Du Bois announced portentously that the war then raging should be fought in the hope that a result might be the enhancement of the independence of colored peoples, including Indians, a result that would enhance the otherwise dreary lives of African Americans (Horne, 2008).

He was to be proven wrong in the specific—for as Du Bois knew better than most, this was an unjust war, a war grounded in the division of colonial spoils, that could hardly eventuate in a just result. But he was correct in general—African Americans began to realize that a crucial factor in determining their fate was precisely what was occurring in the world at large.

6

A Life of Conflict

Rather quickly, Du Bois's support for United States' entry into what was then called the Great War was proven to be deeply flawed. This fundamental error, combined with his feud with Marcus Garvey, who had sought to seize the mantle of the now-departed Booker T. Washington, cast a shadow over Du Bois's subsequent career—among the Black left as a result of his misjudgment of the war and among Black nationalists as a result of his confrontation with the bombastic migrant from Jamaica.

On the other hand, those so bold as to oppose the war often found themselves harassed, under indictment, or, in the case of immigrants, deported. As an officer of the NAACP, already under siege, adopting positions beyond the mainstream on such a fundamental matter as war and peace was not easy. A strategic objective of the Association and its erudite staffer was the inclusion of African Americans at all levels of U.S. society, not least the military—but did this mean backing every goal of a military, which at that point was brutally occupying Du Bois's ancestral homeland, Haiti?

This issue came to the fore in the case of Charles Young, one of a very few Black graduates of West Point and a friend of Du Bois from the 1890s, when both were teaching at Wilberforce. During an often tense twenty-eight years of active duty, Young had served the U.S. Army in the U.S. West, in Haiti, in Liberia, and during the revolutionary tumult in Mexico. Then, after much agitation by the NAACP and its allies, in 1917 the War Department established a center for the training of Negro officers in Des

---

LIBERIA

In "The African Plymouth Rock," Du Bois analyzed the founding of Liberia at the intersection of the industrial revolution, the spread of European economic imperialism in Africa, and the rise of the Cotton Kingdom in the United States. Liberia was settled in 1822 by the American Colonization Society "as a dumping ground for America's Negro problem"—that is, to resettle free African Americans who threatened the continuation of the U.S. slave system. They were joined by enslaved Africans who had been captured from smugglers by American war ships.

Liberia became an independent nation-state in 1849, though the United States did not recognize it as such until after the Civil War. From the outset, it was imperiled by British and French economic interests. At the 1885 Berlin Conference, Liberia protested for Africans' natural right to the land and condemned imperial attempts to impede the ability to "build up a Negro nationality."

Despite European insistence that Liberia was undeveloped and that Africans were unfit to rule themselves, the new nation-state continued to defend its sovereignty. Struggling from lack of capital investment, predatory loans from England, and ineffective efforts to export sugar and coffee, the troubled Liberian economy temporarily recovered in 1909 when, with the help of African Americans, it procured financing and protection from the United States. Nonetheless, throughout the first half of the twentieth century, the country remained dependent on foreign trade and aid, and it continued to be pressured by imperial powers to cheaply surrender its natural resources and labor.

Moines, Iowa. Young, by then a lieutenant colonel, was generally expected to be the officer in charge. But that spring, at forty-nine years old, Young was subjected to a medical examination that uncovered high blood pressure. This revelation excluded Young from serving as the officer in charge. In the face of pressure from African Americans and persistent efforts by Young himself (he rode on horseback from Ohio to Washington, DC, to demonstrate his physical stamina), the spotlight was shone brightly on his troubling case. This demonstration was to prove wanting, despite Du Bois's adamant intervention (*Crisis* 14, Oct. 1917, 286; 14, 1918, 165).

But the larger question was this: Was there an inherent tension, if not contradiction, in Du Bois's and the NAACP's stance of integration and the tasks performed by those doing the integrating? Could one demand inclusion of Negroes in the military without conceding that the military had a role to play that often was deleterious? Black nationalists of Garvey's stripe began to resolve this tension by reconsidering the entire notion of Negro inclusion into what many saw as a bankrupt society; instead, Garvey and others called for repatriation to Africa or otherwise building a Negro nation. From the affluent sailor Paul Cuffe funding a small group to settle in Sierra Leone in the early nineteenth century to the organization of the Liberia Exodus Arkansas Colony in 1877 to Bishop Henry McNeal Turner helping to convince over five hundred African Americans in the 1890s to emigrate to Liberia through the American Colonization Society, "Back-to-Africa" movements and schemes have been a staple of Black history. A return to the Africa, proponents believed, resolved a host of issues, including the inability of whites and Blacks to exist on an equal footing, the potential extinction of the Black race if they remained in the United States, the deplorable socioeconomic conditions of African descendants, and persistent white supremacist violence and terrorism. Thus, organizations like Garvey's Universal Negro Improvement Association and African Communities League and Mittie Maude Lena Gordon's Peace Movement of Ethiopia worked to garner resources—even from the very racists they sought to escape—to ensure a better life in Africa (see Blaine, 2018).

Ultimately, Du Bois's tenure with the NAACP was to run aground because of a similar tension: How did one oppose racial segregation and push for inclusion through the vehicle of organizations that were often based on tight Negro unity? Thus, Du Bois and the NAACP were elated when, in the midst of war preparation, 700 Negro men were commissioned as officers while others were given high appointments in the Departments of War and Labor. The Red Cross followed suit by promising to employ Negro women as nurses, though they later reneged. Moreover, Du Bois was influenced by the pro-war attitude of his NAACP colleague, Joel Spingarn. It was in that context that Du Bois made a decision that was to bring him a maelstrom of criticism, especially from the Black left and Black nationalists, for years to come: in June 1917, Du Bois was asked to serve in a projected special bureau whose purpose was, supposedly, to "satisfy" the grievances of Negroes but was justifiably seen by his critics as little more than intelligence gathering for U.S. authorities. In fact, the agency of the U.S. General Staff for which Du Bois would work was notorious for harassing both African Americans and radicals.

This was the background for his infamous July 1918 *Crisis* editorial "Close Ranks," which Spingarn had encouraged Du Bois to write to increase his chances of being appointed a captain in military intelligence. The contentious editorial contained the fateful sentence: "Let us, while this war lasts, forget our special grievances and close our ranks shoulder to shoulder with our own white fellow citizens and the allied nations that are fighting for democracy." It would have been bad enough if he had stopped there, but in a rhetorical flight, for which he was well-known, Du Bois—who more than most had reason to resist the anti-Berlin hysteria—asserted, "that which the German power represents today spells death to the aspirations of Negroes and all the darker races for equality, freedom and democracy."

Many Black Americans had a hard time swallowing this approach. One comrade of William Monroe Trotter was "amazed beyond expression. I believe that we should do just the reverse of what you advise"; actually, said Byron Gunner, the war "was the most opportune time for us to push and keep our 'special grievances' to the fore" (Aptheker, 1973, 228). The most vociferous critic of "Close Ranks" was Trotter's comrade Hubert Harrison, "grand organizer" of the antiwar National Liberty Congress to be held in June 1918 and one of the most important Harlem Black radicals of the early twentieth century. Encouraged by Major Walter Howard Loving, the lone Black officer in military intelligence, Harrison excoriated Du Bois in a July 25, 1918, editorial titled "The Descent of Dr. Du Bois." He argued that Du Bois had sacrificed his commitment to racial equality to collaborate with the War Department and that "Close Ranks" encouraged the race to be acquiescent and subservient. Most egregious of all, according to Harrison, was Du Bois's instruction for Black people to "forget their special griev-ances" because this would require them to cede their life, manhood, and political liberty to white domination. Moreover, the editorial represented the moral downfall of another leader who chose to genuflect to white authority rather than ethically represent the race's consciousness. As such, Harrison proclaimed, Du Bois had failed African Americans, who no lon-ger trusted him and now rejected his leadership (Perry, 2010, 385–390).

Just as the Red Cross' promise of hiring African-American women had been withdrawn, so too was the offer of an intelligence post to Du Bois, due in no small part to Harrison's withering critique of him. Nonetheless, the controversy continued, and for good reason. How could it not? How could the Du Bois of the "African Roots of War," the Du Bois who condemned the U.S. occupation in Haiti, the Du Bois who sternly denounced Jim Crow and any accommodation to it, become the Du Bois of July 1918 who offered to make a "constructive attempt to guide Negro public opinion by removing pressing grievances of colored folk which hinder the prosecution of the war"? (Aptheker, 1973, 227–228). Decades later it remains difficult to com-prehend altogether Du Bois's attempt to reverse field and contradict much of what he had espoused. On the other hand, James Weldon Johnson, who was the chief administrator of the NAACP, had served in the U.S. diplomatic corps in Central America at a time of great turmoil, which suggested that a precedent had been set for NAACP leaders toiling on behalf of Washington and, more precisely, extending the battle for inclusion of Negroes to all levels—including the inner sanctums of power. Again, the larger question—which would erupt in the 1960s when "integration" became the watchword of the Black Freedom Movement—was, in the phrase of the brilliant writer James Baldwin, should one choose to "integrate" a burning house?

In that vein, Du Bois continued his pro-war drumbeat. In August and September 1918, the *Crisis* implored, "This is Our Country. We have worked for it, we have suffered for it, we have fought for it; we have made its music, we have tinged its ideals, its poetry, its religion, its dreams." What the *Crisis* failed to ask was, how could an unjust war for redivision of colonial spoils benefit African Americans? This issue may have occurred to Du Bois himself, for hard on the heels of his misbegotten effort to enlist in military intelligence, his beaver-like energy turned in the opposite direction: the fate of the colonized, particularly in Africa, as a result of the war, began to rivet his imagination. Even before this juncture, Du Bois had addressed the cosmopolitan readers of the *New York Post*, warning them that the silence about Africa's future was ominous for those who wished a democratic outcome of the war (*New York Post*, Sept. 22, 1917).

With Africa in mind, in early December 1918 Du Bois headed eastward across the swirling waters of the Atlantic, destined for Paris. He had been preceded by President Woodrow Wilson, who was headed to Versailles with the aim of forging a peace settlement for a conflict that had led to the deaths of 21 million civilians and combatants. Du Bois, on the other hand, was on a mission for the NAACP to serve as special representative with the portfolio of ensuring that what occurred at Versailles was not disadvantageous to those of African descent. This would include convening another Pan-African Congress, though, unlike the earlier conference, it would be clear who was in charge: Du Bois. This congress would also include an investigation of the treatment of Negro soldiers, including 200,000 African Americans, as reports streamed in concerning their maltreatment during the recently concluded conflict.

Upon arriving in France, the Du Bois who had attempted to work on behalf of U.S. military intelligence had vanished, supplanted by the Du Bois who had become the very apostle and tribune of Black liberation. He informed NAACP members about his proposal for moving Africa away from European domination and toward control by Africans themselves, which would open the door to mass migration by African Americans to Africa, an idea that Garvey, ironically, came to embody. Du Bois, however, denied that this was a "'separatist' movement" because, he counseled, "the African movement means to us what the Zionist movement must mean to the Jews, the centralization of race effort and the recognition of a racial fount" (*Crisis* 17, Feb. 1919).

As it turned out, only a handful of the fifty-eight delegates from sixteen nations, protectorates, and colonies that attended the Pan-African Congress had intimate day-to-day knowledge of Africa. Even Du Bois, the convener, had yet to visit the continent—and at this gathering, he was not alone in this deficiency—though it was heartening that Haiti was well represented, given its historic role as a Pan-African citadel. Still, the opening session was quite impressive with the delegates seated at long green tables attired in business suits and frock coats (*New York Evening Globe*, Feb. 22, 1919).

Du Bois was buoyed by his presence in France, which soon was to become a site of exile for a generation of African-American intellectuals and artists it embraced, including Josephine Baker, Richard Wright, Ollie Harrington, and James Baldwin. "Vive La France!" chortled Du Bois as he hailed France's public celebration of the role of African soldiers most notably in preventing her defeat, after the French had almost wholly ingested propaganda about German superiority, a notion eroded in the battlefields of Marne and Verdun (*Crisis* 17, Mar. 1919). France's hospitability, however, did not necessarily extend to the Pan-African Congress, a congress that was thought to have anticolonial overtones, held on its soil. The "American Secret Service [was] at my heels," Du Bois complained later, though Europe, presumably, was beyond their remit. Yet the Pan-African Congress was held nonetheless, and "the world fight for black rights is on," he exclaimed. Rather ambitiously, he proclaimed, "[W]e plan an international quarterly, 'Black Review,' to be issued in English, French and possibly in Spanish and Portuguese." Du Bois expressed hope about the formation of the League of Nations, sensing that if appeals to Washington went unheeded, the league might lend a willing ear. As for his other mission, Du Bois—who only recently had urged Black Americans to "close ranks" in support of the war—now expressed shock at how Negro troops were being mistreated. Already it seemed that Du Bois was edging and inching away from his startling pro-war stance, observing that "under similar circumstances, we would fight again. But by the God of Heaven, we are cowards and jackasses if now that the war is over, we do not marshal every ounce of our brain and brawn to fight a sterner, longer, more unbending battle against the forces of hell in our own land" (*Crisis* 18, May 1919).

No doubt Du Bois was chastened by what he discovered concerning the brutishness directed toward Negro troops: even the most ingenuously trusting naïf would have had difficulty in supporting a war in which men were treated so horribly (*Nashville Globe*, May 1919). To his credit, Du Bois did not let his initial error infect his subsequent actions, for he collected documents about this scandal and dutifully published them for the benefit of a wider audience. Readers of the *Crisis* learned that Paris was informed that their citizenry's less-than-hostile attitude toward U.S. Negroes was a threat to Washington's security. Rather angrily, the U.S. authorities announced that "the French public has become accustomed to treating the Negro with familiarity and indulgence." The authorities argued that such solidarity had to end as it was an "affront" to U.S. "national policy"; Washington was "afraid that contact with the French will inspire in black Americans aspirations which to them [Euro-Americans] appear intolerable" (*Crisis* 18, May 1919, 7–11).

Thus, if Du Bois committed an egregious and fundamentally flagrant error in requesting African Americans to "close ranks" on behalf of this war in an effort to gain a military intelligence post, it is striking that within months, he sought to make amends, advising Negro soldiers who only recently had wielded weapons: "We Return. We Return from Fighting. We Return Fighting" (*Crisis* 18, May 1919). Yes, they did—because they had to—for Negro troopers were at times murdered in their uniforms as the former slave South leaped to reassert its dominance over those who might have imbibed "subversive" ideas in the freer air of France and had the effrontery to act likewise. Dixie's worst nightmare took place in August 1917 when armed Negro troops in the Jim Crow bastion that was Houston, Texas, went on a rampage, attacking white police officers and others in retaliation for real and imagined provocations. What ensued thereafter was the Red Summer of 1919, as pogroms were launched against Black men and women in Chicago, East St. Louis, and elsewhere.

The great migration from the Deep South to these industrial sites was unfolding, driven by the war's need for labor to staff industrial plants and the difficulty faced by the traditional source—European migrants—in crossing the submarine-infested Atlantic. The war's end also meant there was no longer a need to maintain any kind of diplomacy toward the quint-essential domestic foe—the Negro—and open season upon them quickly ensued, a direct rebuff to Du Bois's naïve notion that this conflict would bring benefits. Now breathing fire, Du Bois instructed his troops in the NAACP that "when the armed lynchers gather, we too must gather armed." His words rising in intensity, he exhorted, "[W]e must defend ourselves." Fueled with the radicalism that only a trip to Paris, and the witnessing of bloody pogroms, could bring, Du Bois went on to hail the "one new Idea of the World War—the Idea which may well stand in future years as the one thing that made the slaughter worthwhile—is an Idea which we are like[ly] to fail to know because it is today hidden under the maledictions hurled at Bolshevism" (*Crisis* 19, Sept. 1919, 231–232).

Du Bois was reacting to the reality that in the midst of the war, com-munists had seized power in Russia and then pledged to assist Africa in fighting European colonialism. Though he may have had occasional con-flicts with the domestic counterparts of the Bolsheviks in the U.S. Com-munist Party, Du Bois remained a partisan of what became the Union of Socialist Soviet Republics (USSR) from its inception. Du Bois's ties with the USSR were ultimately to lead to the real threat of imprisonment. But Du Bois at that moment could hardly know what fate awaited. In any case, he was then overjoyed at the growth of *Crisis*, which had skyrocketed from sales of 9,000 in 1911 to 104,000 by mid-1919: he must have concluded that he was doing something right (*Crisis* 18, Sept. 1919).

Nevertheless, Du Bois's paeans of praise for Bolshevism cannot be understood outside of the context in which he was operating, that is, the gnawing perception that African Americans had few allies in North

America and were fighting a desperate battle for survival, and, like the United States itself when faced with this daunting prospect in World War II, Du Bois saw no alternative to seeking an ally in Moscow. The events in Elaine, Arkansas, in which scores of African-American sharecroppers were slaughtered and hundreds jailed after they protested against their cruel fate, further substantiated the desperate plight of those Du Bois was sworn to serve. With aching precision, Du Bois took to the pages of the mainstream press to plead on their behalf, but at a certain point, he had to wonder if justice could actually be achieved in a nation founded on the principle of African enslavement (*New York World*, Nov. 28, 1919).

* * *

By 1918, Du Bois was fifty years old and increasingly viewed as the preeminent intellectual among African Americans. To be sure, he was spending ever-increasing amounts of time away from his spouse and seemed to be married in name only—yet, his public persona seemed to be reaching for the stratosphere. Yes, there were bumps in the road, the failed attempt to join U.S. military intelligence being foremost among them. But, ironically, the perfervid essence of Jim Crow, which automatically cast African Americans unilaterally into the profoundest depths of Hades, made it difficult for the talented among them—such as Du Bois—to be embraced by the dominant society. Such rejection converted them, whether intentional or not, into dissidents of various types.

Such brutal ironies inexorably drove an intellectual like Du Bois to his typewriter. *Darkwater*, his sixth book, was published in 1920, though the final draft was actually completed in 1918 on his fiftieth birthday. It captured nicely the essence of its creator in that it was a curious mélange of autobiographical reflections, trenchant commentary, poetry, fictional musings, and the like. Yet among the odds and ends, standing out starkly in these pages was his pivotal essay, "The Damnation of Women," a heartfelt assault on the centuries-long brutalization of African-American women in particular. This essay, emerging at a time when the right of women to vote was about to be ratified, was quite timely.

Yet it could not be denied that some among his constituency had lost confidence in Du Bois because of his dalliance with U.S. military intelligence, and such doubts not only created an opening for the rise of one Marcus Garvey but also created fertile soil for a raging debate between the two—a debate that has survived the passing from the scene of both men. Garvey, a Jamaican, was deeply influenced by Du Bois's former sparring partner, Booker T. Washington, but it would be an error to see their conflict as simply a replay of what had occurred at the turn of the twentieth century. To the contrary, Du Bois and Garvey had much in common, which may have made their contretemps all the more ferocious. Both men had a deep and abiding interest in Africa. They recognized that the destiny of the diaspora was tied intimately to the fate of continent—that African Americans would receive better treatment if Africa itself were to revive, and this meant that both men placed a premium on anticolonialism, which brought both into conflict with London, Paris, Brussels, and Lisbon.

Another commonality of the two men was their roots in the Caribbean basin. Garvey's rise was difficult to separate from the mass migration of those from the so-called British West Indies (Jamaica, Trinidad, Barbados, etc.) to New York City in particular, where they came to comprise a significant portion of the overall Black population. Emerging from small islands where those of African origin were the overwhelming majority, West Indians including Richard B. Moore, Cyril V. Briggs, Claudia Jones, and Claude McKay brought a determined militancy to the United States as many were unaccustomed to taking a racial backseat.

Their relationship commenced innocently enough. Garvey, who was born in Jamaica in 1887 and died in 1940 in London, first visited the United States in March 1916. A year earlier, he had been in correspondence with Booker T. Washington, who urged the journey, but ominously, by the time Garvey arrived, Washington was dead. Though he was nonplussed, one of Garvey's first efforts in the United States was to hold a meeting, with a lecture by himself and musical entertainment, at Saint Mark's Hall at West 138th Street in Harlem. The lecture concerned Jamaica, and the meeting's purpose was to help Garvey's nascent organization form industrial farms. Thus, on April 25, 1916, Garvey visited Du Bois's office but found him out of town, so, quite graciously, he left a note asking if the famed intellectual would "be so good as to take the 'chair' at my first public lecture." Du Bois just as graciously declined (Aptheker, 1973, 214–215).

By mid-1920, Garvey's forces had grown exponentially, and he then paid Du Bois the ultimate compliment: "At the International Convention of Negroes to be held in New York during the month of August," he told his soon-to-be bitter rival, "the Negro people of America will elect a leader by the popular vote of the delegates from the forty-eight States of the Union. This leader, as expected, will be the accredited spokesman of the American Negro people. You are hereby asked," Du Bois was informed, "to be good enough to allow us to place your name in nomination for the post" (Aptheker, 1973, 245). This was during an era of good feeling between the two, as Du Bois referred glowingly to Garvey as "an extraordinary leader of men" and one who had "with singular success capitalized and made vocal the great and long-suffering grievances and spirit of protest of the West Indian peasantry." At this juncture, Du Bois was evidently moved by the spectacle of Garvey's Universal Negro Improvement Association and African Communities League (UNIA), which had been organized in Jamaica in 1914 with the goal of uplift of Africa and Africans. However, a premonition of Du Bois's increasing

BOLSHEVIK REVOLUTION

In February 1917, the Romanoff Czars, in power since the beginning of the seventeenth century, were ousted from power. The regime had been routed by Japan in the previous decade, and in the context of World War I, a bourgeois democratic revolution led by Alexander Kerensky seized power from the weakened dynasty and established a provisional government. In October 1917, the Bolsheviks—Russian Marxists organized under Vladimir I. Lenin—took control of the revolutionary situation. Seizing power from the bourgeois revolutionaries, they demanded peace, basic necessities, the end to imperialist war, and a worker-peasant alliance. They did so to prevent counterrevolution and to consolidate popular power in the form of the United Soviet Socialist Republics (USSR).

The Bolsheviks sought to organize industry and production in the interest of workers and to fundamentally redistribute income and wealth. They installed a "dictatorship of the laboring class" and soon wiped out adult illiteracy, democratized land use, increased wages, improved working conditions, expanded housing, improved food access and quality, and gave peasants modern machinery to till the land. The period of 1921–1925 was the period of rehabilitation; 1926–1932 was the period in which the foundations of the socialist economy were laid; and the period of 1932–1938 saw the restructuring of the socialist economy completed and socialism consolidated.

The rapid development of the USSR was made possible by rational planning; the full utilization of material and human productive resources; the elimination of periodic crisis, demand creation, and competition; and the rapid increase in production and the propensity to accumulate.

skepticism toward Garvey and the UNIA is reflected in his polite but terse response that, "I thank you for the suggestion but under no circumstances can I allow my name to be presented," to which he added, "However, I desire to publish in the *Crisis* some account of you and your movement" (Aptheker, 1973, 245–246).

But just as Du Bois stubbed his toe on the boulder that was military intelligence, Garvey too had his flaws, which caused the NAACP leader to pursue him with a determined ferocity. For although, like Du Bois, Garvey had spoken highly of the Bolsheviks and Irish anticolonialists, unlike Du Bois, the Jamaican had sought an alliance with the terrorist Ku Klux Klan on the premise, inter alia, that both would be satisfied if African Americans decamped en masse from North America (Du Bois, "Back to Africa," 1923). Thus, despite their commonalities, Du Bois went to some length to distinguish himself from the Jamaican, particularly differentiating his brand of Pan-Africanism from Garvey's version (*New York Age*, May 28, 1921).

Ultimately, Garvey ran afoul of the U.S. authorities and was tried for and convicted of mail fraud, spending time in federal prison before being unceremoniously deported. This led to the still resonant charge that Garvey's misfortunes were a product of the purported rivalry between him and Du Bois and their two organizations, respectively—a charge Du Bois rejected with contempt. "It is absolutely untrue that the NAACP is a rival organization to the UNIA or instigated the charges against Garvey," he contended. He conceded that the *Crisis* had published articles about Garvey and his organization and that he "furnished" these to the Department of Justice. But, he maintained, three of the articles in his journal were simply "expository and on the whole friendly," though admittedly, the fourth was "severely condemnatory" but "was not published until after his conviction and because of the propaganda which he was sending out against our organization and against all Negroes in the United States who were standing up for their rights as American citizens." As Du Bois saw things, Garvey's troubles "originated in two ways. First because of suits brought against him by members of his own organization who had invested in the Black Star Line under false representation and secondly by the effort of the state and city of New York to make Garvey stop violating the law in his issuing and selling of stock. The prosecuting members," Du Bois emphasized, "in every single case were former members of Garvey's organization or officers of the law. Not a single member or officer of the NAACP appeared as witness against Garvey" (Aptheker, 1973, 317–318; see also Du Bois's contribution to "A Symposium on Garvey," *Messenger* 4, Dec. 1922, 551; *Crisis* 21, Dec. 1920; 21, Jan. 1921; 24, Sept. 1922; 28, Aug. 1924).

This was no doubt true, but this could not obscure the sharp differences that had arisen between the two, with Garvey commenting derisively more than once about the interracial nature of the NAACP and what he saw as the preponderance of light-skinned Negroes within their ranks. There was probably an ethnic component to the conflict as well, as the controversy between the NAACP and UNIA erupted simultaneously as migrants from the Caribbean basin at times encountered conflict in integrating seamlessly into the boroughs of New York City. African Americans had a tendency to express anti-Caribbean and nativist sentiments, while Caribbean immigrants felt compelled to form their own cultural and political organizations to distinguish themselves from the despised African Americans. Some African Americans believed that the difference between the two groups stemmed not only from national and cultural divergences but also from the fact that West Indian immigrants were stealing American jobs, were submissive and litigious in nature, and believed themselves to be superior to African Americans. Radicals like Wilfred Adolphus Domingo, who hailed from the Caribbean, warned that such stereotyping undermined intraracial solidarity, created undue hostility toward West Indians, and opened them up to state repression. Nonetheless, African Americans across the political spectrum, from the socialist Chandler

Owen to the conservative Kelly Miller, accused West Indians of being politically deviant, especially susceptible to foreign ideology, and blind followers of Garvey due to ignorance and emotionalism. In turn, African Americans were accused of prioritizing the leadership and views of the Black bourgeoisie over and above the working class and of subjecting poorer, less educated African Americans to elite domination. These issues of nationality and class exacerbated the conflict between Garvey's UNIA and the Du Bois's NAACP (Makalani, 2011, 105–109).

Thus, in January 1922, Garvey was arrested by federal authorities and charged with using the mail to defraud, and it was at this point that his ideology began veering in a more conservative direction. He was tried in May 1923 before Judge Julian Mack, a contributor to the NAACP, which convinced many of his followers that the NAACP's hand in his conviction and imprisonment was not exactly benign or minor. Earlier, eight prominent African Americans—including William Pickens and Robert W. Bagnall of the NAACP—had petitioned the U.S. Attorney General to "push the government's case against Marcus Garvey" (Essien-Udom, 1967, xxvi). Rather promptly, Garvey was convicted and received a five-year prison term, although three codefendants were acquitted. President Calvin Coolidge commuted the sentence in 1927, and in December of that year, Garvey was deported to Jamaica, though this hardly ended the conflict between himself and Du Bois.

Given the circumstances, it was believed far and wide in Black America that Du Bois helped to manipulate the prosecution and deportation of his political rival—an allegation that the NAACP leader was compelled to deny more than once. "I beg to say," he announced resolutely after the initial conviction, "I have never written any letters to the District Attorney or Judge Mack or anyone else in authority with regard to Marcus Garvey, nor have had anything whatsoever to do with the prosecution of the case against him" (Aptheker, 1972, 271–272). But Du Bois's detractors were disbelieving. Among this proliferating group was Ida May Reynolds. Du Bois's presumed anti-Garvey posture, she said, was "unmanly and cowardly"; moreover, she insisted, "the methods used by you and your organization were . . . uncalled for" and "will always reflect to the discredit of you and your associates and cause everlasting enmity between the West Indian and the American Negroes which feeling will take a long time to eradicate" (Aptheker, 1973, 271–272).

There was reason for Ms. Reynolds to be skeptical of Du Bois's rationalizations, for what he had written in his journal about Garvey was quite lengthy—and pointed. Du Bois saw Garvey's movement as being expressive of the exploited peasantry of the Caribbean. Du Bois saw Garvey himself as "an honest and sincere man with a tremendous vision, great dynamic force, stubborn determination and unselfish desire to serve." Yet, Du Bois also perceived "very serious defects of temperament and training: he is dictatorial, domineering, inordinately vain and very suspicious." Moreover, "the great difficulty with him," said Du Bois of Garvey, "is that he has absolutely no business sense, no *flair* for real organization and his general objects are so shot through with bombast and exaggeration that it is difficult to pin them down for careful examination." Yet, Du Bois was struck by the point that Garvey had "become to thousands of people a sort of religion. He allows and encourages all sorts of personal adulation" (*Crisis* 21, Dec. 1920).

Du Bois was also struck by the point that Garvey had "never published a complete statement" of the income and expenditures of his organization. Nevertheless, Du Bois was taken by the fact that Garvey had "put vessels manned and owned by black men on the seas and they have carried passengers and cargoes." Du Bois could hardly disagree with the "main lines" of Garvey's program (as they mirrored his own): "American Negroes can, by accumulating and ministering their own capital, organize industry, join the black centers of the South Atlantic by commercial enterprise and in this way ultimately redeem Africa as a fit and free home for black men. This is true," said Du Bois (*Crisis* 22, Jan. 1921).

Du Bois continued to be haunted by Garvey, even as his various campaigns bore fruit. Thus, along with the *Crisis*, it was Garvey's newspaper, *Negro World*, that pioneered in providing a venue for the Harlem Renaissance—and early Black left politics of organizations like the African Blood Brotherhood—to flourish, and it was Garvey, despite his shortcomings, who put forward the idea of closer relationships between African Americans and Liberia, which Du Bois saw fit to emulate.

But from Du Bois's viewpoint, it was not just that Garvey was not expert in the art of execution or that he saw fit to consort with the Ku Klux Klan or express distaste for the lighter-skinned—a tension that, if pursued, could have torn Black America asunder. Du Bois recognized that in some ways, Garvey—his emphasis on Africa notwithstanding—represented an update of the program of Booker T. Washington (the man who brought the Jamaican to these shores in the first place), and, years after the Wizard had left the scene, Du Bois remained concerned about the impact of his ideas. As Du Bois saw things, both Garvey and Washington represented an evasion of the necessity to confront U.S. elites on their home turf—the former by looking longingly toward Africa, the latter by dint of his myopic stress on building businesses in Black America. It was in mid-1923 that Du Bois summed up his differences with Washington, asserting that his "weakness" was the "assumption that economic power can be won and maintained without political power." Garvey, too, evaded the central question of political power in the United States itself, even though this power could just as easily follow one to Africa, as the case of Liberia exemplified.

"No Negro dreams today," stressed Du Bois, "that he can protect himself in industry and business without a vote and without a fighting aggressive organization" (Aptheker, 1973, 266–267).

Still, it would be a mistake to view this conflict without a consideration of the context. That context was a sharp escalation of postwar racism, driven by apprehensions about the concomitant rise of the New Negro, that is, those who no longer saw the need to smile when nothing was funny, or shuffle when a confident stride would suffice, or confront white supremacy forcefully, if need be. The New Negro emerged out of a historically specific conjuncture of internationalism, antiracism, anticolonialism, and Black modernism between the two world wars. Though African Americans resided in a world that continued to be defined in Eurocentric and white supremacist terms that rationalized Black exploitation, after having "closed ranks" in World War I, they were far less willing to accept their second-class position, not least because international mobilization and connection had directly impacted their consciousness.

Hence, the New Negro was both an offensive and defensive subjectivity predicated upon the political and cultural drive for self-determination, self-sufficiency, economic development, and race pride. Through racial modernization in all areas, including art, science, economics, literature, and music, the New Negro sought to challenge white supremacy, inequality, dehumanization, and intimidation. New Negroes asserted their capacity for equality and citizenship through cultural creativity; analyses linking U.S. racism and Jim Crow to colonial and imperial oppression; and explorations of alternative modes of socioeconomic organization. They sought to challenge the narrative that African descendants were culturally backward because they had no history or civilization, a narrative that had historically legitimized racial domination, from enslavement to segregation to colonization.

On the one hand, the postwar era witnessed the rise of the second iteration of the terrorist and racist Ku Klux Klan, which actually dominated the political scene in Indiana, among other states, during this rabid era. On the other hand, the Klan was confronted by the rise of the New Negro's own Harlem Renaissance, which was a remarkable flowering of artistic merit, symbolized by the creativity of figures such as Langston Hughes, Jesse Fauset, Aaron Douglas, and James Weldon Johnson. Interestingly, Du Bois was at the center of this initiative as it was the journal he edited that gave many of these writers an opportunity to strut. Actually, this efflorescence stretched far beyond Harlem, as exemplified by Leopold Senghor, who led independent Senegal and before that had established an estimable reputation as a poet writing in French, and Nicolas Guillen of Cuba, whose wonderful poetry in Spanish was translated by Hughes.

This transnational effort was buoyed as well by Du Bois's continuing labor on behalf of the Pan-African Congress, which provided a rationale for these cross-border collaborations and linkages (*New York Age*, May 28, 1921). After the 1919 gathering in Paris, Du Bois convened yet another during the summer of 1921, this time in London (with the Labour Party participating) and Brussels (headquarters for, perhaps, colonialism at its most brutal: the Congo) with rapt attention paid to Paris (whose pretension to being a great power was based largely on its empire in Africa) and Lisbon (whose colonies, in Mozambique and Angola particularly, had contributed immeasurably to enslavement in the Americas) (*Manchester Guardian*, Aug. 30, 1921).

But even in this admirable effort, Du Bois revealed troubling signs that he may have been too busy peering over his shoulder at the presumed challenge from Garvey. For on the occasion of this congress, he informed Secretary of State Charles Evans Hughes—previously governor of New York, later chief justice of the U.S. Supreme Court, and therefore a member in good standing of the U.S. ruling elite—that his Pan-African Congress "has nothing to do with the so-called Garvey movement." Du Bois sought to reassure the fretting that his own movement "contemplates neither force nor revolution in its program. We have had the cordial cooperation," he stressed, "of the French, Belgian and Portuguese governments"—though in a real sense, this admission was discrediting in the eyes of many of the colonized (Aptheker, 1973, 250–251).

Nevertheless, it would be an oversimplification to dismiss Du Bois's handiwork peremptorily, for to do so would mean dismissing the extraordinary "Manifesto [to] the League of Nations" that was submitted by him in the aftermath of this Pan-African Congress. His "three earnest requests" included the farsighted demand that the needs of African workers be made the concern of a special section of the International Bureau of Labor; that a person of African descent be appointed a member of the Mandates Commission, which had taken jurisdiction over Germany's former colonies in Africa; and that the League itself "take a firm stand on the absolute equality of races and that it suggest to the colonial powers" that there should be formed an "International Institute for the Study of the Negro Problems and for the Evolution and Protection of the Negro Race." That this manifesto was trumpeted in the mass circulation *Crisis* ensured that it would receive wide dissemination (*Crisis* 23, Nov. 1921). Shortly thereafter, forces emanating from the congress pushed to have a special commission established by the International Bureau of Labor (*Crisis* 25, Mar. 1923).

Moreover, Du Bois continued to persevere on behalf of Liberia. Along with Ethiopia, Liberia stood as a lodestar among African Americans as African nations that had managed to escape colonialism. As 1923 dawned, Du Bois felt compelled to contact Secretary of State Hughes once more, this time because he was "alarmed at the failure of Congress to confirm the Liberian Loan." What was at play? It was "an open secret," argued Du

Bois, "that the British and French governments have only been held back in their aggression on Liberian territory, by the interest of the United States and by the prospect of her active aid," and if Washington failed to follow through, this beacon of African hope would "practically become a British protectorate with complete absorption looming in the future." One alternative proposed by Du Bois, which, once more, mirrored ideas then propagated by Garvey, "would be to establish a direct commercial intercourse between America and Liberia under a small company in which colored people [U.S. Negroes] had representation." Again, in case the influential Hughes had not noticed, Du Bois chose to bring Garvey into this field of vision, reminding him that the Jamaican's similar plan failed because he "was not a business man and turned out to be a thoroughly impractical visionary, if not a criminal" (Aptheker, 1973, 260–261). Du Bois was referring to Garvey's most ambitious commercial plan, the creation of the Black Star Line: the burly Jamaican raised hundreds of thousands of dollars, and four ships were ultimately obtained, though no business was ever actually conducted, at least not to any significant degree.

Unfortunately, the conflict with Garvey was not the sole relationship that rocked Du Bois's world. Walter Francis White, born in 1893, was a 1916 graduate of Atlanta University, and his family was well known to Du Bois when he resided in Georgia. At Du Bois's recommendation and with his urging, White, as a young man, served alongside James Weldon Johnson, the chief administrator of the NAACP. White was to take the helm of the association in 1931 and remain until his premature death in the mid-1950s. He was a man of no small talent, having authored numerous articles and several books of both fiction and nonfiction (e.g., his autobiography, White, 1948). Light-skinned enough to be able to pass as white, he did so at times in order to investigate lynchings. White had a black belt in the dark arts of bureaucratic infighting, which allowed him to oust Du Bois from his NAACP position twice—first in 1934 and then again in 1948. Their differences were stylistic but, as will be seen, also deeply political and, at their root, as consequential as Du Bois's differences with Washington and Garvey.

7

A Life in the Talented Tenth

When Du Bois stepped off a ship at the dock in West Africa in 1924, he recognized instinctively the potent importance of his arrival. Finally, he had arrived on the continent that had electrified his dreams and whetted his imagination. After spending so many hours of musing about Africa, he had arrived—but this was a bittersweet moment (Du Bois, "The Primitive," 1924, 675–676). "When shall I forget the night," he waxed, "I first set foot on African soil—I, the sixth generation in descent from my stolen forefathers." Yet the poverty and misery that greeted him was bracing during this 15,000-mile journey that took him to four African islands and five African colonies (*Crisis* 27, 1924).

This was part of Du Bois's largely successful attempt to escape the cloister that cocooned all too many scholars. For just before this punishing and protracted sojourn, Du Bois had embarked on a lengthy lecture tour in the United States that took him from Massachusetts to Minnesota, Oklahoma, Louisiana, and back to his home in New York; all in all, he spoke before over 20,000 people. His lectures were not only meant to enlighten but also to recruit for the NAACP, then in the midst of a membership drive.

These tours of Africa and the United States exemplified the contrasting aspects of Du Bois's life and career as he entered the second half of his life: a slashing indictment of white supremacy while in the United States and a less forceful approach in Africa, which was a virtual precondition to gaining admission to a continent—admission often denied to African Americans.

For as his minuet with U.S. military intelligence exemplified, Du Bois had difficulty in reconciling the apparently contrasting ideas of African Americans inclusion at all levels of U.S. society and representing a nation whose record abroad was considered questionable by some of his closest colleagues. Of course, when he accepted an offer by President Coolidge as special envoy to represent the United States at the inauguration of President C. D. B. King of Liberia in 1924, he had the added incentive, as noted, of seeking to block London and Paris's incursions into this rare independent African nation. Certainly, traveling with the imprimatur of Washington gave Du Bois added credibility when he arrived in Monrovia (the capital named after U.S. president James Monroe), though in retrospect, his journey illustrated once more that he and Garvey shared similar ideas when it came to Pan-Africanism.

For Du Bois insisted in language that could have been uttered by Garvey that Liberia "needs the aid of American Negro capital and colored technical experts to help Liberians in the development of agriculture, industry and commerce" (Aptheker, 1973, 279–280). But, unlike Garvey, Du Bois had another agenda, which did not necessarily reflect well upon him: he was an emissary of Washington and, thus, was carrying his nation's portfolio in a way that the anticolonial Jamaican did not. Thus, Du Bois argued that Liberia should favor capital infusions from the United States—in contrast to, for example, capital from Britain and France—since "if white Americans invest in Liberia and if they do not treat Liberia fairly and they try and get the United States Government to back up their demands, the Negroes of America [unlike the Negroes of London and Paris] have enough political power to make the government go slowly"; thus, "as between these three great countries, Liberia should apprehend least danger from American capital" (Aptheker, 1973, 279–280). This argument was no doubt pleasing to those in Washington.

The available menu of choices was decidedly unappetizing, Du Bois thought. After returning to the United States, he told Harvey Firestone, whose eponymous rubber company was to make a major fortune in Liberia, "I have seen parts of British and French colonial Africa and have come in close contact with those who know colonial conditions in other parts of Africa. In all these cases," he asserted, "with the exception of the French, the procedure has been to enter the black country with entirely white personnel, to use the natives as laborers with the lowest wage and to use imported whites as the personnel in control." He warned Firestone against replicating this distasteful pattern in Liberia by dispatching there "whites used to 'handling' colored laborers" who "get results by cruelty and browbeating alternating with pandering to drunkenness, gambling and prostitution among the blacks." Du Bois also requested that Firestone recruit "American Negroes" for his enterprise, seemingly unaware that the pattern was to keep this group as far away as possible for fear they might influence Africans toward sedition (Aptheker, 1973, 320–322).

Certainly, this equivocating approach was not Garvey's, but Du Bois's words, which the Jamaican would vilify, were a response to the abject weakness of Africans and African Americans at this moment. Garvey's approach, in a sense, ignored this weakness amid a farrago of verbiage about "up you mighty race!" while Du Bois—at this point—was seeking to leverage U.S. nationality in a positive manner, which was considered naïve, and not only by the cynics. Moreover, Du Bois's position carried more nuance than that of Garvey. Thus, he argued, there was "only one power" that might prevent Firestone Rubber from repeating "in Liberia all the hell that white imperialism has perpetrated heretofore in Africa and Asia," and "that is the black American with his vote" (Du Bois, "Liberia," 1925, 326–329). Du Bois was vainly seeking to play a weak hand strongly. Meanwhile, he reprinted in his journal an italicized letter from Ernest Lyon, Liberian consul general in the United States, who stated bluntly that "no person or persons leaving the United States under the auspices of the Garvey movement in the United States, will be allowed to land in the Republic of Liberia," a response to the perception that rather than seeking to assist this small West African nation, the UNIA was seeking to take it over (*Crisis* 28, 1924). This was a perception shared by Du Bois, who observed that "Liberia discovered that the Garvey organization was practically setting up a government within a government"—though, to be fair, Garvey's aim seemed to be anticolonial in nature, which ruffled the feathers of London and Paris, forcing Monrovia to act (Aptheker, 1973, 317–318).

Yet, to Du Bois's credit, this African initiative was not his only approach. He sought to forge an alliance with Moscow, which was also interested in destabilizing colonialism in Africa as a way to weaken a formidable foe in Europe. Unlike Garvey, he also sought to build domestic alliances beyond the mainstream. This was the import of his attempt over the years to ally with the Socialist Party. And, consequently, in 1924, he supported the third-party candidacy of Robert La Follette—the noted and influential Wisconsin leader of the left (as did, by the way, both the NAACP and the American Federation of Labor). He issued an appeal to his fellow Negro voters, urging them to do likewise, though he lamented the fact that the graying orator with a lion's mane, despite his positive platform, bowed to Jim Crow dictates and avoided any direct reference to the plight of African Americans (*New York Times*, Oct. 21, 1924; *Crisis* 28, 1924). On the other hand, La Follette had condemned the Klan and promised "to free Haiti," and, after all, a bit of a loaf was better than none at all (*Crisis* 29, Nov. 1924).

But this positive gesture illustrated the weakness that characterized Du Bois's position, because La Follette performed poorly at the ballot box in a nation that had extended its bigotry from African Americans to European immigrants. About 2 million African Americans cast ballots, with, most likely, about 1 million for Coolidge the Republican and half a million each for the Democrats and La Follette—which was something of a break-through from the time that the great Frederick Douglass proclaimed that the GOP was "the ship, all else is the sea." In Texas, the Negro vote defeated the Klan candidate for governor—though the Klan won important victories in Indiana, Kansas, Oklahoma, and Colorado (*Crisis* 29, Dec. 1924). Du Bois knew that as long as labor organizations were reluctant to embrace workers of all stripes, the most debilitated workers of all—African Americans—would be perpetually weak (Du Bois, "Worlds," 1925).

Hence, when his fellow intellectual, Kelly Miller, convened a meeting of the best and the brightest, the Negro Sanhedrin, to ponder the plight of the Negro, Du Bois was disappointed with the outcome. For their denunciation of unions and "economic radicalism" was "most pitiful," he thought. "Union labor has given the modern worker . . . whatever he has of decent wages, and hours and conditions of work" said Du Bois. As for "economic radicalism," now a live issue in light of events in Moscow, there "lies," said Du Bois "the only hope of the black folk" (*Crisis* 28, May 1924). Nonetheless, Du Bois was not naïve about the potential of these radicals as he knew that they very often functioned without even being aware of the special and awful oppression of over 12 million Negroes. Radicals' willful ignorance meant, whether they knew it or not, that their programs would remain stymied. "It is absolutely certain," he pronounced, "that the future of liberal and radical thought in the United States is going to be made easy or impossible by the way in which American democracy treats American Negroes" (*Crisis* 29, Mar. 1925).

As a result of such thinking, Du Bois hailed the organization in 1925 of the Pullman porters into a union under the leadership of A. Philip Randolph, born in 1889. Though they had endured sharp differences in the past, Du Bois was elated with his success. For the Brotherhood of Sleeping Car Porters, a union of mostly Negro men, also served as a communications network as they traveled by rail from city to city, often transmitting news and dropping off bundles of journals that might be unwise to send through the mail—such as the *Crisis* itself (*Crisis* 31, Dec. 1925; for more editorials by Du Bois urging support of Randolph's campaign, see *Crisis* 33, Jan. 1927; 34, Dec. 1927).

Still, Du Bois was above all an intellectual, and (jaunts to West Africa aside) this was what had come to occupy a good deal of his waking activity. Thus, the year of his first visit to Africa appropriately witnessed the publication of his still worthy book, *The Gift of Black Folk: Negroes in the Making of America.* This book was copyrighted by the Knights of Columbus in 1924 and was written at the request of that predominantly Catholic organization. This otherwise staid grouping was moved to this effort because of the anti-Catholicism and nativism that had reached a zenith during the 1924 election, spearheaded largely by the Ku Klux Klan, which had expanded its agenda beyond the traditional target—African Americans—to those who were Jewish and Catholic. A few years earlier in Georgia, Leo Frank, a Jewish factory manager, had been lynched in retaliation for his alleged killing of a young Christian woman; this outrage had spurred many Jewish Americans to join the NAACP on the accurate premise that anti-Semitism would rise or fall in the United States, depending on what fate befell African Americans. Many Catholics were arriving at a similar conclusion; hence the Knights of Columbus' sponsorship of Du Bois's new book. *The Gift of Black Folk*, carrying chapters on such matters as "Black Explorers," "Black Labor," "Black Soldiers," and, one of Du Bois's central preoccupations, "The Freedom of Womanhood," also carries reflections on music, art, and literature (Du Bois, *The Gift*, 1924).

Nevertheless, despite this collaboration with the Catholics, Du Bois was not blind to their liabilities, noting subsequently that "because Catholicism has so much that is splendid in its past and fine in its present, it is the greater shame that 'n*****' haters clothed in Episcopal robes should do to black Americans in exclusion, segregation and exclusion from opportunity all that the Ku Klux Klan ever asked" (*Crisis* 30, July 1925). In fact, he continued, "in over 400 years the Catholic Church has ordained less than a half dozen black Catholic priests either because they have sent us poor teachers or because American Catholics do not want to work beside black priests and sisters or because they think Negroes have neither brains nor morals enough to occupy positions open freely to Poles, Irishmen and Italians" (Aptheker, 1973, 309). The Catholic Church was a powerful institution in Louisiana particularly, where Jim Crow seemed to have no bounds. This body, thought Du Bois, "stands for color separation and discrimination to a degree equaled by no other church in America, and that is saying a very great deal" (Aptheker, 1973, 311). Lest anyone think that Du Bois was singling out the Catholics for a special critique, he went on to note that the mostly Protestant YMCA (Young Men's Christian Association) may have been worse, that "the Negro race" could "teach" the YMCA a "good deal about Christianity" (Aptheker, 1973, 313).

So there it was: although the 1920s may have been roaring for some, African Americans faced a dull roar of lynchings, exclusion, and the like. With rare exception, radical organizations were not sufficiently radical to take up their cause, and religious bodies were not sufficiently divine to counter this exclusionary tendency. In response, Du Bois was reduced to approaching those who desired to exploit Africa—like Firestone—with modesty and deference. The NAACP continued to plod along, though there were already disturbing signals that, like Villard before him, Walter White had severe doubts about the autonomy of their chief journal and its editor.

American Negro Labor Congress

The American Negro Labor Congress (ANLC) was organized in Chicago, Illinois, on October 25, 1925, by the Communist International (Comintern) and the Workers Party (WP). It was formed at the behest of the WP's Negro Committee to agitate for the complete economic, political, and social equality of Negroes in the United States; to launch a sustained campaign against segregation, lynching, race riots, and imperialism; and to extend communist efforts into the South. The ANLC also established a paper, *Negro Champion*, to voice the experiences and concerns of the Black masses.

Though the WP and other national Communist Parties were generally indifferent about the "Negro question," the Comintern supported the initiative of Black communists like Otto Huiswoud and Richard B. Moore to recruit Black workers from noncommunist organizations. The American Federation of Labor and the Brotherhood of Sleeping Car Porters, among others, were hostile to the ANLC because of its affiliation with the Soviet Union. Despite this Red-baiting, the ANLC gained the support of workers on Chicago's Southside through its attention to issues confronting Black Chicagoans and its support of anticolonial struggles in places including Haiti, Puerto Rico, and the Philippines.

Black Communist Lovett Fort-Whiteman's inept leadership hampered the ANLC's efforts to sustain a mass base and build an international network. Nonetheless, its work on behalf of the "working and farming classes" had some successes in key urban areas like Cleveland, Philadelphia, and Harlem. The ANLC was dissolved in 1929 and superseded by the League of Struggle for Negro Rights.

In short, things seemed rather bleak, which drastically circumscribed Du Bois's available options. One response he did develop was the notion of the Talented Tenth, or a cadre of the "best and the brightest" who would, somewhat selflessly, serve African Americans. Du Bois was one of those rare individuals who did not become more conservative as he grew older but rather more radical (most leaving radicalism behind with their departed youth), and eventually, he was to discard the idea of the Talented Tenth as unreflective of the reality of how easily the United States could seduce the talented with various emoluments. But by the time the 1920s arrived, he was still smitten with this notion, which seemed to reach stunning heights with the advent of the Harlem Renaissance, the emergence of an incredibly talented array of artists and cultural workers.

The Harlem Renaissance was a movement that offered an alternative narrative of modernity by harnessing race and culture for the purpose of achieving full equality for African Americans and combatting discrimination. This artistic formation, which lasted throughout the 1920s, conveyed that Black people were indeed modern, that the poor social conditions of

Black people were neither natural nor permanent, and that a reconstruction of the image of Blackness was possible through cultural production. This was a militant critique of inherent Black inferiority that legitimated Black dispossession; it posited that the *image* of Blackness—not Blackness itself—was the problem. The caricature of Black people in the sciences, film, and popular culture meant that aesthetic production was an essential site of struggle. To manipulate the image of Blackness was to manipulate reality, so the Harlem Renaissance aimed to craft a New Negro to combat pervasive pejorative stereotypes, from the licentious rapist presented in David Llewelyn Wark Griffith's *Birth of a Nation* to the stupid and complacent "Sambo" that was ubiquitous in American popular art of the time.

According to Alain LeRoy Locke, the "dean" of the Harlem Renaissance: "This deep feeling of race is at present the mainspring of Negro life. It seems to be the outcome of the reaction to proscription and prejudice; an attempt, fairly successful on the whole, to convert a defensive into an offensive position, a handicap into an incentive" (Locke, 1925, 11). The production of New Negro art was meant to gain white recognition of Black creative genius to achieve full inclusion, citizenship, and equality. Through cultural creativity, Black artists sought to insert themselves into the public sphere on their own terms by reconstructing and reconstituting Black images and representations. The Harlem Renaissance challenged white supremacist and Eurocentric assertions that Black people had no history or civilization and were therefore incapable of producing culture. It brought forth a historical connection between Blackness and modernity by establishing Black cultural creativity as a form of reason and rationality. Likewise, the Harlem Renaissance, according to Locke, was an assertion of Americanness that demanded the inclusion of Black people in the "American scene." By asserting Blackness as presence, the Harlem Renaissance as the artistic and creative space of Black development and self-realization produced a radicalized version of the American civilization narrative that, through cultural accumulation, included the New Negro as full citizen.

As early as 1903, Du Bois began to lay out more systematically what he meant by the talented tenth—the quintessential New Negroes. As he was beginning to think more deeply about his differences with Washington, he announced, "The Negro race, like all races, is going to be saved by its exceptional men." Obviously, this notion was not attuned to gender and was evasive about the class interests of the "exceptional." Still, Du Bois continued, "men we shall have only as we make manhood the object of the work of the schools—intelligence, broad sympathy, knowledge of the world that was and is, and of the relation of men to it . . . on this foundation we may build bread winning, skill of hand and quickness of brain, with never a fear lest the child and man mistake the means of living for the object of life." The character of past leadership is traced down to "the present—a day of cowardice and vacillation, of strident wide-voiced wrong and faint-hearted compromise; of double-faced dallying with Truth and Right." In this context, he emphasized, education must be stressed: "[T]here must be teachers, and teachers of teachers and to attempt to establish any sort of a system of common and industrial school training, without *first* (and I say *first* advisedly) without *first* providing for the higher training of the very best teachers, is simply throwing your money to the winds" (Du Bois, "Talented," 1903). The Harlem Renaissance, which featured the ascendancy of university-trained intellectuals such as the paradigmatic figure, poet, and playwright Langston Hughes—of Columbia and Lincoln University in Pennsylvania—was, thus, emblematic of the rise of the Talented Tenth that Du Bois had envisioned. "I'm always proud of *The Crisis*," Hughes told Du Bois, "and proud when you print me there." Hughes's praise was understandable, as the poems that appeared there helped both to propel Hughes's career and the Renaissance that he symbolized (Aptheker, 1973, 374; Hughes's poetry in Du Bois's journal remains worth perusing: see "The Childhood of Jimmy" and "Song for a Dark Girl" in *Crisis*, May 1927; "Ma Lord" in *Crisis*, June 1927; "Tapestry" in *Crisis*, July 1927; "Freedom Seeker" and "Being Old" in *Crisis*, Oct. 1927; "Montmartre Beggar Woman" in *Crisis*, Nov. 1927; "Johannesburg Mines" in *Crisis*, June 1928).

In short, Du Bois sought to bolster those with sufficient talent to aid a beleaguered African-American community. Foremost among these was the novelist Jesse Fauset, who, like Hughes, was university trained, in her case at Cornell, where she studied German and French among other subjects. Du Bois thought so highly of her that he invited her to join the staff of the *Crisis*, an invitation she accepted. The publication of her novel *There Is Confusion* and Jean Toomer's *Cane* were said by Du Bois to "mark an epoch." Enthusiastically, he pointed to the work of five poets (Hughes, Countee Cullen, Georgia Johnson, Gwendolyn Bennett, and Claude McKay) and two essayists and critics (Eric Walrond and Walter White) as being emblematic of the Renaissance then being bruited (*Crisis* 27, Feb. 1924).

Du Bois was also a critic of some of the work that emerged from this protean era. This included Claude McKay's novel *Home to Harlem*, which brought the demimonde and the underworld of Black New York to a wider audience (McKay, 1928). McKay, who was born in Jamaica, had migrated to the United States, where he attended college in Manhattan, Kansas, and became quite close to the Communist Party. Though Du Bois found the writing to be both "beautiful and fascinating," with "all the materials of a great piece of fiction," overall, he was less than impressed. Actually, Du Bois confessed, the book "nauseates me," as the NAACP leader felt McKay seemed to "set out to cater [to] the prurient demand on the part of white folk." As Du Bois saw it, a "number of New York publishers" were encouraging such fiction, work that was marked by an "utter absence of restraint."

Predictably, McKay was displeased with Du Bois's evaluation. Writing from Barcelona—McKay was a habitual traveler and a veritable permanent exile—he took particular umbrage at the notion that Du Bois published his review in the same edition of the journal that carried some of McKay's poems. McKay was outraged, telling Du Bois, "I should think that a publication so holy-clean and righteous-pure as the 'Crisis' should hesitate about printing anything from the pen of a writer who wallows so much in 'dirt,' 'filth,' 'drunkenness,' 'fighting' and 'lascivious sexual promiscuity'" (Aptheker, 1973, 374–375).

McKay seemed to forget that Du Bois was of the view that all art was "propaganda," not in the pejorative sense of this phrase but in the sense that a beset population of Negroes had a special need for art that was uplifting, not degrading, just as this population desperately needed artists who spoke to and of their deepest and most heartfelt needs—a Talented Tenth, in other words. "All art is propaganda," Du Bois thundered, "and ever must be," adding angrily, "I do not care a damn for any art that is not used for propaganda." Again, what he meant was that art conveyed ideas—for better or for worse—and the oppressed were desperately in need of uplifting ideas (*Crisis* 32, Oct. 1926).

Du Bois also thought that the Negro had a peculiar contribution to make to the arts. The "Negro as a race," he announced, "has always exhibited peculiar artistic ability." To flourish, he opined, this art required freedom for the artist to perform and create. It also required support from an audience that would allow the artist to produce. Their overarching theme—the Black experience—provided these artists "an astonishingly fertile field," which was a positive way of evaluating the dialectic of oppression (*Crisis* 34, May 1927).

Thus, Du Bois saw art and creativity not as trivial frivolity but an essential component of the uplift of an oppressed people, and to execute this important task, a Talented Tenth was absolutely necessary. The Harlem Renaissance, therefore, reflected a flowering of Du Bois's own vision. It is often difficult to conceptualize eras and epochs as they are unfolding, precisely because they are so close to one's own eyes. Despite this natural handicap, in 1926, as the Harlem Renaissance was still taking shape, Du Bois began to analyze this phenomenon, observing that beginning about 1910, there commenced "something that can be called a renaissance," and since then there had appeared a "more careful consideration of the Negro's social problems." In the field of history, he pointed to the trailblazing work of Benjamin Brawley and Carter G. Woodson. Yet, their eye-opening work notwithstanding, "the true renaissance," said Du Bois, "has been a matter of spirit," which was manifested most effectively among the poets, dramatists, and novelists—not to mention musicians such as J. Rosamond Johnson (Du Bois, "Negro Literature," 1926, 110–111). Du Bois could well have added the development of blues and jazz, particularly the work of W. C. Handy, Scott Joplin, Louis Armstrong, Sidney Bechet, and Buddy Bolden.

Given his pivotal role in helping to give rise to a wildly riotous outpouring of creativity, it should not be overly surprising that Du Bois decided to try his hand at novel writing. It was in 1911—just after he had noticed a "renaissance" in creativity among Negroes—that his novel *The Quest of the Silver Fleece* was published. And it was in 1928 that his next effort in this realm appeared. *Dark Princess: A Romance* featured a worldwide conspiracy of the colored peoples—led by a princess hailing from the India—to forcibly overthrow the evil machinations of white supremacy (Du Bois, *Dark Princess*, 1928). The conspiracy never reaches the point of actual attempt, but in the process of developing the theme, Du Bois discusses the intricacies of Chicago politics and upper-class life among Negroes (though Du Bois personally was not affluent, his position with the NAACP and his intellectual candlepower meant that he became conversant with these circles). Still, it is working-class Negro life that Du Bois portrays with the utmost sympathy. This novel may have been prompted by his tours of Europe, where he had met people from the colored world who had proposed—for example—a military attack on Europe via North Africa and through Spain (not unlike what had occurred hundreds of years earlier at a time when Islam was spreading globally). Du Bois also had met Asian women who bedazzled him with their pulchritude and brilliance. As World War I was winding down, San Francisco was the site of a lengthy trial—the so-called Ghadr conspiracy trial—of South Asian revolutionaries who had been plotting to overthrow the rule of the empire in what was referred to as British India. One can detect in these novels suggestions that this trial did not escape Du Bois's attention. In this "romance," he was seeking to signal to those who held white supremacy dear that there was a raging discontent against this praxis that soared far beyond the precincts of Black America.

And by placing an Indian character at the center of his narrative, he was also paying homage to the crowning jewel in the British Empire—India—a nation to which he long had looked for inspiration. Early on he struck up a friendship with L. L. Rai of Lahore, a journalist, historian, and political activist—that is, a man not unlike Du Bois in profile—with whom he corresponded frequently and whom he escorted during Rai's journey to the United States (Horne, 2008). As for the paramount leader, Mohandas K. Gandhi, Du Bois was effusive, speaking of him generously as a "a man who from sheer impeccability of character and extraordinary personality and from loftiness and originality of doctrine and ideas, takes rank at once among the great men of the world" (*Crisis* 23, Mar. 1922).

But in addition to his crusade to mobilize art and creativity via the Talented Tenth on behalf of Black liberation, Du Bois—as his novel demonstrated—also sought to take advantage of tumultuous events world-wide; and in the 1920s, that meant taking the measure of Moscow. The Communist International, also known as the Comintern and the Third International, was formed March 2–6, 1919, after its first congress was convened in Moscow, Russia. Its creation stemmed from Bolshevik leader Vladimir I. Lenin's belief that socialist revolution would only be successful if it arose throughout the world. Delegates from thirty-four countries, including Russia, Poland, Hungary, Germany, and Latvia, attended the first congress, at which representatives gave reports of the revolutionary situation in their home countries and formulated a policy statement that articulated the foundations of the Comintern. The main propositions included the eradication of capitalism and its suppression by communism, the overthrow of bourgeois governments by proletarian revolutionary struggle, and the dismantling of the bourgeois state and its replacement by a proletariat state based on the Soviet model. An executive committee was elected by the entire body, and the coordinating bureau was elected by the executive committee. On September 21, 1919, the Communist Labor Party—formed out of the left-wing faction of the Socialist Party—became the first U.S. organization to apply for membership in the Comintern (Adler, 1983).

Du Bois had his doubts to begin with. Claude McKay, an early proponent of the Bolshevik Revolution of November 1917, queried Du Bois in late 1921 as to why he seemed to neglect or sneer at the result of the Czar's overthrow. Taken aback, Du Bois replied that he did not wish to sneer at the Russian Revolution: "Russia is incredibly vast," he offered, and while he thought there were positive developments occurring, he was quick to observe that he had been "hearing of other things which frighten us." Du Bois was elated with the declaration emerging from Moscow that placed emphasis on freeing Africa and Asia from colonial tyranny as a priority, which Du Bois as a socialist could only applaud. But he rejected the "dictatorship of the proletariat" and observed dryly that he was "not prepared to dogmatize with Marx or Lenin." Though a professed socialist himself, Du Bois was concerned about the applicability of this philosophy to the United States, as he was doubtful if the white working class in particular could ever be prevailed upon to overcome its racism. In any case, he informed McKay that the immediate program of the NAACP, focused on voting rights and antilynching, should not be ditched in favor of repatriating to Africa (yet another shot at Garvey) or joining a revolution that "we do not at present understand." At the same time, Du Bois noted, "as McKay says, it would be just as foolish for us to sneer or even seem to sneer at the blood-entwined writhing of hundreds of millions of our whiter human brothers" (*Crisis* 22, July 1921).

Overall, however, Du Bois had severe doubts for much of his lengthy life as to whether white workers could ever come to break from the grip of white elites and ally with laborers of the same class, yet of a different color. It was not just the Bolsheviks coming to power in Moscow; the fact was that unlike London, which featured a strong Labour Party, or France, Germany, and Japan, all of which had relatively strong political parties with substantial support from trade unions, the United States simply had no equivalent. And, as Du Bois saw things, racism was a major reason. Du Bois was not purblind. He recognized the greatness of Eugene Debs, the Terre Haute–born U.S. socialist leader who was jailed for his antiwar views and who ran for president from a prison cell. At Debs's passing in 1926, Du Bois praised him for realizing that "no real emancipation of laboring classes in the United States can come as long as black laborers are in partial serfdom" (*Crisis* 33, Dec. 1926).

Yet, just as there was a discontinuity between Du Bois's thunderbolts launched at white supremacy in the former slave South and his comparatively soft-spoken approach to the likes of Harvey Firestone, there was also a discontinuity between his relative pessimism about the prospects of socialism in the United States and his bright-eyed optimism elsewhere. This came clear most dramatically during his first trip to Russia in 1926. Alone and unaccompanied—once again leaving his spouse and daughter behind—the aging leader walked through half a dozen of the larger cities there. He was in the region at a time when Leon Trotsky, a Soviet founder, was under siege by the ultimate winner in their power struggle, Joseph Stalin, as the nation writhed in turmoil in the face of a concatenation of unforced errors and hostile encirclement that followed the premature death of Lenin. But Du Bois, who was bent on finding an ally against his antagonists, did not focus on this matter (just as the United States itself did not when it was seeking allies against Berlin and Tokyo a few years later). Instead, he seemed ecstatic at what he had witnessed: "I stand in astonishment and wonder," he enthused, "at the revelation of Russia that has come to me. I may be partially deceived," he conceded, "and half-informed. But if what I have seen with my eyes and heard with my ears in Russia is Bolshevism, I am a Bolshevik" (*Crisis* 33, Nov. 1926). During this journey, the peripatetic Du Bois had passed through Antwerp—"to see Rubens," confessed this patron of the arts—before reaching Cologne, Frankfurt, and Berlin, past German haunts. But always the center of the journey was Soviet Russia (*Crisis* 33, Dec. 1926). This fascination was to bring him much grief during the early Cold War when Moscow-Washington relations suffered a profound downturn, and Du Bois refused to repudiate his position.

Yet there were parallels between Du Bois's faith in the ability of a Talented Tenth to lead Black America to the promised land and his abiding faith in what had been wrought in the Soviet Union, for similar to the Talented Tenth, the revolutionary vanguard was a slice of the population that had pledged to lead the nation. In the vanguard's case, they pledged to lead the nation beyond the merciless misery that had afflicted czarist times. Du Bois also saw an intimate tie between the hysteria in the North Atlantic generated by the rise of communist parties and the possibility of pushing back vigorously against Jim Crow terrorism. When Moscow and its surrogates in the United States began making vigorous appeals to African Americans at a time when Washington itself was challenged by a nation whose territory spanned the richest and most populous continents (Europe and Asia), an opening was created that Du Bois rushed to exploit. Almost from the moment the Bolsheviks seized power, Washington began raising a clamor about real and imagined human rights violations that were besetting this vast land. But how could the United States credibly point the finger of accusation at Moscow about, for example, extrajudicial executions when there was a similar phenomenon in place in the United States in the form of lynchings, which Washington claimed the federal government had no power to stop, because the regulation of justice was purportedly the province of the individual states?

Moreover, when Du Bois began to look positively toward Moscow, he was both exemplifying a long-term trend in Black America to seek allies abroad and to find them in nations that had problems with Washington. Thus, just as more enslaved Africans fought with the British during the eighteenth-century war that led to U.S. independence than fought with the victors, thousands more Negroes fled to British lines during the War of 1812, many of whom decamped afterward permanently to Bermuda, Trinidad, and elsewhere within the Empire (see Schama, 2006). London abolished slavery well before Washington did, which meant that the enslaved of North America often fled in droves to British soil, be it Canada or the Bahamas—all the while tensions between the Empire and the United States did not abate, with one reason being this draining capital loss in human "commodities" (see Horne, 2014). As Japan began to rise as a power and sought leverage in North America, Tokyo too developed a robust relationship with African Americans—and vice versa (see Horne, 2007; Horne, 2004; Horne, 2018). This was not peculiar to African Americans and Washington: Palestinians in the Occupied Territories looked to Moscow during the Soviet era at a time when both were in conflict with Israel; the Quebecois in Canada often looked to Paris; such was the nature of diplomatic statecraft to which African Americans were not immune.

Thus, Du Bois was merely walking in the footsteps of those who came before; furthermore, his growing fascination with Moscow was not sui generis. In fact, a good deal of the Talented Tenth that Du Bois had helped in part to propel—including Hughes and McKay, the leading luminaries—had a similar orientation, with both of these skilled artists spending considerable time in the Soviet Union. Even the NAACP, whose leadership was often at odds with its feisty editor, consented to allowing staff member William Pickens to sail to Belgium in order to participate in the International Congress of the Oppressed Nations, whose very title was a telling indication to Washington that Moscow was deeply imbedded in this campaign (*Crisis* 33, Jan. 1927). At the time, the official ideology of the United States was white supremacy—infused with apartheid—while the Soviet Union was proclaiming officially that it would provide material assistance for those fleeing from colonialism in Africa and moral support for opponents of Washington. It was therefore not that difficult a choice for those of Du Bois's stripe to lend an ear.

During the same year that he visited the Soviet Union, the *New York Times* reported worriedly about "Communists Boring into Negro Labor." No less provocatively, Du Bois replied that if there was a true desire to stop Negro interest in communism, then more aggressive steps should be taken to halt racism (*New York Times*, Jan. 17, 1926). This became a repetitive theme of his. Indeed, at least since 1919, Black communists in the United States had been instrumental in formulating Comintern policy on the "Negro Question," which combined a critique of capitalist exploitation with a critique of white supremacy. It was they who influenced Lenin's 1920 formulation of American Negroes as a dispossessed nation within the borders of the United States and CPUSA leader John Reed's argument that the explosion of racial consciousness among Black workers, along with their demands for full social and political equality, should be understood as one aspect of the struggle for worldwide socialist revolution (Lenin, 1971, 435; Reed, 1921).

Prominent Black communists such as Harry Haywood, Grace Campbell, James Ford, and Claudia Jones helped to theorize the special character of Black oppression—that is, superexploitation—that required a special approach. They argued that Black people were oppressed on the basis of race; subjugated as workers; imprisoned in plantation systems in the South through sharecropping, tenancy, and land dispossession; and extremely marginalized in the textile and other industries. Moreover, the Black masses occupied the worst forms of employment, endured the most dangerous and unhealthy work conditions, were paid unequal wages, and lacked even the most basic civil rights. These convergences gave Black oppression its national character. In addition, Black communists understood superexploitation as a function of imperialism. Harry Haywood, for example, characterized the relationship between Northern absentee corporate and financial entities and the "Black nation" in the Black Belt as "industrial imperialism." Features including the financing of Southern plantations by eastern banks' credit systems; the control of the majority of coalfields in the South by capitalist families like the Mellons, Fords, and Rockefellers; and Northern financial institutions owning the natural gas and electric companies in the South, underscored Haywood's position (Haywood, 1976, 55–59).

Responding to the hysteria in the press about the purported rise of Bolshevism among Negroes, Du Bois pointed to the profusion of bigotry targeting them as a reason for their disenchantment with the United States (*Crisis* 34, Aug. 1927). This was during a time when the communist-led American Negro Labor Congress was thought to be making gains in organizing, which generated no small amount of consternation. It was "unjust of white men and idiotic of colored men to criticize" such efforts, Du Bois concluded. As for their presumed patrons in Moscow, he argued with no less provocation that "we should stand before the astounding effort of Soviet Russia to reorganize the industrial world with open mind and listening ears" (*Crisis* 31, Dec. 1925).

Moreover, when Du Bois and others within the Talented Tenth reached out to Moscow, this was part and parcel of a larger global initiative to place excruciating pressure upon Jim Crow. After the founding of the League of Nations following World War I, Du Bois advocated that Black Americans should seek permanent representation at their headquarters in Geneva, Switzerland. After the founding of the United Nations in the aftermath of World War II, Du Bois pioneered the search to place the plight of the Negro before this august body. In the pages of the *Crisis*, he pondered the applicability of various international conventions to African Americans, although these were ostensibly designated with the colonized in mind (*Crisis* 33, Jan. 1927). Seeking solace in global bodies a fortiori meant seeking support from those who might be enemies of Washington—and, of course, that included Moscow.

It is worth noting that Du Bois's global initiatives, notably the outreach to Moscow, did not win him many friends even among liberal constituencies that may have been predisposed to back his cause. But this was only a reflection of a deeper dilemma faced by Black Americans as a whole: descendants of slaves, stigmatized and despised, they were reduced to seeking succor from Talented Tenths, at home and abroad.

8

A Life of Departure

Though Du Bois hardly recognized it at the time, from the time of his journey to the Soviet Union in 1926 all the way to 1934, he was on a death march to being sacked by the organization he had helped to found, the NAACP. This was not inevitable, and it was not exclusively a product of Du Bois's stated sympathies toward Moscow; after all, at this juncture (and unlike his second sacking in 1948, after his 1944 return) the board of the organization was hardly a fortress of anticommunism. Some of it had to do with his perceived prickliness. Just as he had clashed with Oswald Villard, as his tenure was winding down with the NAACP, his relationship with Walter White was deteriorating at warp speed. But looming above all these issues in explicating why Du Bois parted company with the NAACP in 1934 was, ironically, the question of whether he had come to embrace unduly the philosophy of a man with whom he had jousted so famously: Marcus Garvey.

This was not an ideal moment for this dustup to occur, for the buildup to Du Bois's exit from the NAACP occurred simultaneously as a series of disasters bombarded Black America. The Great Mississippi Flood of 1927 caused hundreds of deaths and mass destruction over an area of 27,000 square miles due to the failure of levees (not unlike the destruction caused by Hurricane Katrina along the Gulf Coast in 2005). That this catastrophe was centered near what was probably the epicenter of Jim Crow, Mississippi, only complicated the attempt by the NAACP to assist Negro victims.

For example, shortly after the height of this tragedy, Du Bois was contacted by Tillman Jones of Hinds County, Mississippi. He felt compelled to send the letter "under a camouflaged address to avoid the consequences of racial hatred and mob violence." He added ominously that "it is dangerous for the name of Mr. Du Bois or the name of Mr. Spingarn to be seen in this section . . . the eternal danger is highly imminent." He complained bitterly about a "reign of terror" and the "ceaseless toils of whitecap persecution" (Aptheker, 1973, 349–350). Jones's language is probably too mild to capture the humdrum hounding of being forced to abandon the sidewalk for the gutter as a white person approached or not being able to try on shoes or clothes at stores before purchase (and being unable to return them if such did not fit) or the inability to visit restaurants or bathrooms while on a driving trip through the region—and far, far worse.

Then, in October 1929, the stock market collapsed, and soon to follow was the economy as a whole: unemployment lines stretched as far as the eye could see; once-affluent stockbrokers were reduced to selling apples for coins; homeless hoboes stalked the land, riding the rails from town to town. What came to be known as the Great Depression was caused by a number of factors, including declining production, high consumer debt, low wages, and climbing unemployment, all of which were concealed by the artificially high price of stocks. As investor confidence waned, and they began to rapidly sell their overvalued shares, the stock market tanked. What resulted was a slowdown of production; the mass firing of millions of workers; starvation wages for those who remained employed; a meteoric rise in indebtedness, foreclosures, and repossessions; and the failure of countless banks as a result of multiple bank runs. By 1931, more than six million workers were unemployed, and there was no relief in sight. Conditions were far worse elsewhere in the world.

Harlem, where Du Bois resided at 409 Edgecombe Avenue on a bluff overlooking Yankee Stadium in the Bronx (a baseball shrine where stellar African-American stars like Josh Gibson and Jay "Cool Papa" Bell were routinely barred from making a living), was hit hard by this economic distress. As Du Bois strolled to the subway stop to ride the iron horse downtown to his Spartan office, he could not help but notice the growth in panhandling, which was a marker for a community that had been pushed to the edge of survival. Du Bois was most certainly aware of that conjuncture of racist and sexist exploitation dubbed "The Bronx Slave Market" by activist-journalists Ella Baker and Marvel Cooke. The intensification of structural poverty during the Great Depression compelled Black domestic workers to auction their labor on street corners throughout the Bronx. These women were forced to not only accept the "slave wage" of less than thirty cents an hour but also to subject themselves to the indignity brought on by white housewives who often underpaid—or failed to pay altogether—these vulnerable laborers. As Cooke and Baker wrote in their exposé, "[T]he crash of 1929 brought to the domestic labor market a new employer class. The lower middle-class housewife, who, having dreamed of the luxury of a maid, found opportunity staring her in the face in the form of Negro women pressed to the wall by poverty, starvation, and discrimination." Moreover, participants in this "slave market" were susceptible to sexual harassment and sexual exploitation by the fathers, brothers, and husbands of this new housewife class. Given his attention to the specific plight of Black women in writings such as "The Damnation of Women," Du Bois surely understood how this form of labor exploitation was gendered, insofar as domestic work was conventional "women's work," and racialized, insofar as racism reduced African Americans to low-wage, unprotected, contingent labor (Baker & Cooke, 1935).

It was in this context of utter desperation that Du Bois—along with other African Americans—began to contemplate self-help regimes in the midst of conservative nostrums symbolized by the Republican Party many had supported to that point, which abjured any aggressive role for government in economic recovery. The dominant ethos nationally was "do for self" with government aid to the needy seen widely in the United States as worse than blasphemy. The movement led by Marcus Garvey had already demonstrated that it would be unwise for the NAACP leadership to ignore an underlying sentiment among their constituency that, apparently, hungered for approaches that called on Negroes to help themselves. Garvey's relative success in attracting adherents was quickly followed by the rise of the organization that came to be known as the Nation of Islam, which had a similar outlook with the added fillip of devotion to a religion whose roots in Africa—including the regions from which many African Americans had sprung—ran deep.

Du Bois could hardly be immune to these trends. As a lifetime student, he was not above evolving or parsing ideas that were thought to be well-nigh eternal. Thus in 1927 he was queried about the possibility of constructing an all-Negro state somewhere within the bounds of the United States, an idea that had been broached decades earlier by President Thomas Jefferson and that had been adumbrated when Oklahoma was initiated—supposedly as a state for indigenes, many of whom were forced to move from the Southeast. Now the official NAACP policy was to compel desegregation—if not the analytically distinct category of integration—and Du Bois was a founder and most influential member of this organization. While desegregation was predicated upon elimination and negation through the formal removal of legal and social prohibitions, integration was progressive and positive, welcoming Black people to fully participate in and make their imprint on the social, political, economic, and cultural institutions of U.S. society.

Yet, Du Bois—though hedging and hesitating—conceded that the idea of a state for the Negroes was "feasible" (Aptheker, 1973, 359–360). In retrospect, it seems apparent that the ideological momentum created by Du Bois's insistent call for self-determination and self-reliance for Africans, as an antidote to colonialism, inexorably pushed Du Bois in a similar direction in his advocacy for African Americans. In 1928 Du Bois noted offhandedly that "Black America is going to have a voice in Black Africa's fate. Black Africa must and will do the same or die trying," suggesting the everlasting linkage between the two (Du Bois, "Africa," 1928, 420–421).

Du Bois's position on African-American self-determination at the time was not unlike that of the Comintern. As early as 1919, its Black members theorized the "Negro question" as a national question. Their position was predicated on three central points: that Blacks were an oppressed national minority in the South of the United States; that the Black masses possessed the capacity to organize and liberate themselves; and that as a national question, the Black struggle in the United States was part of the international proletarian revolution (Haywood, 1934). In 1920, Vladimir I. Lenin demanded that communists parties support the revolutionary movements of dispossessed nations, which included American Negroes (Lenin, 1971, 435). By 1928, the Comintern, led by Black communist Harry Haywood, had developed a full-fledged position on Black self-determination that it called the "Black Belt Thesis." The Black Belt of the United States encompassed "the old cotton country" that stretched from Maryland to the Mississippi Delta, and contained roughly five million Negroes, or over 60 percent of the Black population (Allen, 1938). The position was predicated on Joseph Stalin's conception of a nation, which he defined as "a historically constituted, stable community of people, formed on the basis of common language, territory, economic life, and psychological make-up manifested in a common culture" (Lenin & Stalin, 1970, 68). Insofar as African Americans in the Black Belt shared a common territory, a common economic system, a common language and culture, and a common history of national development, they fit Stalin's definition. The Comintern argued that "the party must come out openly and unreservedly for the right of Negroes to self-determination in the Southern states, where the Negroes form the majority of the population" (Communist International, 1985, 14).

It was an ever-delicate task to strike the appropriate balance between the rights of African Americans to voluntarily carve out their own path and the necessity to push for equal rights within a diverse polity. Du Bois was accused more than once of hewing too closely to the path of self-determination—as opposed to equal rights—which was ironic indeed in

Scottsboro Case

On March 25, 1931, two white women, Ruby Bates and Victoria Price, accused nine Black boys—Andy Wright, Roy Wright, Haywood Patterson, Eugene Williams, Clarence Norris, Charles Weems, Ozie Powell, Olen Montgomery, and Willie Roberson—of rape.

The "Scottsboro Boys" were initially arrested in Paint Rock, Alabama, for a fight with a group of white boys on a train car. When it was discovered that Bates and Price were present, accusations of rape accompanied charges of assault and attempted murder. On March 31, the Scottsboro Nine were indicted for rape in Gadsden, Alabama. The trial opened on April 6, and Bates and Price reiterated that they had been raped by the defendants. All nine defendants were ultimately found guilty and eight were sentenced to death.

The International Labor Defense (ILD), a Communist sponsored organization, and the NAACP took on the case. Along with appellate work, the ILD launched an international campaign for the boys' freedom. The NAACP focused on persuasive legal argument. Conflict between the ILD and the NAACP hampered legal efforts, though the executions were eventually postponed. Along the way, *Powell v. Alabama* established the right to counsel in 1932, Ruby Bates recanted the rape charges and began testifying for the defense, protests escalated, and petitions circulated worldwide. After countless retrials, four of the defendants were freed in 1937, three between 1943 and 1944, and one in 1946. Haywood Patterson escaped prison in 1948, was captured by the FBI in 1950, and died in prison in 1952.

light of his clashes with Garvey, the embodiment of this purportedly heretical trend. Du Bois's failure to renounce such purported heresy led directly to his departure—at the none-too-tender age of sixty-six—from the organization he had toiled so long to build. Yet instead of gracefully accepting his ouster, Du Bois went on to make some of the most important contributions in his extraordinarily lengthy career.

* * *

Du Bois was far from being the ideal father and husband. Like other renowned men—Nelson Mandela comes to mind—he seemed to be married to the struggle and more devoted to being a father to a people. So, when his daughter, Yolande, chose to marry the famed poet Countee Cullen, he pulled out all the stops, as if in compensation for his lengthy absences during her childhood and adolescence. It seemed to be a marriage made in Talented Tenth heaven, with their union destined to produce progeny primed to engage fruitfully in uplift. Adopted at the age of fifteen by an influential Harlem pastor, Cullen went on to become elected to Phi Beta Kappa while studying at New York University, then to receive an advanced degree at Du Bois's alma mater, Harvard, in 1926 (Guenter in Horne & Young, 2001, 45–46). His blushing bride, born in 1900, had attended the elite British Preparatory Academy, the Bedales School, and later Fisk University, where she graduated with a degree in Fine Arts in 1924. While in school, her father acted the martinet, lecturing her repeatedly about the need to excel academically, sending her one stern letter after another on this topic. Though she was allegedly infatuated with the talented musician Jimmy Lunceford, a pioneer of swing music, this did not halt her rush to the altar on April 8, 1928, accompanied by Cullen as her groom (de Luca in Horne & Young, 2001, 63).

So, just as *Dark Princess*, Du Bois's self-proclaimed romance, was published, he was presiding over an actual romance with potential similar to his fictional creation. Thus it was that the great and the good (hundreds in fact) came uptown to Harlem—the Salem Methodist Church, to be precise—to witness the nuptials. It was an affair to remember. Attending the groom were a virtual all-star team of the Talented Tenth: Arna Bontemps, whose literary contributions were to rival the man with whom he often collaborated, Langston Hughes; W. Alphaeus Hunton, Jr., from a prominent family himself (his sister Eunice Hunton Carter was a prominent Harlem socialite who went on to become the first Black female assistant district attorney of New York), a budding scholar who, like Du Bois, eventually chose exile in Africa in order to escape persecution in the United States; and, among others, Hughes himself. Others watching this spectacle included Du Bois's NAACP comrades James Weldon Johnson and Mary White Ovington.

Two hundred white doves were released during this lavish ceremony that cost hundreds of dollars to produce—no small sum in a time of growing financial distress. The couple honeymooned in Philadelphia, and then it was off to Paris, where Cullen had received a fellowship. But like so many marriages before and since, this one did not last; it was shamefully brief, as there were differences that at the time seemed irreconcilable, though—as so often happens—such were not readily evident. For groom Countee Cullen was a gay man with a lover all his own, a fact which raises crucial questions as to why he chose to marry Du Bois's daughter (Lewis, 2000, 220–228). This love triangle was not revealed immediately, and the notoriously private Du Bois betrayed his New England reserve by broadcasting widely his joy at his daughter's marriage to Cullen and the deep emotion that welled up inside him as a result (*Crisis* 35, June 1928).

Thus, what seemed to be the crowning glory of Du Bois's ambitious plans to embellish in a lively fashion the Talented Tenth turned out to be something else altogether. Homosexuality in Black America—as in the nation as a whole at the time—was not necessarily embraced, and the prolific Du Bois, who seemed to churn out articles, reviews, and essays as if he had a factory of elves toiling on his behalf, chose not to seize the occasion to expound on this fraught matter.

Unfortunately, this was not the only setback Du Bois endured during what was a tumultuous decade. The alarming increase in lynching had not ceased, and in response, he and the NAACP initiated a legislative response. After diligently collecting congressional support, Congressman Leonidas C. Dyer of Missouri introduced antilynching legislation in 1922. Yet the bill quickly collided with the age-old shibboleth of states' rights (i.e., the notion that the Civil War and concomitant constitutional amendments were thought to have resolved that states of the former slave South were "sovereign" to the extent that they could block initiatives from Washington). As early as April 1922, Du Bois contended angrily that if the bill did not pass, it would "end the United States" (Young in Horne & Young, 2001, 67). That the bill did not pass (and the United States did not end) maximized his frustration, causing him to turn his back on both Republicans and Democrats in the 1924 presidential election and back La Follette, while escalating his ongoing effort to build a Talented Tenth.

Although Du Bois's failed attempt to augment the Talented Tenth via the marriage of his daughter was daunting for him, it did not shake what was a bedrock belief for him. As noted, he had introduced this notion as early as 1903, and he argued that he had not constructed this idea from whole cloth, observing that "talented tenthers" [sic] had arisen in the antebellum era in the form of abolitionists, such as Henry Highland Garnet, Sojourner Truth, and Frederick Douglass, among others. The added plus he envisioned for this group was higher education (Horne in Horne & Young, 2001, 203–204). Thus, one of the least discussed, though most successful, initiatives by the talented men and women who Du Bois had slated to lead Black America toward progress was their desire for college degrees, a possession not so common in his day. Black Americans had been admitted to matriculate in colleges like Oberlin before the Civil War, but the number of those who had received higher education by the 1920s was extremely meager. Indeed, what made Du Bois himself stand out—his worthy qualities aside—was the sterling education he had received at Fisk, Harvard, and in Berlin. Du Bois was fortunate to have been born after the Civil War, when the newly freed slaves targeted education as one of their top priorities, and as a result, there was a proliferation of universities and colleges founded during this era, particularly in the South, where the overwhelming preponderance of African Americans continued to reside.

Yet, as Du Bois's notorious confrontation with Booker T. Washington exemplified, there was fierce contestation about the actual role that colleges and universities should play, and this controversy did not die with his death. In one of the earliest editions of the *Crisis*, Du Bois had cited prominently, to great effect, the words of Governor Cole Blease of South Carolina, who growled that "the greatest mistake the white race has ever made was in attempting to educate the free Negro" (*Crisis* 1, Jan. 1911).

In fact, the 1920s witnessed an upsurge of student protest that prefigured a similar wave in the 1960s—inferentially confirming Blease's ominous words. Du Bois and the NAACP were central to the student protests of the 1920s, some of the more important protests of that period. Perhaps unsurprisingly, a particular target of Du Bois's ire was the college once known as Hampton Institute, located in easternmost Virginia. The stress there on industrial education at the expense of the humanities and liberal arts riled him to no end; to him, education that did not embrace the humanities was a concession to the desires of Jim Crow. Thus, in the 1920s, Du Bois took up the cudgels against Hampton as it chose to segregate audience members at cultural performances there—yet continued to be the biggest recipient of white philanthropy. When students went on strike there in 1927, Du Bois became their loudest champion. These students seemed to be illustrating what a Talented Tenth should do and be: struggling to open doors for those other than themselves (Silverman in Horne & Young, 2001, 95–96; see Du Bois, "Hampton Strike," 1927, 471–472; Du Bois, "Negroes," 1926, 228–230).

A key informant about the Hampton strike was Louise Thompson, who was then a faculty member and would later become a member of the Communist Party, a founder of the radical Black women's organization, the Sojourners for Truth and Justice, and the general secretary of the committee formed to defend Du Bois when anticommunist repression was brought to bear on his peace activism. Thompson was thoroughly disgusted by Hampton's racial conservatism and was thus sympathetic to and supportive of the student strike. As an act of solidarity with militant students, she wrote Du Bois on October 17, 1927, to provide details about the two-week strike and to encourage him to editorialize about it in the *Crisis*. She explained that she and other faculty members who were "not afraid to think for [themselves] even at the risk of personal security" had taken it upon themselves to support the students' protest of Hampton's "hypocrisy, racial prejudice, and backwardness" (Du Bois Papers, Oct 17, 1927; Lewis, 2000). She excoriated the white female teachers who attempted to appease unrest with sewing bees and tea parties while ignoring the earnest demands of the Black students. These white teachers, she explained, did not understand why students would be anything but gracious and obsequious toward them. Thompson enjoined the "Negro world" to see the "justice in the students' stand" and to support them in their struggle against the institution.

As its most distinguished alumnus, Du Bois was keenly interested in the destiny of Fisk University. Though it was in the eastern region of conservative Tennessee, and though Nashville was known for its cosmopolitanism, as evidenced by the presence of Vanderbilt University, Fisk did not seem to benefit from this purportedly favorable location. In 1912 Du Bois observed that the General Education Board, which aided Fisk, had made conditions for the receipt of a grant unusually harsh—but he thought that in its parlous condition, the school had no choice but to comply (*Crisis* 3, Jan. 1912). Du Bois cared deeply for his school because, he once said, "it was to me a place of sorrow, of infinite regret; a place where the dreams of great souls lay dusty and forgotten" (*Crisis* 28, Sept. 1924). But caring for Fisk and the wider cause of creating a Talented Tenth by means of higher education did not cause Du Bois to evade the flaws he espied. As student protests were heating up in October 1924, Du Bois tossed down the gauntlet, charging that the university had failed in providing true education to African Americans—in the sense of failing to respect them, to seek to give them the best, to develop their self-knowledge and self-pride. No, charged Du Bois, Fisk had insulted them and, instead, curried favor with the racists who honeycombed Nashville and imposed a brutal Jim Crow that the school was bound to observe (*Crisis* 28, Oct. 1924).

A major source of information for Du Bois concerning events at his alma mater was James Ford. Born in Alabama in 1896, he too was an alumnus but had veered in a radical direction, founding the American Negro Labor Congress in 1925 and joining the Communist Party in 1926, on whose platform he ran for vice president of the United States in 1932, 1936, and 1940. He had left Birmingham in 1913 to enter Fisk, graduating with the class of 1918. He volunteered for service in the U.S. Army in the waning days of his senior year and saw eight months' service in France with the Signal Corps, an experience sufficient to radicalize even the least conscious. "I remember too," said Ford subsequently, "those more vital days of hell in France."

"Now that the exposure of conditions at Fisk has started we must not relent," Ford instructed Du Bois in early 1925. Waxing nostalgic, he recalled his years in Nashville and "the abrogation of the fundamental principles of education and the attempt at suppression of manhood and courage by [the college administration]." For Ford recalled bitterly a time when he had returned from the bloody battlefields of France to address Fisk students: "I sensed that the students were eager for experience and something of the practical contacts of war." Ford graciously complied and "told them something of these contacts; of hope for better conditions thru out the world; and most of all, of the contribution of black men from all parts of the world to this war. This said, I took my seat and to my surprise," said the still-startled Ford, "I was followed by the President [of Fisk] who delayed chapel long enough to make, in a sarcastic manner, the statement that there was nothing to feel 'chesty' about; that we had contributed no more than anybody else." The next day Ford was asked to speak to a class-room of students, and again, he complied. "Again I found," said the dumb-founded alumnus, "the President's private secretary was in the rear of the room taking down everything I said." Ford—and he was far from being alone—was even more incensed in that this occurred at a "Negro Univer-sity with a white president who had, previously, so willingly espoused the cause of democracy and urged Negro students to go to war" (Aptheker, 1973, 306–307).

Consequently, the dramatic 1925 student strike at Fisk should have been a shock only to those not paying attention. For Du Bois, it seemed to be vindication of the faith he had placed in the Talented Tenth, the idea that this group could be the vanguard to lead Black America to the promised land. The heart of the students' grievance was their charge that tyrannical racism was the accepted norm on campus. A delightedly heartened Du Bois announced dramatically, "Men and women of Black America: Let no decent Negro send his child to Fisk until Fayette McKenzie [the President] goes" (*Crisis* 34, Apr. 1925). As things turned out, some of the students had to go, ousted as a result of their militancy. But the sparks from Nashville ultimately helped in setting ablaze campuses far and wide.

Howard University, long regarded as the "Capstone of Negro Educa-tion," was founded in Washington, DC, in 1867, and it quickly distin-guished itself from the model provided by both Hampton and Tuskegee, which meant that it attracted the apt attention of Du Bois. Ralph Bunche, who, like Du Bois, was trained at Harvard (and eventually won a Nobel Peace Prize and served at the highest level at the United Nations), taught there, along with a number of others who fit the Du Bois mold, as did his-torian Rayford Logan; he too taught at Howard, collaborated with Du Bois on the Pan-African Congress movement (acting as the chief translator into French), and conducted pioneering research on U.S.–Haiti relations. When Fisk students in 1925 faced ouster due to their protests there, it was Du Bois who intervened on their behalf, requesting that Howard admit them (Bowles in Horne & Young, 2001, 104–105). Being in Washington, DC, Howard's location meant that students were forced to endure the Jim Crow that was endemic there; such a hostile environment helped create a mili-tant student culture that in some ways exceeded that of Fisk. Unsurpris-ingly, it was at Howard that one of the initial demands of Negro students—that mirrored subsequent demands in the 1960s for more Black faculty—was met when the board capitulated and consented to name an African American, Mordecai Johnson, as president (*Crisis* 32, Aug. 1926).

It was early in 1929 that Du Bois chose to make a tour of campuses and—like a latter-day Johnny Appleseed—sprinkled seeds of dissent all along the way. The choices were in the heart of the Deep South: Virginia Normal in Petersburg, Palmer Institute in Sedalia, Shaw in Raleigh, State

Normal at Fayetteville, and Johnson C. Smith in Charlotte, all in North Carolina; Allen (and Avery High School) in South Carolina; and Bethune-Cookman and Edward Waters College in Florida. The very act of launching this tour involved a leap of faith, as an African-American man attired in a suit and tie traveling through this benighted region then aroused suspicion automatically, and in some areas, if Du Bois had been searched and the purportedly seditious *Crisis* had been found on his person, he might have become the guest of dishonor at his very own old-fashioned necktie party. Thus, friends arranged his transportation with great care and tact, as if he were being smuggled along an updated Underground Railroad. He often moved about surreptitiously, furtively stealing a glance over his shoulder as he ducked into an automobile or the odd train car. The latter was to be avoided, not least because they were segregated rigidly, and the "Negro cars" were often grimy and disgustingly unclean. In Georgia he spoke at the Haines Institute in Augusta. As for his once (and future) hometown, Atlanta, he was palpably unimpressed, finding it "taller and fiercer and richer" than ever—but with "no culture, no humanity, American in the crassest sense."

After an absence of a quarter century, Du Bois entered the lion's den, visiting Tuskegee, and was disheartened with the regimentation he witnessed. He was pleased with the presence there of the National Veterans Hospital ("a miracle"), which employed a number of Negro professionals. However, he would have been outraged if he had lived to hear of the so-called Tuskegee Syphilis Experiment that was to be launched there soon after his departure from the campus, in which some of these very same professionals collaborated in a horrific experiment that left poor Negro men with a sexually transmitted disease untreated—though they were told otherwise—thus jeopardizing their lives and that of their families. If nothing else, knowledge of this episode would have shaken Du Bois's confidence in the beneficence of his beloved Talented Tenth. What Du Bois did see at Tuskegee, on the other hand, was sufficiently noteworthy; he later observed that most of the graduates of this university had become not artisans and farmers—contrary to Booker T. Washington's prognostications—but teachers, professionals, and small businessmen (*Crisis* 38, June 1931).

His journey to Fisk was a kind of homecoming. He found it markedly improved from the time of his tenure there; the freedom of students was greater, not least due to the sacrifice of strikers a few years earlier, and new buildings were desperately needed. Interestingly, only Fisk and Talladega in Alabama dared to select the more daring lecture topics Du Bois had offered (e.g., "The Russian Revolution"). Befitting the more vibrant atmosphere in Nashville—compared to, say, Tuskegee—students from adjacent white universities attended his lecture, as did some visitors from overseas (*Crisis* 36, Feb. 1929).

It was at Howard that Du Bois delivered one of his more important addresses on education, which anticipated his tenure-ending rift with the NAACP. It was June 1930, and the proud young graduates had gathered on a warm day on the hilltop where this lovely campus was sited. Du Bois did not disappoint those seeking intellectual nourishment, for it was there that he argued that neither the industrial education ideas of Booker T. Washington nor his own more enlightened notions had succeeded in addressing the dire needs of Negroes. He therefore called for an agonizing reappraisal of what education for African Americans entailed, a reappraisal that would be driven by the specific needs of this community, rather than what the "American" state required (King in Horne & Young, 2001, 117–118).

Nevertheless, Du Bois needs to be credited for doing well what he chose to do. Months before his daughter's ill-fated wedding, once again he convened what had come to be one of his crowning accomplishments: this version of the Pan-African Congress was better attended than the previous ones, as 5,000 attendees and 208 paid delegates descended on New York City, hailing from twenty-two states in the United States and the District of Columbia, not to mention the Caribbean, South America, much of West Africa, Germany, and India. Uplifting Africans and African Americans was central per usual, but highlighted was "real national independence" for Egypt, China, and India and the termination of Washington's interference in the internal affairs of the Americas—the occupation of Haiti that had begun in 1915 had plodded on murderously. Strikingly, Moscow was "thanked" for its "liberal attitude toward the colored races and for the help which it has extended to them from time to time" (*Crisis* 34, Oct. 1927).

Though the NAACP board was not as far to the left as Du Bois, his positions were not wholly incongruent with theirs—yet it would be hard to see how this organization could lead African Americans into the mainstream as long as it harbored radical views akin to those spouted routinely by its most prominent personality, Du Bois. Though differing views on Negro self-reliance were the ostensible reason for the founder's messy departure from the NAACP, the fact is there were fundamental differences that created the yawning chasm between Du Bois and the board that had controlled the organization, and there was a similar gap between Du Bois and the donors who had helped to generate some of the litigation successes that were beginning to accrue.

Actually, this idea of the differences between Du Bois and his organization were not as simple as suggested at first blush. In 1930, Du Bois placed side by side the programs of the NAACP and the American Negro Labor Congress, "a Communistic organization." The parallels were obvious even to the dimmest of his readers in the *Crisis*: though the latter group stressed the needs of workers, his own group, he said irritably and tellingly, was the "potential leader of a class of small capitalists" (*Crisis* 37, Apr. 1930).

Nevertheless, while the mainstream thought that Moscow was—to put it mildly—on the wrong side of history, in 1928 Du Bois took to the pages of a radical journal to proclaim that the Soviet Union was a "victim of a determined propaganda of lies," as he hailed what "it is trying to do" (*Labor Defender*, Nov. 1928). Then, in May 1933, the *Baltimore Afro-American* blared a headline that must have caused some of the NAACP's more affluent donors to wince, if not blanch: "U.S. Will Come to Communism, Du Bois Tells Conference." It was true that this was during the midst of a devastating economic depression with confidence in the future of capitalism diminishing rapidly, and it was equally true that in this maddening maelstrom, Black Americans were suffering disproportionately—yet, some within the NAACP wondered how politic (or accurate) was their eminent founder's prediction. Still, these words were delivered by Du Bois at a gathering sponsored by the Rosenwald Fund, founded by an affluent Jewish American with a decided interest in Negro uplift, and there were no reports of shoes or chairs being hurled at Du Bois after he spoke, for what he said was being said by many others. This is why the *Afro-American*, not known to be a Leninist newspaper, devoted twelve entire columns to Du Bois's speech, reprinting his remarks in full. Du Bois insisted at this confab that production for private profit was wrong and disastrous and that African Americans in particular should undertake various forms of cooperative and collective efforts, thus helping to prepare the way for, and preparing themselves to be an essential part of, the coming revolutionary transformation (*Baltimore Afro-American*, May 1933). Even the *New York Times* found this important meeting to be sufficiently newsworthy to devote seventy-five words to it (*New York Times*, May 13, 1933).

Du Bois was not above introducing these unconventional views to the readers of the NAACP's prime journal. Du Bois toasted Moscow on the tenth anniversary of the Bolshevik Revolution—and denounced the royal family that had been displaced in the process, a clan that he found notably despicable. Despite mainstream criticism of Moscow, Du Bois exclaimed, "[T]he Union of Soviet Socialist Republics is celebrating today its Tenth Anniversary and here's hoping that this is but the first decade towards its hundred years"—one of many Du Bois wishes that wound up unfulfilled (*Crisis* 34, Dec. 1927).

Yet Du Bois's push toward radicalism was not only influenced by the imminent signs of the economic collapse of capitalism. What was occurring simultaneously was a wrenching political evolution by Black America itself, and when such a rare event occurs, it opens up all manner of alternative possibilities that were barely visible previously. In 1928, Republican Herbert Hoover challenged Democrat Al Smith for the right to occupy the

White House. Hoover, a Stanford-trained engineer, if history was the guide, would receive the bulk of votes from those African Americans who could vote (which excluded the vast majority who were trapped in the former slave South). Yet Hoover seemed strangely indifferent to the distress inflicted upon Black America, demonstrated most dramatically along the Gulf Coast in 1927 when the levees broke. In addition, he seemed embarrassed by the presence of Negroes in his party and did not seem overly concerned when a movement arose to purge them—a movement that claimed as an initial victim Benjamin Davis Sr. of Atlanta, whose son of the same name was a Harvard student who eventually became a prominent New York City councilman and a comrade of Du Bois's in the Communist Party (Horne, 1994). Governor Smith of New York, on the other hand, was a standard-bearer for a party that saw no problem with segregating African-American delegates quite rudely at their quadrennial convention and, perhaps worse, welcomed the Ku Klux Klan into its ranks.

Thus, weeks before the 1928 election, Du Bois argued that those Black Americans who could vote should look toward a party other than the major two. Once that possibility was opened, it was only a short step to looking toward the Communist Party or its patron in Moscow (*Crisis* 35, Oct. 1928). The election, concluding with Hoover's victory after a noticeable bump in anti-Catholic sentiment generated by the prominence of Smith, repulsed Du Bois. This campaign, he said disgustedly, was "the most humiliating" ever experienced by African Americans, which was quite a statement given the opprobrium they routinely endured. Black people, he said, were flagrantly and intentionally ignored by both parties. The situation, again, demanded a search for options. Moreover, as events in the 1920s were beginning to shape the decades to come, Du Bois anticipated what occurred in 1941 when Washington itself found it opportune to ally with Moscow in order to confront Berlin and its allies. It was in 1928 that Du Bois noticed what was evident: that the U.S. press, despite having been so critical of V. I. Lenin, was quite favorable to the epigone of fascism, Benito Mussolini. Du Bois would have preferred the U.S. view of 1941, which reversed this tendency (*Crisis* 35, Dec. 1928).

Thus, when the bottom fell out and Wall Street collapsed, auguring even more woe, Du Bois saw it as "above all, a shaking of the faith of Americans in American industrial organization and in all private capitalistic enterprise"; exposed for all to ponder was "the fundamental weakness of our system" (*Crisis* 37, Jan. 1930).

Too much can be made of this trend in Du Bois's thinking, however, for it does not explain how he could simultaneously be favorable toward the Soviet Union and critical of its domestic surrogate, the Communist Party. In 1931, for example, the case of the Scottsboro nine erupted in Alabama; it involved nine Negro youth charged falsely with the rape of two white women, with the death penalty looming for the defendants before the CPUSA and their allies intervened, galvanizing a global crusade in their behalf. The NAACP too had sought to intervene in this case but were out-maneuvered by the CPUSA; yet it was evident that Du Bois's sentiments rested with his employer (*Crisis* 38, Sept. 1931).

Still, this apparent defense of his parent organization could not obscure the widening differences that separated the two. Finally, in May 1934, writing from Atlanta, Du Bois did the inevitable: he resigned. This was after his journal had opened its pages to criticisms of the NAACP's ada-mant opposition to segregation, something to which the board took strong exception. Du Bois was equally adamant, saying the journal "never was and never was intended to be an organ of the Association in the sense of simply reflecting its official opinion"—and this was the direction in which the Board was now pointing (Aptheker, 1973, 478–479). Differences over the rationale for segregation, or self-help, more precisely, was thought to

---

ANTI-LYNCHING BILL

Throughout the twentieth century, African Americans agitated for the pas-sage of a federal antilynching bill. Those in support of such legislation argued only federal action and investigation would help to stop this act of white terrorism. Ideally, municipal government would apprehend and prosecute perpetrators of lynching; however, these same governments generally shared the prejudices of their communities and defended rather than punished its perpetrators.

Although a federal antilynching bill would not stamp out lynching alto-gether, proponents argued, it would persuade or coerce local authorities to discourage, disclose, and discipline lynch mobs. It would also give the national government the authority to prosecute lynchers beyond the purview of local and district courts comprised of sympathetic peers who might be lynchers themselves. Even if the bill was found unconstitutional—a preeminent con-cern for its supporters and critics alike—it would provide the foundation to either amend the constitution or develop a more definitive law that accounted for noninterstate cases.

In 1918, organizations including the NAACP and the Black women-led Anti-Lynching Crusaders backed the Dyer Anti-Lynching Bill, named for Mis-souri Representative L. C. Dyers who introduced it in Congress. It was defeated in the Senate in 1922 due in large part to a Democratic Party filibuster. Other failed legislation includes an Anti-Lynching Bill introduced in 1926 and the 1934 Constigan-Wagner Anti-Lynching Bill. Success finally came on Decem-ber 9, 2018, when a bill introduced by Black Senators Cory Booker, Kamala Harris, and Tim Scott to make lynching a federal crime was unanimously passed.

be at issue also, but it was not the "main reason" for his resignation, said Du Bois. He recalled the World War I era when at first the NAACP protested the "colored camp" for soldiers in Des Moines, but upon losing this battle, the NAACP sought to make this facility as efficient as possible. There was no contradiction, said Du Bois, between struggling for desegregation of schools and seeking to make those schools (despite continued segregation) work smoothly. Du Bois had wanted to broach these matters in the journal but was forbidden, and now he let loose with full shotgun blasts, asserting that the NAACP "finds itself in a time of crisis and change, without a program, without effective organization" (Aptheker, 1973, 479–481).

Du Bois's resignation left Black America thunderstruck. It was like an otherwise responsible parent abandoning his child. Yet the reputedly bristly Du Bois was known to be rather protective of a journal he had founded, and he revolted at any indication of invasion of his jurisdiction. Besides, he was ascending the scale of age and had reason to believe—given the average or median life-span of Negro men—that he was already living on borrowed time and, perhaps, deserved more change in his life. Moreover, donors and board members were becoming increasingly exasperated with some of the stances of their illustrious founder—for example, his favoritism toward the Soviet Union. Still, Du Bois's departure from the NAACP was as shocking and disconcerting as the controversial departure of his daughter Yolande from her marriage to Countee Cullen.

9

A Life in Wartime

New York City was no prize for the Negro. As late as the onset of the Civil War, it was the metropolis that financed slavery and slave trade expeditions, and this profiting from the misery of Africans trickled down to influence day-to-day attitudes of the populace as a whole. It was no accident that African Americans were sited mostly in segregated neighborhoods, such as Harlem (where Du Bois chose to reside), and were subjected to systemic harassment by often trigger-happy police officers. Yet, with all of its problems, Gotham may have seemed like paradise to Du Bois compared to the Atlanta to which he was returning. Though it prided itself on being the "city too busy to hate," this would have come as a rude surprise to those African Americans forced to endure the hateful Jim Crow that occupied every nodule of the city.

Yet, the job to which Du Bois was returning—professor at Atlanta University—was a symbolic aspect of the rift that had driven him from the NAACP. Du Bois was of the opinion that, yes, the University of Georgia should be desegregated, but in the meantime African Americans should not slacken in building a university that could train the Talented Tenth so necessary for liberation. In any case, the life of the mind was not alien to Du Bois, and beyond training the next generation, he had books percolating in his brain that were yearning to break free, and his job in Atlanta would provide the time and occasion for these to emerge.

Still, Du Bois was not just a thinker; he was also a man of action, and he held firmly to the belief that it was "painfully easy" for one living in a thickly populated city like New York to "mistake it for the nation," and he sought to avoid this error by regularly journeying at length throughout the enormous nation in which he resided. Thus, 1934 was not only a time of transition for him but also a time for exploration as he visited and lectured in a good deal of the South and the West. As ever, he shared his impressions with a wider audience, a service that allowed others to share his experiences. Interestingly, it was in Chicago that he debated with African Americans who were advocates of a separate forty-ninth state for this community; just as interestingly, he opposed this scheme while insisting that where segregation existed, in fact, one had the duty not only to fight it but also to improve whatever institution was so segregated (*Afro-American*, May 5, 1934). Allied with this idea was Du Bois arriving steadily at the conclusion that what was called racial "integration" actually meant an effort to make Negroes a subordinate part of a nation based on exploitation and class division, and he counseled in response more collective remedies for African Americans.

Though he was often at odds with U.S. communists, tellingly, his viewpoint reflected theirs insofar as he, too, often spoke of Black Americans as a "Negro Nation within the Nation." This was not least because white people, he argued, dispossessed Black folk economically, politically, socially, and educationally. Likewise, they had little interest in ensuring African Americans' survival or future if it entailed freedom, self-determination, and equality. The only path to empowerment, he advised, was through, "a concentration of inner Negro forces—a group movement among Negroes, particularly along economic lines, involving increased racial separation and voluntary segregation, taking advantage of every single point that will increase group loyalty" (Du Bois, "A Negro Nation," 1935; see *New York Times*, May 21, 1935; and Du Bois, "Does the Negro," 1935). Thus, in writings including the "The Right to Work," "Does the Negro Need Separate Schools?" "A Negro Nation within a Nation," and "Social Planning for the Negro, Past and Present," Du Bois urged Blacks to plan a separate economy in the spirit of survival, self-preservation, and sustainable struggle.

Also in line with U.S. communists, Du Bois saw Karl Marx, the stern critic of capitalism and advocate of socialism, as a "colossal genius of infinite sacrifice and monumental industry and with a mind of extraordinary logical keenness and grasp." Yet, he added forlornly, "it seems to me [that] the Marxian philosophy is a true diagnosis of the situation in Europe in the middle of the 19th Century," and not necessarily applicable to the United States, where a pike of racism divided the working class racially (*Crisis* 40, Apr. 1933). It was evident that at this juncture, Du Bois harbored a profound pessimism about the ability of Euro-Americans to overcome the obscenity that was racism, which inexorably pushed him toward a firmer advocacy of Black solidarity.

INVASION OF ETHIOPIA

Fascist Italy's invasion of Ethiopia in 1935 was an important historical event for Black people throughout the world because of its colonial, racial, and imperial significance. The invasion prompted Black intellectuals, workers, students, activists, and journalists across the ideological spectrum to critique not only fascism, but also the entire imperial-colonial project.

Throughout the United States, a number of internationalist organizations, such as the Ethiopian Research Council, the International Black League, and the Abraham Lincoln Brigade, were organized in defense of Ethiopian sovereignty. Though the United States officially declared neutrality in 1935 and imposed embargos on both Italy and Ethiopia, the economic support provided to Italy by U.S. corporations and industrial capitalists like Henry Ford represented the country's implicit alignment with the Italian invaders. Likewise, the failure of the League of Nations to defend Abyssinia's sovereignty despite the 1928 Kellogg Briand Pact that committed its members to renounce war as an instrument of national policy, served to underscore to Black people that Italy's invasion of Abyssinia constituted an act of white supremacy against its only African member.

For Black supporters of the Ethiopian cause, the failure of the United States to intervene on behalf of Ethiopia resonated with its historical failure to protect African Americans from racial terror. Experiences of white supremacy in the United States, ranging from individual attacks by the Ku Klux Klan to the structural injustices of Jim Crow, fomented antifascist sentiments and a sense of solidarity with Ethiopians.

For it should be understood that what has been interpreted as Du Bois's endorsement of segregation was actually a creative response to this dilemma sensed by African Americans—that is, the sense that they were bereft of allies—and, thus, there was hardly an alternative to trying to make the most out of a bad situation, that is, improving these segregated institutions. But even as Du Bois was formulating this notion, forces were at play that would cause him to downplay ideas that had caused him to depart from the NAACP. For the Great Depression had led to a rebirth of unions—the primary transmission belt bringing the dispossessed of all colors together, thus serving to undermine the racist segregation to which Du Bois felt he had to accommodate himself. Though on this surface this position could be interpreted as an ironic replay of Booker T. Washington's, it was actually the converse; while Washington believed segregation and group cooperation would ultimately lead to equality among the races, Du Bois was accepting the reality that, because equality of the races was highly unlikely, segregated group cooperation was a dire necessity.

The Great Depression inaugurated the era of industrial unionism, a particularly important moment for Black labor not least because the Congress of Industrial Organizations (CIO) made a concerted effort to organize industries with a significant portion of Black workers. These industries included food processing, tobacco, steel, and mining. Unlike the American Federation of Labor (AFL), which had a long history of racism and Jim Crow locals that dissuaded African Americans from supporting interracial labor organizing, the CIO was much more active in its opposition to these segregationist policies. In 1930, Du Bois noted that while the AFL professed to openly accept African Americans, it in fact only admitted them to federal unions that only had the duty of paying dues and that had no real say or power in the organization. Likewise, some of the skilled unions either openly rejected Black workers under all circumstances, clandestinely rejected them when they attempted to join locals, or accepted only a few exceptional Black workers in areas where a Black skilled union was influential. To this end, Du Bois enjoined: "American Negroes demand justice and fair dealing on the part of organized labor. In spite of the professions of the American Federation of Labor and its constituent unions, the policy of openly or secretly discriminating against Negroes is widespread, as everybody knows. This double-dealing makes real union among laborers impossible, and compels the Negro worker to scab or starve" (Du Bois Papers, 1930).

Due in no small part to its left-leaning, communist, or "fellow traveler" unions, the CIO had noteworthy success in spreading unionization among Black workers. One important reason for the marked increase in unionized Black labor was the CIO's support for civil and voting rights and the convening of local meetings in Black community institutions like churches and lodges. Though the upsurge in unions by no means had a perfect record on race—African Americans were underrepresented in leadership positions, unions didn't always challenge discrimination in hiring and promotion, and sectors like agriculture and domestic service in which Black laborers were overrepresented were largely left out of union efforts—the organization of Black workers during the Great Depression helped to push their needs and concerns to the forefront more than ever before.

Thus it was in the Bronx, New York, in the late summer of 1935 at the National Negro Baptist Convention attended by a massive crowd of 3,000 that Du Bois argued that the salutary impact of President Franklin D. Roosevelt's New Deal lay in the emphasis it gave to the duty of government to provide for the needs of all its citizens (*New York Times*, Sept. 7, 1935). The myrmidons of the former slave South had defeated the antilynching bill—and other progressive legislation—by asserting that the federal government's role should be limited, and it was the obligation of the states to take the initiative, which they inexorably chose not to do. This served as the foundation of conservatism and racism. But with the rise of the Great Depression, the government began to feel that it needed to intervene in the economy and elsewhere forcefully. These policies at once served to erode segregation, the foundation of conservatism, and the need for Du Bois to make the best out of a bad situation.

Consequently, as the Depression marched on savagely, Du Bois continued to refine his thinking on fundamental matters, observing at one juncture that the so-called race problem was at root a socioeconomic one and identical "with the labor problems of the world and with the whole question of the education, political power and economic position of the mass of men," who in some cases happened to be "colored" (*Pittsburgh Courier*, Nov. 14, 1936). The dilemma for Du Bois was that this kind of thinking seemed to lead him inevitably into the embrace of the CPUSA, which had been buoyed by economic devastation. Yet his dearth of faith in the feasibility of class-based coalitions across racial lines made him skeptical at best about the long-term prospects of this organization. Thus, despite the rise of unions—which helped to mitigate his skepticism—he remained staunch in his advocacy of organizations and institutions rooted among African Americans, perhaps because he saw a benefit in providing them with skills that had eluded them in a segregated society. "We must have power," Du Bois insisted in 1933. "We must learn the secret of economic organization." And building cooperatives of various sorts was his preferred solution as it would allow Black Americans to circumvent the bonds of segregation and "stretch hands of strength and sinew and understanding to India and China and all of Asia," not to mention Africa and the Americas. Only with global freedom, Du Bois contended, could "we become in truth, free" (*Crisis* 40, Apr. 1933, 93–94).

In academia Du Bois was the epitome of the scholar-activist, the man of ideas as the man of action. As chairman of the Department of Sociology at Atlanta University, Du Bois approached his old friend and university president John Hope with the idea of publishing a social science journal that would not shrink from publishing articles of literary merit and that would engage the types of issues he was debating in Chicago and elsewhere. Hope's untimely death meant that he was replaced by Rufus Clement, who was not enthusiastic about Du Bois's demarche. Thus, Du Bois queried the leader of his alma mater, Charles Johnson of Fisk, who was more enthusiastic about initiating a quarterly journal that would rival Carter G. Woodson's *Journal of Negro History* and Charles Thompson's *Journal of Negro Education*. With a mere thousand dollars and the promise that more would be solicited, *Phylon: A Quarterly Review of Race and Culture* was launched. Johnson ultimately pulled back, and the initial edition emerged in 1940 under Du Bois's leadership. Unlike the *Crisis*, this journal had more of a scholarly patina and was published less frequently. It was a throwback, a continuation of the Atlanta University Studies he presided over from 1897 to about 1914. In his opening words in the opening issue, Du Bois announced that *Phylon* (from the Greek, meaning "race") would "proceed from the point of view and the experience of black folk where we live and work in the wider world." In other words, the journal, under Du Bois's leadership, would specialize in publishing original scholarship on a broad array of matters relevant to the culture and life of peoples of African descent, especially African Americans. Yet, ultimately, the *Crisis* and *Phylon* shared commonalities as much as differences, for it was Du Bois's stinging critiques of the Atlanta University administration—not unlike his opening the NAACP journal to criticism of its leadership—that led to his ouster from the school in 1944 at the age of seventy-six and his return to the NAACP, an organization that had been transformed by the antifascist war then in motion (Lewis in Horne & Young, 2001, 165–166).

But his return to the embrace of the organization he had helped to found was far from his mind in the 1930s, occupied as he was with the economic cataclysm that had descended. This was a complicated moment for Du Bois to return to the reflective groves of academe, for if ever there was a moment when the frontlines of struggle needed a man of Du Bois's caliber, it was the 1930s, when fascism was on the march and financial distress and uncertainty were stalking the land. For African Americans like Du Bois, the fascist danger hit home most dramatically when Mussolini's Italy invaded Ethiopia in 1935. This East African nation had long been a bright lodestar for Black Americans, given its independence—rare for a continent generally in thrall to colonialism—and its ability to beat back the previous attempt at European domination, besting the Italians at the Battle of Adwa in 1896. Though tragically underdeveloped, Ethiopia also provided an outlet for some Black American professionals, as some could flock to Addis Ababa to toil as pilots and doctors at a time when opportunities in the United States were distortedly circumscribed.

Du Bois knew better than most that the relationship between Black America and Ethiopia was bilateral. It was during the time of the Italian occupation of this East African nation that he wrote affectingly about Malaku Bayen, who had been the personal physician of Ethiopia's deposed leader, Haile Selassie. Like so many from Africa and the diaspora, Bayen had been trained as a doctor at Howard University, and, like so many other students from abroad who had matriculated at such institutions, he too married an African American and then went on to serve as a strong link in a sturdy chain of Pan-Africanism (*New York Amsterdam News*, June 1, 1940).

It should come as no great surprise, then, that Du Bois—and African Americans as a whole—were extremely hostile to Mussolini's invasion (Du Bois, "Inter-Racial Implications," 1935, 82–92). This widespread sentiment was manifested most directly at New York's Madison Square Garden in the early autumn of 1935. A positive aspect of this gathering—and the entire movement against Rome's brigandage—was how it helped to bridge the chasm that in the previous decade had pitted African Americans against those of African descent from the Caribbean. Ethiopia provided a common platform on which all could unite. Thus, 10,000 chanting protesters—overwhelmingly with African roots from varying points on the globe—applauded and cheered the stirring words of a range of speakers, including Du Bois's fellow Fisk alumnus and communist leader James Ford, Walter White of the NAACP, and representatives of Garvey's movement and from the Brotherhood of Sleeping Car Porters. In this context, Du Bois was asked why public opinion was so alarmed by this invasion when Europeans overrunning Africa seemed to be a normative event. Du Bois's response revealed that just as the New Deal had challenged the necessity to make the best out of segregation, the complicated global situation was having a similar effect. For he asserted that "the World War has taught most of Europe and America that the continuing conquest, exploitation and oppression of colored peoples by white[s] is unreasonable and impossible and if persisted will overthrow civilization." Colonialism, which was complemented by segregation, was finding it difficult to survive in these altered conditions (*New York Amsterdam News*, Sept. 28, 1935).

That the locus for the central problem confronting the world was headquartered in Berlin provided Du Bois with a special challenge, as he had long been a close student of Germany and had spent some of his most fruitful days there. It was in 1936 that he applied for a grant from the Oberlaender Trust—part of the Carl Schurz Memorial—to study developments in education in Germany. He won this grant and sailed for Germany in June. On this lengthy journey, Du Bois also visited England, Austria, the Soviet Union, China, and Japan. He returned to his professorial perch in Atlanta in early 1937. It was an enlightening adventure, as he found time in London to dine with the famed novelist and futurist H. G. Wells and the celebrated anthropologist Bronislaw Malinowski; his other ports of call were just as intriguing (*Pittsburgh Courier*, Sept. 5, 1936).

One reason Du Bois spent so much time abroad was precisely because he felt that generally, Black Americans were treated better abroad than at home; however, there were signs of increasing racism in England, as he recounted saddening stories of what had befallen Paul Robeson, his fellow African American and noted actor and activist, who had decamped to London some years earlier in order to escape bigotry at home. Yet, Du Bois acknowledged, what befell Black Americans overseas was small potatoes compared to what they encountered at home (*Pittsburgh Courier*, Sept. 5, 1936).

As he wandered the streets of Berlin, Du Bois found himself appalled by what he saw. Adolf Hitler had come to power in 1933, and it was unclear to some—particularly governments in the North Atlantic—what devastation would be wrought by his rule. Du Bois, on the other hand, was not fooled: he reported that Hitler's party, the Nazis, had constructed a tyrannical state of breathtaking proportion replete with storm troopers, devious spies, brutal police, and a bloodthirsty military. He saw in Hitler's petit bourgeois German Austrian background the basis for his personal appeal and suggested that this leader's ordinary experiences as an artisan (Hitler thought of himself as a painter of note), war veteran, and worker who— supposedly—had to confront the economic interests of those who were Jewish made him a leader with whom many Germans identified, which was then translated into votes (Fikes in Horne & Young, 2001, 100–102).

Du Bois's harrowing experience in Germany helped to solidify his appreciation for the travails of Jewish Americans, who had played such a pivotal role in the founding of the NAACP and the struggle for equality generally. This tie eventually led him to be in the vanguard of those who endorsed the idea of a Jewish state, which came to fruition in 1947–1948. Thus, when he sought to justify his ideological conflict with the NAACP, he resorted to pointing to the formation of the United Hebrew Trades of the late nineteenth century, which was seen widely at the time as a form of so-called self-segregation but whose aim was to break down the anti-Semitism that prevailed in the trade union movement as a whole (*New York Amsterdam News*, Nov. 25, 1939).

Du Bois was received in Germany with proper courtesy, which obviously contrasted sharply with how those who were Jewish were then being treated. This was a reflection of larger phenomena: as their brutal colonial past in the nation now known as Namibia suggested all too accurately, Berlin was not necessarily gentle to those who appeared to hail from Africa. The point was, however, that those like Du Bois were not central to Nazi racism at home in Germany in the same way that those who were Jewish tended to be. Thus, the tremendous African-American athlete, Jesse Owens, had a similar experience during the Berlin Olympics of 1936. In fact, Owens confessed that while in Germany, his hosts "bent [over] backward in making things comfortable," which included inviting him to "the smartest hotels and restaurants." This was a reflection of another reality with which Du Bois was all too familiar, the operation of which served preponderantly in eroding Jim Crow: that is, those nations with seemingly insoluble problems with Washington saw an advantage in not maltreating those thought to have their own grievances with the United States, that is, African Americans (Horne, 2004).

Despite being treated relatively well, Du Bois had good reason to be concerned with the scenes he witnessed in Europe. Like others, he was overwhelmed by the tragedy that was befalling Spain, a reality that was difficult to ignore on the continent, as refugees from there were pouring into various capitals. The duly elected republican government in Madrid was under siege by fascist elements backed avidly by Berlin and Rome in a precursor of what was to overcome the entire continent rather shortly. Official support from Washington, London, Paris, and other Western European powers was glaringly absent, not least because these nations felt that to back the republican government was to aid in the spread of communism.

The Spanish Civil War attracted Langston Hughes, Ernest Hemingway, and hundreds of volunteers from the United States who went to fight, arms in hand, under the rubric of the Abraham Lincoln Brigade. Black women dedicated to socialism and antifascism, including Thyra Edwards, Salaria Kee, and Louise Thompson, also threw their support behind the Spanish republican cause. They saw the defeat of fascism in Spain as a blow against European colonialism, as a step toward freeing Ethiopia from Italian rule, and as a challenge to the degradation and oppression of women that fascism promoted (McDuffie, 2011, 102–110). According to Edwards: "Just now the Spanish people happen to be symbolic of all the rest of us. And certainly there

---

AFRICAN AMERICANS AND THE SPANISH CIVIL WAR

The Spanish Civil War erupted in 1936. The Nationalists, the conservative stratum comprised of most elements of the Spanish Roman Catholic Church and the military, landowners, and businessmen revolted against the Republican government with support from Nazi Germany and Fascist Italy. The Republican faction, comprising urban workers, agricultural laborers, the intelligentsia, and sections of the middle classes, were aided by the Soviet Union and International Brigades from all over Europe, the Caribbean, Latin America, and the United States in their defense of the government.

This fight against fascism in Spain inspired many African Americans to get involved not least because it represented the struggle against European imperialism and colonialism more broadly. Likewise, African Americans linked the defeat of General Francisco Franco's forces in Spain to the defeat of Benito Mussolini's troops in Ethiopia. Those who traveled to Spain to observe or participate in the war effort linked with volunteers in International Brigades from throughout the African Diaspora, which honed their transnational, Pan-African, and Black Internationalist sensibilities. For Black women like Louise Thompson, Esther V. Cooper, Salaria Kee, and Thyra Edwards, the struggle in Spain represented a challenge to women's oppression given the ways that subordination of women operated under fascist regimes.

By 1939 the Republicans were defeated, an outcome that had broad implications. It was in Spain, for example, that Italy and Germany tested new methods of warfare that would be perfected during World War II. Likewise, the Spanish Civil War was seen as one battle in the international struggle between fascism and antifascism.

isn't going to be any freedom and equality for Negroes until and unless there is a free world" (Edwards, 2011, 101). Du Bois concurred: "There is no working class in the world that is not intimately and definitely interested in the outcome of this battle" (*Pittsburgh Courier*, Oct. 24, 1936).

His presence in Berlin provided Du Bois with an inkling of what would occur to others—those in Spain not least—if Hitler's minions were to prevail. It was true that Du Bois was treated courteously (which was more than could be said for his experiences in the states of the Old Confederacy), but while he was in Berlin, his mail was opened, and he was subjected to other forms of espionage. Sadly, despite the obvious tragedy that was ensnaring the Jewish population, Du Bois had reason to believe that many Germans were supportive of Hitler. "And yet," he added, "in direct and contradictory paradox to all this, Germany is silent, nervous, suppressed." He could not help but notice that "there is a campaign of race prejudice carried on, openly, continuously, and determinedly against all non-Nordic races but specifically against the Jews, which surpasses in vindictive cruelty and public insult anything I have ever seen and I have seen much," said this man who then resided in Jim Crow Georgia (*Pittsburgh Courier*, Dec. 5, 1936). Particularly disturbing to Du Bois was the perception that what had propelled the Nazis forward—bigotry and hatred of Moscow—was achingly present in his own nation (*Pittsburgh Courier*, Dec. 12, 1936).

Perhaps because he thought that the logic of Germany's xenophobia—extermination—could conceivably be followed in his own nation, Du Bois did not stint in limning the disastrous consequences of what came to be known as the Holocaust or Shoah and, in that regard, was one of the more far-sighted, visionary, and perspicacious of U.S. nationals who were witnessing this catastrophe. "There has been no tragedy in modern times," he cried, "equal in its awful effects to the fight on the Jew in Germany. It is an attack on civilization, comparable only to such horrors as the Spanish Inquisition and the African Slave Trade." Du Bois, fluent in German, was outraged by the bile and vitriol spewed by certain newspapers; such attacks echoed with his own experience. One journal he observed was "the most shameless, lying advocate of race hate in the world," and "it could not sell a copy without Hitler's consent," meaning that this racism was sanctioned officially and was no accident (*Pittsburgh Courier*, Dec. 19, 1936). As early as 1933, not long after Hitler's ascension, when the full import of his rise had not been recognized by many, Du Bois was launching thunderbolts across the Atlantic in the direction of Berlin. "Race prejudice," charged Du Bois, "is an ugly, dirty thing. It feeds on envy and hate," of which Germany then had a surplus. "One has only to think of a hundred names like Mendelssohn, Heine and Einstein, to remember but partially what the Jew has done for German civilization" (*Crisis* 40, May 1933).

This rigid opposition to anti-Semitism was not wholly selfless, as Du Bois knew that this poison was of a piece with anti-Black racism, with which it enjoyed a symbiotic relationship. "The Nazis made a mistake in beginning their propaganda in New York," he said in late 1933, as "they should have started in Richmond or New Orleans. Their whole philosophy of race hate [has] been so evolved in our own South," he added sardonically, "that Hitler himself could learn a beautiful technique by visiting us" (*Crisis* 40, Dec. 1933).

Nevertheless, as riveting as his journey to Europe might have been, it was his first journey to China that enchanted him; it was "inconceivable," he said wondrously. "Never before has [a] land so affected me," not even Africa: he found the vastness, the hundreds of millions of people, its venerable civilization, all remarkable (*Pittsburgh Courier*, Feb. 20, 1937). In Shanghai he was struck by the pervasive influence of European colonialists who had carved out their own sectors, where they ruled supreme in the heart of this populous city, amid a terrible differentiation in terms of how the rich and poor lived (with the colonialists disproportionately among the former, while the poverty among the latter was overwhelming). Aghast and disgusted, Du Bois expressed in pungent remarks why revolution was erupting in this Asian giant even as his eyes were overpowered by what he saw. He observed that "three things attract white Europe to China: cheap women; cheap child-labor; cheap men" (*Pittsburgh Courier*, Mar. 6, 1937). His journey to China acquainted him with a land that he visited again more than two decades later after the communists came to power (which they did in 1949) precisely because of the misery that moved him so.

Yet, perhaps more than Germany or China, it was his first trip to Japan that may have been the most controversial—and most enlightening—part of his long journey. In the period before World War II, there was little doubt that Japan was the nation most admired by Black Americans, not least because its very existence exploded the convenient fiction that only those of European descent could construct an advanced society. If Japanese could do so, why not Africans? was the weighty question that was posed. In return, like any other nation that endured tensions and conflict with Washington—Moscow comes to mind—Tokyo painstakingly cultivated African Americans, a task that was reciprocated (Horne, *Race War*, 2003). Hence, Du Bois found Manchuria—Chinese territory seized and colonized by Japan—to be exceptional as a form of colonialism purportedly devoid of racism—a conclusion reached by few other observers who denounced Tokyo's aggression. Du Bois was moved by the hospitality shown him in Japan, which he saw as a diplomatic gesture from one colored people to another, and "for this reason," he added gratefully, "my visit is not to be forgotten" (*Pittsburgh Courier*, Mar. 20, 1937).

Through his travels to Nagasaki, Yokohama, Kobe, Kyoto, and Tokyo, Du Bois's admiration for Japan seemed to increase with each mile traversed, as he was treated like a visiting dignitary. At a well-attended press conference in Tokyo, he speculated that it was white racism in the United States in the form of anti-Japanese immigration sentiment that helped politicians in the U.S. West and South strike a deal to squash antilynching legislation that he championed. He also had the opportunity to meet the young author who was translating *The Souls of Black Folk* into Japanese. Upon departing this nation, which was about the geographical size of California (though today it has a population of 110 million), he informed his African-American audience back home that "it is above all a country of colored people run by colored people for colored people. . . . Without exception, Japanese with whom I talked classed themselves with the Chinese, Indians and Negroes as folk standing against the white world" (Fikes in Horne & Young, 2001, 111–113).

Du Bois's fondness for Japan extended to the point where it seemed that he wanted China to renounce its anticolonial struggle against Tokyo. During his time in Shanghai, he recalled "sitting with a group of Chinese leaders at lunch." Rather "tentatively," he told them that he could "well understand the Chinese attitude toward Japan, its bitterness and determined opposition to the substitution of Asiatic for an European imperialism." Yet what he "could not quite understand was the seemingly placid attitude of the Chinese toward Britain." Indeed, he thought "the fundamental source" of Sino-Japanese enmity resided in China's "submission to white aggression and Japanese resistance to it." The Chinese, he concluded acerbically, were "Asian Uncle Toms of the same spirit that animates the 'white folks' n*****' in the United States." With a wave of the hand, Du Bois dismissed concerns about violations of Chinese sovereignty by Japan. "In 1841," he argued, "the English seized Hong Kong, China with far less right than the Japanese had in seizing [Manchuria]" (Horne, 2004, 111).

It is difficult to comprehend Du Bois's apparent dearth of solicitude for the travails of the Chinese languishing under the heavy hand of Japanese colonialism without an acknowledgment of his suspicion of those in the corridors of power in Washington and London who railed against Tokyo while remaining deathly silent about European misdeeds. These elites, he charged, were creating "quite a dither" about China, but that was only because they wanted to feast exclusively on this Asian carcass (*New York Amsterdam News*, Dec. 23, 1939). Moreover, Du Bois was alarmed when a movement seemed to be forming around the dangerous ideas of Charles Lindbergh, the famed pilot who in 1927 had defined celebrity when he flew an airplane unaided across the Atlantic. Lucky Lindy, as he was called, was among a "number of voices," Du Bois warned, who were calling for the so-called white nations to stop fighting each other and to join hands in war

AFRICAN AMERICANS AND THE NEW DEAL

For W.E.B. Du Bois, one of the central questions of Franklin D. Roosevelt's "New Deal" was whether efforts would be made to simply restore previous prosperity or to progressively restructure the country's economic relations. The former provided little hope for African Americans who, he analyzed, would go back to tenant farming, casual agricultural labor, low wages, and precarious employment. Blacks and the majority of workers would benefit most if the relationship between industry and labor was fundamentally readjusted.

The New Deal, heavily influenced by chief advisor Harry Hopkins, combated unemployment, provided loans to failing banks, imposed wage and price controls, offered farm subsidies, controlled production, and reorganized and regulated business and industry. While the Supreme Court moderated some of these efforts, much of the New Deal persisted in applying public funds to alleviating extreme poverty, improving public welfare, empowering consumers and workers to share in private profit, and curbing corporate excess.

African Americans benefited far less than whites from programs including the Federal Emergency Relief Administration and the Works Progress Administration. Reasons included their exclusion by organized labor from public works; local white administrators' racist distribution of relief funds to Black farm laborers and sharecropper; white women's displacement of Black women from domestic and mill work; National Recovery Act codes that often resulted in depressed wages for Black workers; and the prioritizing of white over Black families on relief rolls. With the onset of World War II, the New Deal—especially its regulation of business—was largely halted and reversed.

against the colored peoples of the world (*New York Amsterdam News*, Feb. 3, 1940).

Nevertheless, it would be a mistake to see Du Bois's fondness for Tokyo as wholly and purely blind. He was impressed with its modernization but was not as enthusiastic about the capitalism that had produced this result. By this juncture, Tokyo feared London, and this was driving her toward expansionism as a way to counter the latter's strength in Hong Kong, Singapore, and other critical nodes. But "worst of all," lamented Du Bois, "this alliance of Japan with fascism sets her down as an enemy of Russia," whose assistance to anticolonial fighters in Africa he admired most of all (*Pittsburgh Courier*, Mar. 27, 1937).

Du Bois worried endlessly about the fate of the Soviet Union. Ultimately, Moscow was to be driven into an alliance with London and Washington in order to confront Berlin, Tokyo, and Rome; this antifascist alliance both saved the planet from the Nazi scourge and carried the seeds of the Cold War that was to follow quickly after the conclusion of World

War II. Since visiting Moscow a decade earlier, Du Bois had developed a deeper analysis of this self-proclaimed socialist state. He viewed Joseph Stalin as a "tyrant" but coupled this denunciation with the idea that he "expected" the Soviet Union to "stagger on in blood and tears toward their magnificent goal with many a stumble and retreat." Thus, he announced even before the antifascist alliance made such statements less controversial, "I still believe in Russia" (*New York Amsterdam News*, Feb. 24, 1940). Articulating views that have become no less controversial decades hence, Du Bois asserted, "I believe that the Russian Revolution in its essence and depth of real meaning was greater than the French Revolution, with more vivid promise of healing the ills of mankind than any movement of our day; and [I] believe this despite the murder of [Leon] Trotsky and dozens of great Russians who dared to disagree with Stalin" (*New York Amsterdam News*, Oct. 4, 1941).

Yet the complexity of this global conflict that was unfolding before his very eyes as he traipsed from Europe to Asia confounded Du Bois. As he put it, "if Hitler wins," this means "down with the blacks!" But "if the democracies win," well, "the blacks are already down" (*New York Amsterdam News*, May 31, 1941).

Du Bois returned to the United States, traveling eastward via Hawaii and arriving after President Roosevelt's smashing victory over the Republicans in the 1936 election, which extended the New Deal's lease on life. Roosevelt's victory also meant a continuing upsurge of growth in unions, particularly in the industrial heartland, where a number of African Americans resided (in cities like Detroit, Gary, Cleveland, Chicago, and St. Louis). The growth in unions had the effect of increasing their incomes, just as their political clout was likewise growing, as Black Americans jumped ship from the GOP and cast their fate with FDR. This brought them face-to-face with the Dixiecrats, who theretofore had dominated this party, and hastened the day when their influence would be eroded. For Du Bois, this was part of a gradual process that served to give him reason to believe that, perhaps, the white working class was not hopelessly deluded; and therefore, the desire to strengthen rather than dismantle automatically all-Negro entities began to lose its original rationale.

A transformed Du Bois returned to the classroom in Atlanta. He was approaching the age of seventy, a time when lesser mortals would have chosen retirement. But for Du Bois, in many ways, his best years were ahead of him. In 1933 Du Bois was engaged in intensive study of Marxism, not least because he thought that every engaged intellectual should be doing so. Out of his study came two leftist courses to be taught at Atlanta University: "Karl Marx and the Negro Problem" and "The Economic History of the Negro." The Marx course, which was to include a study of *Das Kapital* and *The Communist Manifesto* and assignments that applied

Marxism to the Negro problem in the United States, was the first of its kind at Atlanta University and one of the first to be taught in U,S. college and universities. He insisted that the radical economist Abram Harris (who himself had just completed a new interpretation of Marx) rush him a list of works "which the perfect Marxian must know." Most of Harris's recommendations, including *History of Economic Doctrines* by Charles Gide and Charles Rist and *The Essentials of Marx* by Algernon Lee, ended up as required readings for the Marx course or in the classroom library on socialism and communism, which, Du Bois boasted, was likely the most comprehensive in the South at the time. For "The Economic History of the Negro," he used *The Black Worker,* coauthored by Harris and Sterling D. Spero, as the primary textbook ("Courses in Atlanta University, Second Semester, 1933"; "Summer School at Atlanta University," 1933; "Memorandum to Dr. Whittaker," n.d. [1933]; W.E.B. Du Bois to James Whittaker, Sept. 14, 1933; "Library List," n.d.; Abram Harris to W.E.B. Du Bois, Jan. 7, 1933; "Memorandum to President Hope from W.E.B. Du Bois," Mar. 9, 1933, Du Bois Papers).

At the same time that he was ensconced in the study of Marxism, he published perhaps his most significant historical work: *Black Reconstruction in America: An Essay toward a History of the Part Which Black Folk Played in the Attempt to Reconstruct Democracy in America, 1860–1880.* Befitting its lengthy title, it was his magnum opus, his landmark on a major topic. This profoundly thoughtful book forced readers of that era—and this one too—to rethink fundamentally one of the more contentious eras in U.S. history, namely, the period following the Civil War. Theretofore, as represented in the shockingly popular Hollywood blockbuster *The Birth of a Nation*, this fecund era was commonly seen as a disaster, an orgy of Negro misrule visited upon their beset former masters. Through diligent research and a visceral rejection of the racist stereotypes that too often characterized the writing of U.S. history, Du Bois emblazoned a new trail of scholarship that continues to reverberate, and, in some ways, his efforts have revolutionized the historical profession itself. Though acknowledging the earlier contributions of Carter G. Woodson, John R. Lynch, Frederic Bancroft, and a raft of other historians, Du Bois undoubtedly made a great leap forward in the historiography. This book also stands as a document of another time when many major libraries and archives, in the South particularly, were closed to African Americans, and, as an unfortunate result, there were numerous documents that Du Bois was unable to examine. Sadly, this lacuna hindered his ability to construct a timeless narrative.

On the other hand, *Black Reconstruction* stands as an outline, leaving plenty of room for other scholars to fill in the blanks, which has happened in succeeding generations, thereby vindicating his original insights. The emphasis in this book, as in much of his work, is on the agency or active engagement of ordinary people, mostly African Americans, in the face of racist violence (much of it spearheaded by the Ku Klux Klan), fraud, and the like. The monumental final chapter, "The Propaganda of History," continues to be a classic denunciation of the rampant chauvinism that to that point had been hegemonic—and, to a degree, has not dissipated altogether.

Despite the strain and time consumption of teaching, Du Bois also found time to publish while in Atlanta yet another classic, *Black Folk Then and Now: An Essay in the History and Sociology of the Negro Race*, which was, in a sense, an update of what he had written in his justly praised book, *The Negro*, published over two decades earlier. The later book contains sixteen chapters and an extensive bibliography, with the first nine chapters offering a history of Africa and its early civilizations, the coming of modern slavery and the slave trade, and the movement for the abolition of both. Two chapters treat those of African origin in the United States and Europe contemporaneously, while four chapters treat Africa, particularly landownership, the plight of subalterns, and systems of political control and of education. Here again he repeats his archetypal phrase that the problem of the century is the "problem of the color line."

Finally, it was in Atlanta that Du Bois completed his insightful *Dusk of Dawn: Essay toward an Autobiography of a Race Concept*. While *Souls* and *Darkwater* "were written in tears and blood," Du Bois wrote that while *Dusk of Dawn* was "set down no less determinedly," it was written with "wider hope and some more benign fluid," hence the title, which he saw as optimistic. Until the publication of his more official autobiography, published posthumously, this book was the most basic source for biographical data about him. Also displayed here—and quite typically—was a luscious and affecting writing style of a type that is all too rare nowadays. Herein is likewise revealed his positive attitude toward Moscow and his skeptical attitude toward domestic communists. This attitude received a stern, stiff challenge once Nazi Germany attacked the Soviet Union in 1941, quickly followed by Japan's bombing of Pearl Harbor, Hawaii. "Again the tragedy of the Negro American soldier festers," he lamented, "as it did in the Revolution, the Civil War, the Spanish War and the first World War. The sore will never heal," he moaned, "so long as we fight for a Freedom and Democracy which we dare not practice" (*New York Amsterdam News*, Sept. 13, 1941).

What Du Bois came to see was that the dynamic unleashed by the antifascist war served to erode the encrusted bigotry of Jim Crow that had ruined the life chances of so many African Americans and the colonialism that had handcuffed Africa. That is, it became difficult for Western European countries to argue that they did not merit domination by Germany while they continued to dominate Africa. African and African-American soldiers shed blood in buckets (as they had throughout World War I), providing them with a further rationale to demand justice. Washington's alliance with Moscow served to undermine biases that associated the left—of which Du Bois was a constituent member—with a demonized Soviet Union, which led to an undermining of numerous Jim Crow barriers that he had railed against for decades.

It was in this radically altered atmosphere that a reconciliation took place between Du Bois and the NAACP. Its leader, Walter White, recognized more than most how the changing global environment could radically determine the fortunes of African Americans, and with this idea firmly in mind, he invited Du Bois to return to Manhattan in 1944 as a kind of "Minister of Foreign Affairs," not just for the NAACP but also for Black America as a whole.

10

A Life of Radicalism

Du Bois had departed from the NAACP in 1934 because of a dispute with the group's leadership. This led to his return to Atlanta University, from whence he had departed a quarter of a century earlier to play a leading role in Manhattan in the NAACP. But like a human yo-yo, he departed Atlanta University in 1944 to return to Gotham—again, to play a leading role in the organization he had helped to found (substantiation for the following pages can be found in Horne, 1986; Burden-Stelly, 2019).

Why would Du Bois return to an organization with whose leadership he had feuded quite famously? The short answer is that there were both push and pull factors. By 1944, Du Bois was seventy-six years old and, given actuarial projections for African American men, was thought to be soon headed to the nearest mortuary; moreover, he had come into sharp conflict with the administration of Atlanta University—a contretemps that was in some ways fiercer than his previous dustup with the NAACP leadership— and returning to New York City seemed suddenly more attractive than enduring the routine indignities of Jim Crow that Atlanta offered.

In fact, Du Bois was unceremoniously dismissed from Atlanta University for old age. Though he had been past the retirement age of sixty-five when he was rehired by his friend John Hope, after the latter's death in 1936, Du Bois had come into increasing conflict with the administrations at both Atlanta University and Spelman College. Du Bois suspected that his leftist courses, especially the Marx course, "eventually stirred up opposition" from Spelman President Florence Read. Years earlier, she had attempted to keep out his "radical influence" by delaying his full appointment to Atlanta University's faculty and by stymieing his attempts to start *Phylon*. In 1944, with the support of Rufus Clement (who had assumed the presidency of Atlanta University upon John Hope's death), she continued her campaign against Du Bois by moving to have him retired; the Atlanta University trustees complied. Years later, when *Freedomways* magazine was preparing a memorial issue in tribute to Du Bois, his widow roundly rejected any input from Clement, whom she accused of attempting to destroy her husband's work with the abrupt retirement. She considered the latter not only a personal assault on Du Bois but also an attack on research and study on behalf of Black people more broadly.

But why would the NAACP leadership see fit to ask him to return, considering that their top leader—Walter White—was still in office and continued to be decidedly immune to Du Bois's charms? White was responding to a global climate in the midst of a war against fascism and militarism that was profoundly different from the environment that existed in 1934 when he and Du Bois had last feuded. For after Nazi Germany invaded Soviet Russia in June 1941, followed swiftly by militarist Japan bombing Pearl Harbor, Hawaii, in December of that same tumultuous year, the United States felt compelled to ally with its former antagonist in Moscow, a decision that substantively altered the situation inside the United States. Now that Washington was allied with a nation that many had seen theretofore as the embodiment of an "evil empire," there was a felt desire to reduce the intensity of anticommunism, which was now seen as an impediment to prosecuting successfully a war for survival. Thus, Hollywood—partially at the behest of President Franklin D. Roosevelt—began shifting from its previous portrayal of the Soviet Union as the epitome of evil to more benign portraits (e.g., Horne, *Final Victim*, 2005). Inexorably, this climate influenced how Du Bois—a man with socialist convictions who was not unfriendly to Moscow—was perceived. This changing climate heightened the need for the NAACP to have on staff someone with expert knowledge about the state of the world. More pointedly, in seeking someone to fill a post that amounted to Black America's "Minister of Foreign Affairs," White and the NAACP were hard-pressed to find someone more qualified than Du Bois, who did not require intensive study to get up to speed on the intricacies of the international situation and the politics of Russia, China, Europe, and the African and Caribbean nations whose independence was deemed a high priority emerging from the war.

Such circumstances led to the NAACP offering, and Du Bois accepting, the job. The Association itself was in a growth spurt, affording it the increased dues payments—and the concomitant increased budget and ambitions—that would allow it to turn its sights more intently on a world at war in which (once more) African-American soldiers were being forced to shed blood and treasure. In 1940, the NAACP had about 40,000 members; by the time Du Bois came on board, membership had grown tenfold. Part of this phenomenal expansion was driven by the tireless labor of two women on the NAACP's staff—Ella Baker and Shirley Graham—the latter of whom Du Bois had come to know quite well.

Explicating this growth also sheds light on how and why Du Bois would be invited to return to the NAACP: again, those with whom the United States was now in a battle to the death—principally Nazi Germany, with its insidious nostrums of racial superiority—seemed all too similar to those who stood as the major proponents of Jim Crow. The idea was growing that unless the NAACP took a more active role in combating bigotry abroad, it would be disadvantageous to the antiracist struggle at home. Moreover, in recent decades, Japan had made pointed overtures to Black America, playing adroitly upon their bruised racial feelings and assuring one and all that if Tokyo prevailed, African Americans could be assured that the hated Jim Crow would simultaneously suffer a death blow (Horne, 2004). In short, racism was very much at issue during this war, and the U.S. authorities had little choice but to retreat from the more egregious aspects of white supremacy.

It was in such an environment that, for the first time since the end of Reconstruction—a period about which Du Bois had written so eloquently—minority voting rights were expanded. An indication of the growth of the left that accompanied this retreat of ossified racism—which made Du Bois's return to Manhattan possible—was the election in 1943 of a Black Communist to the New York City Council. Ben Davis Jr., yet another son of Atlanta who had moved northward to secure a niche, succeeded his good friend Adam Clayton Powell Jr. when the Harlem minister was elected to Congress (Horne, 1994). In sum, the period from 1941 to 1945, an era suffused with massive bloodletting and untold agony, also marked a sharp break from the recent past, creating an opening for the left, for African Americans, and, not least, for Du Bois.

At the same time that the United States was retreating from de jure segregation and African Americans were experiencing some political success, the government was also keeping close tabs on African-American radicalism, not least because it suspected that much of this group's agitation was foreign-inspired. On July 2, 1942, FBI Director J. Edgar Hoover commissioned the *Survey of Racial Conditions in the United States* (RACON) to investigate the causes of Black rebelliousness during the war. Its aim was to curb African-American protest and racial tension that had been taking off since 1940. What resulted was a file consisting of 77,000 pages covering a range of topics, from Black worker militancy to Japanese influence on Black antiwar sentiment to CPUSA efforts and membership in Black communities. The initial target of Hoover's investigation was the Harlem-Based

PEEKSKILL RIOT

The Peekskill Riot took place on August 27, 1949, at a scheduled Civil Rights Congress concert in Peekskill, New York. When Paul Robeson showed up to sing, a vicious mob assaulted attendees and burned a five-foot cross on the concert grounds. Instead of defending the civil rights of the largely left-wing crowd that had been savagely attacked, authorities deceitfully blamed the violence and lawlessness on the victims by construing the concert as a "communist plot."

Dissent against Paul Robeson had been mounting since he delivered an angry speech at the World Peace Conference in Paris earlier that year. Press reports indicated that he found it unthinkable that American Negroes would go to war for a country that had historically oppressed them (the United States) against a country that treated African Americans with full dignity (the Soviet Union). Thus, in the context of the Cold War and increasing anticommunist hysteria, he was construed as disloyal, traitorous, and a "stooge" of Moscow.

Concert attendees, including Du Bois, Robeson, and Louise Thompson Patterson argued in a letter to President Harry Truman that the attack at Peekskill was a form of state-sanctioned "anti-Negro" and anticommunist mob violence against persons deemed "un-American" because they supported constitutional rights for all people, the end of colonial rule, and durable peace.

Ethiopian Pacific League, headed by Robert Jordan, which the FBI sought to prosecute under the Espionage Act for loyalty to Japan that undermined the internal security of the United States. Surveillance soon spread to all organizations and individuals that purportedly had pro-Axis or pro-Communist affiliations, manifested in racial disturbances, demonstrations, and agitation. Prosecution was a priority, and during World War II, eighteen African Americans were ultimately convicted of sedition or conspiracy to commit sedition. In addition, the FBI's Security Division prepared a report of its findings on August 15, 1943, that it presented to Hoover on September 10 of that year, and which served as the foundation for the broader counterintelligence apparatus used against African Americans, communists, and other radicals in subsequent decades (Hill, 1995, 1–72).

Du Bois's journey northward was no simple matter; in fact, it was a major logistical exercise to move the 883 miles that separated Atlanta from Manhattan. For over the years, he had accumulated thousands of volumes that needed to be moved and a number of file cabinets bulging with files and letters that stretched back to his teenage years. Naturally, his personal library was especially strong when it came to the most neglected of continents—Africa. His collection on socialism and communism was also quite extensive, but he also was a fan of the Welsh writer Dylan Thomas and the British novelist Agatha Christie (Du Bois Papers, Jan. 7, 1933). He had to cart away numerous musical albums—his favorite was Beethoven's Ninth Symphony, though he was also a devotee of Vivaldi and Tchaikovsky. Naturally, he had a deep appreciation of the old Negro spirituals, as even a casual glance at his classic *The Souls of Black Folk* would reveal. He was a subscriber to numerous publications, particularly those concerning colonized Africa, though he also kept a close eye on publications from the Caribbean (a region he visited repeatedly over the years, particularly the land in which he had roots—Haiti—and its neighbors, Jamaica and Cuba). Naturally, he carefully read the numerous newspapers that covered Black America, notably the *Pittsburgh Courier,* for which his good friend P. L. Prattis served as editor. He subscribed to the *New York Times* and the communist *Daily Worker,* indicative of his open-mindedness and ecumenical approach. Yet somehow, he was able to move this intellectual fortress that accompanied him from South to North and quickly settled into what he saw correctly as a major task: helping to shape Black America's position on a major issue of the war, that is, how to bring freedom to a world that remained largely colonized. In brief, Du Bois had to convince the major powers why it was wrong and irrational to assert that it was unjustifiable for them to be ruled from Berlin and Tokyo, but it was justifiable for Africa, the Caribbean, and a good deal of Asia to languish under a colonial system administered principally from London and Paris.

Being a man of action and a man of thought, Du Bois chose to pursue this lofty goal on two major fronts. Shortly after his arrival at the NAACP, he published a thoughtful book that provided an intellectual and political framework for his newly minted activism. *Color and Democracy: Colonies and Peace* was a tour de force, at once an indictment of the white supremacy that had buoyed Berlin and had provided Tokyo with a basis for appeal (Du Bois, *Color,* 1945). Suggestive of the importance of this topic to him was the fact that he placed the title of this book as an emblem on his stationery. This small planet, Du Bois contended, was simply unsustainable as long as the multitudes of Africa and Asia were doomed to be colonial appendages of the major powers. In some ways, this book-length essay was an extension of his famed essay on the African roots of war that sought to explain the explosion that was World War I as flowing from jousting and contestation by the major powers—in this case, Germany—for their various places in the colonial sun and their share of colonial booty. Yet suggestive of the changed atmosphere brought by the antifascist war was the fact that the U.S. Navy alone brought a hefty 2,400 copies of this militant anticolonial tract for distribution within its ranks, as this now controversial book was viewed widely as reflecting common sense rather than the grinding of a political axe.

Rarely one to allow intellectual endeavors—no matter how laudable—to become the alpha and omega of his labor, upon arriving at the NAACP, Du

Bois immediately began to organize the Fifth Pan-African Congress, to be held in Manchester, England. This European metropolis was an appropriate site for serious planning for an anticolonial world. Its looms had once been fueled by cotton from the former slave South of the United States, which in turn had been picked by legions of enslaved Africans. Now in August 1945, just as the war was arriving at an exclamation point with the atomic bombings of Hiroshima and Nagasaki, the elderly Du Bois—a father of Pan-Africanism—arrived in Britain, a nation that had been devastated by this bloody conflict and contained numerous subjects who were now yearning for a path that diverged sharply from the empire that had brought so much misery to so many.

Because of his towering intellectual accomplishments, it is sometimes forgotten that Du Bois was an organizer of no small talent. Surely, his approach to this Manchester gathering dispelled any doubts that may have existed. Though his fracases with the leadership at Atlanta University and the NAACP may have led the unsuspecting to conclude that he was hopelessly cantankerous, his skill and efficiency in building consensus for what amounted to a global conference belied this easy notion. In plotting his course, he brought onboard the actor-activist Paul Robeson; Amy Jacques Garvey (spouse of the late Jamaican-born leader and an adept organizer in her own right); and Max Yergan, the North Carolina-born activist, who had lived in South Africa and served alongside Robeson as leader of the Council on African Affairs until his treacherous descent into ardent anticommunism. Also essential to this effort was George Padmore; born as Malcolm Nurse in Trinidad, he had attended Howard University and joined the Communist Party—which he subsequently abandoned after a dispute with the Comintern over its commitment to anti-imperialism in the midst of the rise of fascism—before decamping to London, where he became a principal contact point for African and Caribbean anticolonial leaders as the date for the congress approached.

Du Bois also wasted no time in briefing the NAACP leadership, though already he had detected that they were not as enthusiastic about this gathering as he was. Contradicting the commonly accepted idea that with age comes a slowdown in energy, Du Bois took it upon himself to organize an anticolonial conference in Harlem to complement the Manchester meeting. It was at the Schomburg Library at 135th Street—in the midst of a neighborhood whose very congestion and deterioration spoke loudly as to why the racism that underpinned colonialism had to be defeated—that scores of delegates from India, Burma, Africa, and elsewhere met to debate the nature of the postwar world. Kwame Nkrumah, the future leader of Ghana who was to invite Du Bois to reside in his homeland, was generally pleased with this gathering at which he played such a prominent role. He insisted, though, that it should have been more adamant in its call for anticolonial independence, for many at the meeting were reluctant to part with the increasingly antiquated vision of a continuing role for the major powers in colonized lands.

As noteworthy as this Harlem gathering was, it proved to be a mere dress rehearsal for the impressive opening of the Pan-African Congress in Manchester in August 1945, the culmination of a series of gatherings that had begun decades earlier. With the battering absorbed by fascism and militarism, it was recognized by one and all that a momentous turning point had been reached in the epic battle against racism and colonialism and that Du Bois's pronouncement that the century's problem was the color line was more accurate than once supposed.

Present at the Manchester congress were nearly 200 delegates from sixty different nations. Du Bois was one of seven elected to chair sessions and was ultimately chosen as permanent chairman of the entire body, suggestive of the esteem in which he was held. The man with whom he was to be linked in coming years—Nkrumah—set the tone by stressing militant action: strikes, boycotts, and the like, a course of action that was realized in Africa most notably as the war concluded, which paved the way for the retreat of the colonial powers. This congress differed sharply from previous efforts in that it was dominated not as much by intellectuals like Du Bois but more by trade union advocates. It was at Manchester that Du Bois first met Jomo Kenyatta, who was to lead Kenya to independence in 1963.

Yet amid the self-congratulation and celebration, there were somber notes. There was reluctance at the highest levels of the NAACP to endorse this gathering, a fact that stunned Du Bois as it seemed to be consistent with the organization's mandate. As a result, when he returned from Manchester, he found obstruction when he sought to organize a follow-up meeting and publish pamphlets about anticolonial struggles in Africa. Even though the antifascist war was just ending, a new era was beginning— the Cold War—and militant anticolonialism was rapidly being seen by some as no more than a front for the soon-to-be primary foe, communism. The Cold War was predicated on the idea that capitalism in the United States and socialism in the Soviet Union were fundamentally incompatible and that each threatened the other's existence. Each side used geopolitical maneuvering, economic blockades, technical and military aid, and propaganda to weaken its adversary and to gain the allegiance of newly decolonizing countries. The Cold War carried with it the constant threat of nuclear war, proxy wars throughout Asia and Africa, anticommunism and red-baiting, and the continuation of imperialism and neocolonialism in the Third World.

Undeterred, Du Bois pressed on; 1945 was also the year that the United Nations was organized, and, as Du Bois saw it, forging a group that purported to bring under one roof all of the nations of the planet, when a good deal of the world was colonized, was not only unsustainable but deeply flawed. Thus, Du Bois the organizer took it upon himself to assemble an African American delegation to intervene in this process and contacted the National Council of Negro Women, the National Bar Association, and many other groups in this vein.

Du Bois and White arrived in San Francisco, where the United Nations was being planned, and raised the prickly matter of including in this body's charter specific provisions concerning human rights. To that end, Du Bois sought to make alliances with delegates from Moscow and New Delhi, but he also did not neglect rallying his base, for it was during this jaunt to the West Coast that he spoke to clamorous and cheering throngs of supporters in Oakland, Los Angeles, and the city by the bay, San Francisco. Suitably impressed with his effort, the NAACP Board voted to send a copy of his favorably received *Color and Democracy* to every member of the U.S. delegation in San Francisco. Returning home from this triumphal journey, Du Bois detoured to Washington, DC, for an appearance before the Senate Foreign Relations Committee, where he provided measured praise for the UN Charter that emerged in California—though he expressed deep disappointment with the body's approach to colonialism.

Yet despite—or perhaps because of—this stellar debut, the tension between Du Bois and White, which had seemed to dissipate due to the necessity of war, was now rearing its head again as this conflict receded in the rearview mirror. Du Bois saw White as a narrowly educated manager. White saw Du Bois as overbearing and arrogant. Ideologically, Du Bois was a socialist on a path toward the CPUSA. White was a pragmatist, unafraid to join the gathering anticommunist crusade. As so often happens, their initial disputes were about nothing so high-minded as ideology; their disputes were about matters mundane—office space. Du Bois complained that his 12′ × 20′ office housed three workers, 2,500 books, two desks, a typing table, a balky Dictaphone contraption, and six four-drawer file cabinets. He wondered if cattle in rail cars were entitled to more space. There were also questions about whether he was allowed to attend the board meetings of the NAACP (where policy was crafted). To not be invited to attend the meetings of the organization to which he had been so instrumental was quite a setback.

For their part, White and his deputy, Roy Wilkins, thought Du Bois operated as if he were an independent agency, a reprise of his previous experience with the *Crisis*. They could not understand why Du Bois balked at having his mail opened centrally, along with that of other leaders of the NAACP. Actually, the NAACP—perhaps because of the tense atmosphere in which it had to operate, filled with Jim Crow, lynchings, and the like—was a seething cauldron of tension as leaders bickered endlessly, irrespective of ideological clashes. Thus, the group's leading lawyer—Thurgood

Marshall—feuded with White, while the board itself was split by various conflicts. The NAACP structure, which featured considerable power invested in White's post and, according to critics, insufficient power accorded to the branches and annual convention, may have exacerbated these conflicts. On top of all these rifts was a fractious drive to organize the group's staff into a union, a battle in which Du Bois stood with the workers, while his internal opponents did not. This, too, did not lead to an era of good feelings.

Similarly, the changing political climate in the United States did little to assuage internal tensions, for—not coincidentally—external ructions intruded. Indeed, Du Bois's return to the NAACP not only coincided with the war, it also overlapped that conflict's end and the resultant rise in tensions between Washington and Moscow. Almost in metronomic fashion, tensions correspondingly rose between the NAACP leadership symbolized by White and Du Bois. White and Wilkins did not take kindly to Du Bois's growing friendship with Paul Robeson, the actor and activist, who saw fit to launch an international movement against lynching that was quite embarrassing to Washington, which sought to focus the world on human rights violations in Moscow. At this time Robeson was probably closer to the CPUSA than Du Bois. In any case, when the leadership of this group was placed on trial in 1948, supposedly for teaching and advocating insurrection, Du Bois joined Robeson in rising to their defense—but the NAACP chose not to do so. During this same fateful year, a new political grouping came into being, the Progressive Party, which launched a stiff challenge that threatened the Democratic Party of President Harry Truman, who had become quite close to the NAACP leadership, White in particular.

This political-cum-ideological rift was a token of yet another rift: the NAACP was involved in more than litigation, but, as symbolized by the critical role played by Thurgood Marshall and other attorneys of note, the organization certainly tended to privilege litigation over mass mobilization. This was understandable at a time when repression reigned supreme in the South, where most African Americans continued to reside, and was accelerating in the North and West as civil liberties began to fall victim to anticommunism. Yet Robeson, as symbolized by his crusade against lynching, and Du Bois, who joined him, thought that lawsuits could only take flight when buoyed by a mass movement—a lesson later exemplified by Dr. Martin Luther King Jr., who also had his differences with the NAACP leadership. Du Bois took exception to what he viewed as the overly centralized structure of the NAACP, which did not create favorable conditions for the ascension of grassroots activism.

This setup facilitated the rise of a Faustian bargain that was to define Black America for decades to come: Truman spearheaded certain concessions on the civil rights front (e.g., the retreat from a racially segregated army in 1948), and in return the Black leadership backed his anticommunism, including the prosecution of CPUSA leaders (e.g., the Harlem City Councilman Ben Davis Jr.) and the decision to involve the nation in 1950 in the civil war in Korea. When the NAACP began to purge its ranks of real and imagined communists, it was inevitable that their attention would be diverted to the suspected Red on their staff: Du Bois.

A catalyst for this process occurred when Du Bois led in filing a petition at the United Nations charging the United States with human rights violations against African Americans. At a time when Washington was seeking to indict Moscow on similar charges, this petition was not accepted with equanimity in the Oval Office—or the inner sanctums of the NAACP. Actually, Du Bois had laid the foundation for this initiative in his book, *Color and Democracy*, which suggested that a wide audience existed for indictments of white supremacy. It was in August 1946 that Du Bois formally proposed to White that a petition be submitted. Strikingly, this effort was sanctioned, as the import of the rising Cold War had yet to be comprehended altogether by the NAACP leadership.

With typically efficient haste, Du Bois moved swiftly to set this petition in motion, conferring with the UN leadership in Manhattan, enlisting the editorial aid of such luminaries as the future Nobel Laureate, Ralph Bunche; the scholar Rayford Logan; and the attorney Earl. Soon the international community was mulling over Du Bois's handiwork. Despite its lengthy title—*An Appeal to the World: A Statement on the Denial of Human Rights to Minorities in the Case of Citizens of Negro Descent in the United States of America and an Appeal to the United Nations for Redress*—this work was a tightly written ninety-four-page indictment covering history, law, politics, economics, and related topics.

Like the Fifth Pan-African Congress and the San Francisco meeting that founded the United Nations itself, Du Bois again displayed his formidable organizing skills, as hundreds of organizations endorsed this petition, including the fraternity Kappa Alpha Psi, founded in 1911, and the National Medical Association. Remarkably, this indictment of the rulers of the United States was endorsed by mainstream organizations, signaling a growing disaffection at home with Washington's Jim Crow. Similarly notable was the deafening response abroad, particularly in Africa and the Caribbean. Such an indictment gave momentum to their own anticolonial efforts and raised severe questions about whether millions would align with Washington or Moscow as Cold War tensions waxed. Unavoidable was the fact that it was the Soviet Union that brought the petition before the United Nations. Candidly, Attorney General Tom Clark, who hailed from Jim Crow Texas, confessed that he was "humiliated" by the Du Bois–Moscow collaboration. Yet, his concrete response was to enlarge and strengthen the Civil Rights Division of the Justice Department, reinforcing the notion that this kind of collaboration was eminently useful.

Unsettled by this turn of events was the NAACP's own leadership, which included Eleanor Roosevelt, who was a member of the powerful board of directors, as well as the UN's Economic and Social Council. She was not pleased with this petition, and rather quickly, her attitude became the consensus within the NAACP leadership.

When this petition was then followed by Du Bois's support for the left-leaning Progressive Party challenge to Truman in 1948, the NAACP leadership came to believe that his left-wing initiatives were inconsistent with the organization's attempt to seek mainstream backing for civil rights concessions. The Progressive Party, which was led by former U.S. Vice President Henry Wallace, challenged Jim Crow in the South directly, which prodded the Democrats to act similarly, rather than run the risk of defection of droves of African-American voters from their ranks. For the Progressive Party placed the largest number of Black candidates ever selected to run for an office on a single ticket since the days of Reconstruction. The Progressive Party launched a form of guerilla warfare against Jim Crow, refusing to hold racially segregated rallies, defying the law in the process, thereby hastening apartheid's end and serving as a harbinger of the 1960s upsurge.

As the November 1948 election approached, it was evident that Du Bois was not operating in sync with the NAACP leadership. For though he never missed an opportunity to utter high praise for Wallace and the Progressive Party, his NAACP comrades acted similarly on behalf of Truman and the Democrats. The problem was that the latter party was in thrall to a Dixiecrat wing in the South that considered Jim Crow laws to be holy writ, and thus the Democrats were highly vulnerable to Du Bois's charge that they countenanced segregation. As it happened, the 1948 election witnessed the greatest turnout of Black voters to that point. Sensing that the African American vote, which they had come to rely on, might be slipping away, the Democrats borrowed liberally from the Progressive platform, particularly as it concerned civil rights.

Yet the battling between these two parties was dwarfed in animosity and intensity by the internal wrangling that engulfed the NAACP in the dueling personalities of Du Bois and White. Ultimately, the 1948 election, a significant turning point in the struggle for equality, also was the prompting factor that led to yet another turning point in the torturous history of Black America: the ouster, yet again, of Du Bois from the organization he had rejoined only four years earlier. Ignoring their own constant drumbeat of support for Truman, the NAACP leadership accused Du Bois of violating the group's ban on partisan political activity by backing Wallace so avidly. So, he was fired.

This personnel decision proved to be of monumental significance. It lubricated the path for Black America's tightened alliance with the Democratic Party and the liquidation of nascent attempts to build a left-wing alternative to this party that had such a strong Dixiecrat wing. Ultimately, the Dixiecrats were to bolt from this party in the 1960s and join the ranks of the GOP, giving the Republicans a stranglehold on the votes of the white South that was to endure for decades to come and providing them with an automatic advantage in presidential elections. In the short term, when Black America's leading organization—the NAACP—embraced the Democrats so wholeheartedly, it also felt compelled to swallow their foreign policy agenda, favoring the waging of hot wars in Korea and Vietnam and a Cold War globally, which not only demonized anticolonial movements as "communist" but also drained the federal budget that could have addressed pressing needs in housing, health, and education.

As Du Bois was sacked, the NAACP launched simultaneously an internal witch hunt for real and suspected communists that weakened the organization and settled the dispute over whether the organization would favor litigation or mass mobilization in favor of the former. This slowed down the struggle for equality and dissipated the energies unleashed by the 1948 election—a struggle that did not regain momentum until the arrival on the national stage of Dr. Martin Luther King Jr., who also found himself in conflict with the NAACP and who also was accused of being all too close to the dreaded communists. Nevertheless, despite the weighty significance of the foregoing, perhaps the most profound aspect of the sacking of Du Bois was the fact that a triggering factor—beyond the 1948 election—concerned the petition to the United Nations. Taking Black America off the global agenda was certainly a victory for Washington, though it was not as certain that it was a victory for the constituency that the NAACP was sworn to protect.

Sensing the deeper meaning of the routing of Du Bois, a committee of his supporters was formed in an attempt to reverse this decision—though to no avail. It included such dignitaries as Robeson and glittering intellectuals like E. Franklin Frazier, Alain Locke, and Horace Mann Bond (whose son, Julian, was to serve as NAACP Chairman in the late twentieth and early twenty-first century). This committee was to take this dispute to the pages of the press—particularly the African-American press—and to the broader left; the latter sensed correctly that the purging of Du Bois was a loud signal foretelling a wider ouster from influence of all those who refused to toe the anticommunist line. They recognized that if a man of Du Bois's importance could be barred from an organization he had helped to found simply because of a political dispute, then the entire nation was headed in a conservative direction that would make life quite uncomfortable for those unwilling to go along.

A bruised Du Bois, now an octogenarian, was forced to move his many books and file cabinets once more, this time to the office of the Council on African Affairs (CAA), another Manhattan-based organization. Founded in 1937 as a vehicle through which U.S. citizens could intervene more directly in the thorny matter of colonialism in Africa, it was seen in the public mind as the lengthened shadow of one of its founders, Robeson. This was not altogether accurate, and Du Bois's arrival on the scene as vice chairman indicated that the NAACP's loss was CAA's gain. The CAA was not a mass membership organization but more of a lobby that concentrated on producing newsletters and educational materials. The intellectual firepower that graced this group's leadership was formidable: the Los Angeles–based journalist and publisher Charlotta Bass; the famed music producer John Hammond, who, like another CAA leader, Frederick Field, was the scion of a major fortune; the leading academics Ralph Bunche and Mordecai Johnson; and the jurist Hubert Delany rounded out this lineup. There was also the anthropologist and Pan-Africanist Eslanda Goode Robeson, who, in early 1937, at the behest of Max Yergan, became the first contributor to the CAA, donating 300 dollars. The key staff person was W. Alphaeus Hunton, Jr., who held a doctorate in English literature.

Yet it seemed that Du Bois had departed the frying pan only to land in the fire, for it was not long before the CAA was torn by a left-right split not unlike that which had occasioned his hasty and unceremonious departure from the NAACP. In this case, the role of Walter White was played by Yergan. Yergan had toiled for years in South Africa on behalf of the YMCA. Like White, he too had a dalliance with the left, but, if anything, his associations were deeper and more far-reaching, as he was suspected widely of being a communist. But like the NAACP, some within the CAA—notably Yergan—quickly sensed that the U.S. alliance with the Soviet Union, compelled by the exigencies of global war, would become inoperative once this titanic conflict ended. Also like the NAACP, the Yergan-induced split of the CAA, which caused a number of its leaders to depart for greener pastures, severely weakened the attempt to build anticolonial solidarity within the United States. For his part, Yergan executed a dizzying transition from left to right, quickly becoming a favorite anticommunist witness before Congress and an avid supporter of apartheid in South Africa, while leaving a terribly weakened CAA in his wake. These "turncoats" compelled more radical members, such as Eslanda Goode Robeson, to go on the offensive. In an open letter written on April 17, 1948, for example, she defended the CAA's left-wing members, including her husband, Du Bois, Hunton, Doxey Wilkerson, and Ferdinand Smith, and condemned anticommunism as "frightening and very un-American" (Robeson in Du Bois Papers, Apr. 17, 1948).

As for Du Bois, he faced a real dilemma: with every political dispute in which he became ensnared, it became painfully more evident that the political course that had governed his life and career to that point—left of center with a tilt toward socialism—had become incongruent, inconsistent, and incompatible with the dominant course now being followed by the place of his birth. His options were few: he could tack to the prevailing winds and live a more comfortable life at the expense of his deeply held principles, or he could continue to sail fearlessly into the teeth of the bitter gales that now buffeted him. For a man who never had accumulated considerable income and was now elderly, this was no small matter—yet he opted for the latter course.

He chose a global stage on which to make an implicit announcement of this decision. The Cultural and Scientific Conference for World Peace was convened at the posh Waldorf-Astoria Hotel in late March 1949. Du Bois, the adroit organizer, helped to plan this meeting that brought progressive and left-leaning forces from around the world to midtown Manhattan to raise grave alarms about the growing tensions between Moscow and Washington that had frightening nuclear overtones. In the face of scurrilous attacks from the U.S. press, 2,800 people gathered, with thousands turned away because of a lack of space. Appearing alongside Du Bois was a sparkling array of leading artists and intellectuals, including the physicist Albert Einstein, the actor Marlon Brando, the playwright Arthur Miller, the musician Leonard Bernstein, the writer Lillian Hellman, and the architect Frank Lloyd Wright. Messages of solidarity were received from the actor Charles Chaplin, the poet Pablo Neruda, the novelist Alan Paton, and artists Diego Rivera and David Siqueiros.

The zenith of this gathering occurred when 20,000 people congregated in Madison Square Garden in Manhattan to hear Du Bois speak about the ominous clouds of war that had descended. Du Bois had long sought to yoke the ostensibly domestic matter of civil rights for African Americans to a larger Pan-African and global agenda of liberation of Africa. His ouster from the NAACP and the split in the CAA that greeted his arrival had materially hampered this ambitious agenda. Now, with the deterioration in relations between Moscow and Washington that spelled the possibility of a nuclear war that could mean the extinction of humankind, he shifted ground to stress the necessity for détente between and among the great powers, as this liberalization would at once disarm the conservative hawks who were the major impediment to world peace, anticolonialism, and equality. From standing on a civil rights platform and reaching out to the world, he was now standing on a world platform and reaching back to his homeland.

This came clear when he cochaired the World Congress for Peace, which convened in Paris weeks after he spoke to cheering throngs in Manhattan. Present were over 2,000 delegates from seventy nations representing 700 million people. Yet what overshadowed press coverage of this historic gathering in the United States were controversial remarks made by Du Bois's good friend and frequent collaborator, Paul Robeson, who cast doubt on whether African Americans would fight on behalf of the United States in a war with the Soviet Union. When Du Bois actually traveled to Moscow to reiterate the calls for peace and disarmament that had become an essential component of his rhetorical armament, angry accusations erupted in his homeland suggesting that he had become a traitor—or worse.

Yet the travails that Du Bois had to endure during 1949 and early 1950 paled into insignificance when war erupted on the Korean peninsula in June 1950 in a conflict that ostensibly pitted communists against their foes—the latter of which were backed avidly by Washington. Increasingly, anticommunists were wondering why the United States should travel thousands of miles to fight communists abroad, when suspected communists like Du Bois continually and repeatedly challenged Washington's foreign policy. The result was predictable and inevitable: Du Bois was indicted, put on trial, and slated for a lengthy prison term, which, at his advanced age, would be the equivalent of a death sentence.

11

A Life on Trial

A familiar nostrum nowadays is that with age comes conservatism, a dismissal of past radicalism as so much youthful posturing. This did not hold true for W.E.B. Du Bois. During the Cold War, the United States—a nation then approaching its second century of maturation—moved to the right and away from previous positions. Du Bois, almost half as old as the nation in which he lived, either moved to the left or adhered to his previous positions. This was bound to create friction—and it did, to the point where Du Bois faced the distinct possibility of spending his remaining days in a dank prison cell.

The immediate cause for many of his troubles was his crusading against nuclear weapons. The dropping of atomic bombs on Japan in August 1945, which instantly incinerated tens of thousands of civilians, horrified many, including Du Bois. But unlike others, he decided to try to do something about this menacing weaponry; hence his 1949 trip to Moscow, which was thought to be a likely target for nuclear detonation if obtaining trends persisted. His antinuclear stance sheds light on why he organized the World Congress of Partisans for World Peace and invited Pablo Picasso to the United States to confer about what steps to take to ban the bomb. Washington responded by denying this acclaimed artist and activist a visa.

His campaign against atomic weapons was further evidence that Du Bois remained intellectually nimble, able to pivot and attack new menaces that arose. But Du Bois was also able to remain true and consistent, for as his move to the headquarters of the CAA suggested, his devotion to the beleaguered continent continued unabated. One of his principal duties there was as an intellectual resource, a fount of information for those interested in news from Africa at a time when U.S. newspapers and diplomats often routinely paid little or no attention to the impoverished continent. Thus, in his early days there, he analyzed in depth the onset of apartheid in South Africa (which had been proclaimed formally only in 1948) and the vexing matter of Ethiopia and its troublesome province (Eritrea). Above all, he hammered home a point that was his trademark: as long as Africa was colonized, it contained the seeds of war as the major powers jousted to take advantage of its vast wealth.

But the hallmark of Du Bois's last years was clear: as he continued to lean to the left—which had been a key characteristic of his entire career—during this same period, the nation in which he resided came to approximate, some contended, the very fascism it had defeated years earlier. And with that, Du Bois found himself increasingly isolated. The Cold War conflict with Moscow compelled Washington to adopt positions that were to hamper the nation for some years to come; thus, as the Soviet Union stressed control by the state of the commanding heights (if not the entirety) of the economy, the United States felt compelled, in contrast to many of its European allies, to emphasize the primacy of private enterprise, even in spheres where a leading role for government seemed reasonable (e.g., health care). This was just one more indication of the political and psychological investment that had been made in the Cold War, and as a result, when Du Bois began to raise his insistent voice against a course of action that seemed normative and positive to most, the backlash against him became all the more fierce.

There was a silver lining in the cloud of vexation that had descended upon Du Bois as the second half of the twentieth century began to unfold. As Washington began to point the finger of accusation at Moscow for human rights violations of various types, it was forced to respond forcefully to its own weaknesses in this realm—Jim Crow most of all. Remarkably, African Americans came to learn that they could escape the most egregious aspects of Jim Crow if they simply steered clear of the left wing that Du Bois had come to symbolize. But, as the saying went, Negroes gained the right to eat at restaurants and check into hotels but not the wherewithal to pay the bill. For as civil rights were in the process of being expanded, unions, which Black Americans, a mostly working-class population, had come to rely upon, were being pulverized. Simultaneously, the right to association generally—for example, to be it in unions, to join political parties, or, in some cases, to even belong civil rights organizations—was being constricted.

Du Bois was one of the few individuals who, in oracle-like fashion, was able to foresee this course of events, but as early as 1950, his was a voice that many were coming to disdain. As a man of thought and action, Du Bois not only articulated an alternative course of action but proceeded to embody and actualize it. In this he became a leading—and lonely—symbol of opposition to the Cold War—a project that would eventually cost his homeland trillions of dollars and countless lives, and that would also give rise in Afghanistan to a form of religious fundamentalism that was to bedevil the United States indefinitely.

The utter seriousness of the Cold War became clear in 1950 when war erupted violently and terribly on the north-south divide of the Korean peninsula. That same year saw the efflorescence of the Peace Information Center (PIC), which Du Bois had helped to bring into existence; its first meeting was held at his office, with Shirley Graham and Paul Robeson present. Their first activity was sponsoring the Stockholm Peace Petition, known colloquially as the "ban the bomb" initiative. Perhaps signed by more individuals globally than any other petition before or since, this campaign also was able to garner significant support from African Americans, which was no easy matter at a time when signing one's name to such a document was known to bring—minimally—added scrutiny from the government. Charlie "Yardbird" Parker, the innovative saxophonist from Kansas City, and Pearl Primus, the talented dancer and anthropologist, were among those who affixed their signatures to this petition (see, e.g., Intondi, 2015).

When war exploded in Korea in late June 1950, Du Bois sought to galvanize the antiwar sentiment evident among African Americans, which lurked beneath the surface as this community was being asked to give their lives purportedly for freedoms that they most certainly did not enjoy. As Paul Robeson's comments in Paris suggested, raising disconcerting issues about whether Black Americans would stand by the United States during a war was guaranteed to bring a forceful response. And so it was that on July 13, 1950, Secretary of State Dean Acheson bitterly denounced Du Bois's PIC. Du Bois responded with a reciprocal asperity in the *New York Times* as the infant industry of network television besieged him for interviews—but the more typical response was that the Manhattan landlord of the PIC demanded that they vacate the premises. Undeterred, Du Bois called on Acheson to promise that the United States would "never be first to use [the] bomb"—a request greeted with stony silence in Foggy Bottom (*New York Times*, June 17, 1950). Shortly thereafter, the Department of Justice demanded that the PIC register as agents of a foreign power. Who this power might be was left unsaid, but the impression was left that it was Moscow; in other words, to favor banning nuclear weapons meant you were either a communist, a fellow traveler, or a dupe of the Reds.

So prompted, petitioners were subjected to a reign of terror and violence, battered from coast to coast for their activism. In the midst of this vortex of fury, the elderly Du Bois—at a time when most of his venerability had chosen a comfortable retirement—accepted the American Labor Party's invitation to run for the U.S. Senate seat from New York held by the powerful and affluent Herbert Lehman. Only the dire circumstances that the nation and world faced in 1950 could compel the aging Du Bois to cast the state of his health to the winds and take on the responsibility of a grueling election campaign. He received a formidable dose of the abuse heaped on candidates who veered beyond the realm of Democrats and Republicans when he campaigned ceaselessly for the Progressive Party in 1948. New York was one of the bastions of left-leaning thinking generally in the United States, and as a result, the American Labor Party—a local affiliate of the Progressive Party—had arisen, which had sunk deep roots in New York City particularly. Though Du Bois knew that his chances of prevailing in this race were slim, at least a campaign platform provided an opportunity to raise certain issues concerning peace and civil rights that might otherwise be downplayed or ignored (*Chicago Globe*, Oct. 28, 1950).

This bold maneuver was made more complicated by Du Bois's abject refusal to endorse the reigning notion that the Soviet Union was the "evil

---

APARTHEID

Apartheid was a white supremacist system in South Africa that completely subjugated nonwhite populations to the white minority. It was formally instituted in 1948 by the National Party's Daniel François Malan. An array of legislation codified apartheid, including the Mixed Marriages Act that criminalized marriage between whites and nonwhites, the Population Registration Act that compelled the racial identification of all persons over the age of sixteen, and the Group Areas Act that delimited where each racial group could reside and own property. There were also laws that relegated nonwhite labor, stripped African trade unions of their power to strike and collectively bargain, and barred the African population from most forms of skilled labor.

"Natives" were met with extraordinary violence and punishment for contesting the white minority's hegemony and authority. Under the guise of anti-communism, the apartheid regime criminalized the right to assemble and to demonstrate against the government, banned the publication and dissemination of critical newspapers, and arrested and prosecuted African, Indian, and colored leaders of organizations that opposed apartheid. In effect, freedom of speech and freedom of the press were abrogated by legislation like the Public Safety Act, passed in February 1953. As well, raids, searches, and sundry forms of intimidation persisted to crush any form of dissent.

Despite decades of protests, boycotts, and demonstrations by South Africans, the African Diaspora, and the international community, this brutal system of racial subjection persisted until 1994.

empire." In 1949 he made his third visit to this vast land (he had been there in 1926 and 1936), and though he was critical of what he saw, he left once more with a fundamental admiration, not least since he saw this nation as one of the few that chose to assist Africans struggling against colonialism rather than providing tortured rationalizations as to why African protests were supposedly premature or moving too rapidly (*Soviet Russia Today*, Nov. 1949). "The Dark World is moving towards its destiny much faster than we in this country now realize," he said shortly after his return to these shores (*New York Times*, June 2, 1949).

Such heretical ideas became the trademark of Du Bois's uphill climb to the Senate. Early October 1950 found him in old haunts in Harlem, telling a cheering crowd of 1,500 that they should speedily enlist in his antiwar army (*New York Times*, Oct. 6, 1950). Withdrawal from Korea, banning nuclear weapons, liberating Africa, and barring Jim Crow were his call to arms. In the early days of this battleground race, the *New York Times* echoed the sentiments of many when it proclaimed that "Dr. Du Bois is expected to add strength to the Labor Party ticket in Harlem and other Negro sections of the city and state" (*New York Times*, Sept. 11, 1950). At that juncture, this journal may have been selling Du Bois a bit short, as he was expected to add strength to the ticket in college towns like Ithaca and Hamilton and Syracuse, too. In this period before the ouster of dissident voices from the airwaves, Du Bois was regularly interviewed on the radio, declaiming about "peace and civil rights"—the slogan of his campaign. In turn, Senator Lehman unleashed a barrage of commercial advertisements especially on Black-oriented radio stations in New York City, perhaps attempting to erode Du Bois's perceived base of support in this community.

This election race was a hinge moment in Black America, as it pitted a traditional liberal—the incumbent, Senator Lehman—against a man decidedly to his left: Du Bois. One course led away from the Cold War with Moscow and the hot war in Korea and toward peace, and the other in an opposing direction. But many Negro leaders felt that they could hardly move in the same direction as an increasingly marginalized left wing, even if led by the venerable Du Bois. As they saw it, backing Lehman was a step toward long-promised civil rights concessions. Consequently, Mary McLeod Bethune, the leading African-American activist who served alongside Du Bois at the founding of the United Nations, and Channing Tobias, who knew Du Bois well because he served on the NAACP board, were among the leading lights in Black America who supported Senator Lehman avidly. Strikingly, those who turned against Du Bois often raised the question of his real and imagined ties to communists and how this was thought to be "un-American."

Yet, perhaps, even more unsettling than these ties were the blasphemous notions onto which Du Bois had latched that, in their breadth and daring, surpassed virtually everything his capacious intellect had devised to that point. The words he enunciated in November 1950—the month of his defeat for the Senate—seem radical more than half a century since they were pronounced: "Social control of production and distribution of wealth is coming as sure as the rolling stars. The whole concept of property is changing and must change. Not even Harvard School of Business can make greed into a science, nor can the unscrupulous ambition of a Secretary of State use atomic energy forever for death instead of life" (*Chicago Globe*, Nov. 25, 1950). Unsurprisingly, given the political climate and the disparity in campaign funds raised by the various candidates, Du Bois went down to defeat in November 1950. On the other hand, he received 12.6 percent of the total vote in Harlem, not unrespectable given the hysteria about communists that prevailed. Moreover, while the GOP spent $600,000 in this race and the Democrats spent $500,000, Du Bois's party spent a relatively meager $35,000. In other words, the major parties spent one dollar per vote, and the Labor Party spent considerably less.

Yet Du Bois's stirring race for higher office was not supported unanimously. The PIC, which he had helped to bring into being and which spearheaded the landmark crusade against nuclear weapons, was operative for a paltry four months—from April 3, 1950 until October 12, 1950—when, in response to economic and governmental pressures, it went out of existence. Moreover, it proved more than daunting for Du Bois to simultaneously run a Senate campaign and an antiwar office. Yet, perhaps stung by Du Bois's gumption in confronting the Cold War consensus, his adversaries chose not to accept this challenge supinely. On February 9, 1951, he was indicted, along with his coworkers, as an unregistered foreign agent. This dramatic indictment, which threatened to ensure that his last days would be spent in a prison cell, instigated an equally dramatic move on his part. His marriage, which had been drained of emotional content certainly since the death of his firstborn, ended when Nina Gomer Du Bois passed away; shortly thereafter, he married the celebrated intellectual Shirley Graham—not least so that she could have easy access to him because of spousal privilege if he became a prisoner. He was to be acquitted, but the signal sent was clear, as one had to beat only one slave to keep the entire plantation in line.

In some ways, the woman who was to become Shirley Graham Du Bois brought many of the qualities to marriage with Du Bois that were wanting in his first union. First of all, she was an intellectual, perhaps the leading Black woman thinker of her era, and also, like her spouse, a highly motivated political activist (the following is based substantially on Horne, 2000). Born in 1896, the daughter of a preacher, she had a peripatetic upbringing—not unlike her contemporary and fellow radical Louise Thompson—spending time in states including Louisiana, Washington, DC, and Colorado. Like many daughters of this era, she was forced into a maternal role at an early age, helping to raise her siblings; and, it seemed, she sought to escape this drudgery by marrying early. This led quickly to two children, and perhaps, seeing her future fade away before her very eyes, in a challenge to dominant notions of respectable womanhood at the time, she departed her marriage and her children (leaving them with her parents) and decamped to Paris for a lengthy sojourn, where she studied at the Sorbonne and perfected her French, one of the many languages she came to speak.

She returned to the United States by the 1930s and enrolled at Oberlin College, which had been in the vanguard of enrolling African-American students for decades, and there developed real skill as a musician. Eventually, she enrolled at the Yale School of Drama and quickly developed a sterling reputation as a brilliant playwright. It was in the 1930s that she first struck up a surreptitious romance with Du Bois that had difficulty gaining traction, given his preexisting marriage.

As World War II was dawning, she moved to Fort Huachuca, Arizona, to work with Negro troops, soon to be dispatched to fight for freedoms that they did not enjoy. Here she spoke up repeatedly against racist discrimination and justifiably gained an image as an effective and militant organizer, which led her to the NAACP, where, during the 1940s, she presided over the largest spurt in membership this organization has ever enjoyed—before or since. This move to New York City was serendipitous—but not exactly accidental—in that she managed to find herself in the same metropolis to which Du Bois himself had moved in 1944. There their romance heated up once more, and when Nina Gomer Du Bois passed away, followed swiftly by Du Bois's indictment, he came to rely upon her even more, as their relationship deepened. It was Graham, for example, who spearheaded the "Emergency Committee for Dr. W.E.B. Du Bois and the NAACP," which was organized to challenge his dismissal from the Association in 1948. In an article for *Masses & Mainstream*, she lambasted the NAACP for betraying "Negroes all over the world by treating so contemptuously the one man who has been our foremost spokesman, our most immanent statesman for half a century." Moreover, persons well acquainted with Graham, like John Henrik Clarke, and Du Bois, like his long-time friend and confidant Ethel Ray Nance, noted that she had a profound impact on his politics—especially his move toward communism (Burden-Stelly, 2018, 203–205).

When Du Bois's spouse of fifty-five years died at the age of eighty on June 26, 1950 after a prolonged illness, she was buried in his hometown of Great Barrington, Massachusetts, alongside her son. Du Bois had feared that he might die before she did, and, consequently, she would have been bereft of proper care. He paid tribute to her "singularly honest character" and recounted what might have been the most tragic aspect of their marriage, which had shaped it for decades: the devastating death of their first-born (*Chicago Globe*, July 15, 1950).

But, as the saying goes, when a door closes, often a window is opened, and that is precisely what happened when Du Bois's first wife died. A widower, he was free to marry a woman to whom he was, by all accounts, better suited. But this marriage also brought its unique issues, for Shirley Graham was reputed to be a member of the CPUSA, which was not that unusual for African-American intellectuals at the time, but was a factor rapidly being deemed radioactive. Thus, the perception quickly developed that the younger Graham—like Eve in the Garden—was leading Du Bois astray down the primrose path toward the Communist Party. Left unsaid was that, far from being blindly seduced by the siren song of his junior companion, the headstrong Du Bois had a mind of his own and, in any case, reacted negatively to the rightward drift of the nation by clinging even more fiercely to his bedrock positions, which for decades had included an appreciation for socialism.

Du Bois and Shirley Graham were brought closer together as a result of their collaboration with the PIC. Ultimately, 2.5 million individuals signed the Stockholm Peace Appeal in the United States, no small feat in a nation then in the throes of Cold War hysteria. Atomic bombs were viewed as the "winning weapon," the "game changer" that placed Moscow at a decided disadvantage, and the idea that it was U.S. nationals who were in the fore-front of a campaign for their demise was difficult for Washington to swallow. Hence, the indictment pointed to the idea—but did not say explicitly—that Du Bois and his crusaders should have registered as agents of Moscow.

Du Bois was among those stunned by the prospect of imprisonment. After all, despite his politics increasingly being out of step with those of his homeland, he remained an icon, at least in Black America. But that was precisely the problem: Du Bois's popularity was thought to be incongruent with the notion that Black America, in the process of gaining civil rights concessions, had to be wrested away from any identification with the left. Putting him on trial, then, was consistent with the political zeitgeist. The year of his trial, 1951, was not propitious. The nation was bogged down in war in Korea, and the newly installed communist regime in China was making noises about intervening if the forces allied with Washington strayed too close to their borders—and interests.

But as pessimistic as Du Bois had reason to be, even he may have been surprised by being handcuffed when reporting to court. As he was now a distinguished eighty-three years old and hardly a danger to the authorities—at least physically—this manacling of the patriarch of the civil rights movement was sending a loud signal to those who might be so bold (or adventurous) to tread in his footsteps. Such anticommunist intimidation was effective; not a few Black leaders and prominent figures with who Du Bois had been long associated and acquainted either denounced him or distanced themselves. For example, Mordecai Johnson—the first Black president of Howard University whose tenure was due in no small part to the student protest in the 1920s, which Du Bois staunchly supported—and Charlotte Hawkins Brown, the first African-American woman to serve on the national board of the Young Women's Christian Association, had been scheduled to speak at a testimonial dinner for Du Bois's eighty-third birthday; they reneged when he was indicted. The United Nations diplomat Ralph Bunche declined to serve as a sponsor for the dinner, and Du Bois's longtime friend and NAACP colleague Arthur Spingarn refused to serve as honorary chairman (Mordecai, 1951; Hicks, 1951).

Yet, like the operation of a principle in the physical world, the action taken against Du Bois generated an opposite—and perhaps larger—counterreaction. The United States was bombarded with a deluge of protests from around the world, particularly Africa, where he was still viewed popularly and benignly as a father of Pan-Africanism. Moreover, the beleaguered continent was now straining on the leash of colonialism, and it was clear even to the dimmest that foreign domination and exploitation would soon meet its demise—due in no small part to the decades-long anticolonialism of people like Du Bois. And Washington had to wonder what the reaction would be in this Cold War prize if Du Bois were to be accorded a lengthy prison term. This was not only the case for Africa, as Du Bois had for the longest time paid critical attention to the Caribbean, especially Haiti, Cuba, and Jamaica; and this attention paid multiple dividends when he went on trial, and his tormentors were inundated with an avalanche of objections. The same held true for parts of Europe: in the east of this continent, there was a predisposition—given Cold War norms—to lend him support, while in Western Europe there remained strong socialist and communist parties (e.g., in France and Italy particularly) that too were inclined to lend Du Bois's defense a willing hand.

But there was also a spirited protest against the proposed imprisonment of Du Bois from many African Americans—though certainly not all. Many had long memories, and they had yet to forget his yeoman service over the decades from challenging Booker T. Washington, to founding the NAACP, to shepherding Pan-Africanism, to publishing books for the ages. Nevertheless, Du Bois was taken aback when those he had touted—the Talented Tenth—generally headed for the exits when they were asked to support him. Thus imploded one of his earliest theses, that the touting of this well-educated sliver of the population would be the savior for Black Americans generally. What Du Bois did find was that trade unions, particularly unions with sizeable Black memberships, formed the bulwark of his support. The International Longshore and Warehouse Union (the San Francisco–based stevedores), the Marine Cooks and Stewards, and Detroit's Local 600 of the United Autoworkers union all were among those who rallied to his defense. Certainly, the fact that the working class did not stray from his side, unlike the middle-class elements he had hailed in devising the Talented Tenth idea, played a critical role in shaping his thinking as he surveyed the political landscape. In his unjustly neglected book, *In Battle for Peace*, Du Bois details his Cold War travail of the early 1950s (see Du Bois, 1952). In telling this gripping story of how a symbol of Black America's struggles almost became a jailbird, he seems most distressed in sketching the role of the NAACP leadership who spread damaging rumors of his "guilt" as the justification for their refusal to aid his defense. This may have been the most graphic rebuke of his previous hailing of the creation of a Talented Tenth.

Actually, there were some among the Black bourgeoisie who did not turn their backs on Du Bois. Primary among these was Paul Robeson—with degrees from Rutgers and Columbia—whose newspaper *Freedom* became an echo chamber singing the praises of Du Bois. Lorraine Hansberry, who went on to challenge Shirley Graham Du Bois's role as the preeminent Negro playwright of the twentieth century, was among this journal's contributors, as well as John Oliver Killens, whose subsequent novels were among the more revealing of Black life ever devised. In the March 1951 edition *Freedom*'s banner headline exclaimed, "Southern Students Defend Du Bois."

Likewise, Shirley Graham's father was a pastor and, as such, had a network of ministerial contacts who proved effective in mobilizing for Du Bois's defense. These pastors were among those who spearheaded the National Committee to Defend Dr. Du Bois and Associates in the Peace Information Center. Of course, Robeson was essential in this effort, but he was joined by former Minnesota governor Elmer Benson, then a firm advocate of the Progressive Party, and the prominent novelists Dashiell Hammett (whose detective stories like *The Maltese Falcon* helped to create the genre) and Howard Fast. Two radical activists who were instrumental to the committee's formation and endurance were Louise Thompson Patterson and Alice Citron. Thompson Patterson helped to initiate the committee and served as its acting secretary. She drafted letters and circulars, recruited members to the committee, and handled the correspondence. Citron became the committee's permanent secretary and helped to internationalize the case to elicit global sympathy and support for Du Bois and the other defendants. With her encouragement, an international defense committee was established and headquartered in Brussels, international unions like the World Federation of Trade Unions sent resolutions of protest, and women's conferences throughout Europe discussed the case and passed resolutions (Lewis, interview with Alice Citron).

Also helpful to Du Bois and his codefendants were sectors of the African-American press, including the *Pittsburgh Courier*, the *Philadelphia Tribune*, the *Afro-American* (which was headquartered in Baltimore), the *Oklahoma Black Dispatch*, the *Chicago Defender*, and other organs that may have been owned by the Black Bourgeoisie but who depended for their daily bread upon readers who were more likely than not part of Talented Tenth. To these supporters could be added a host of African-American attorneys. There was a trio from Washington, DC, who were critical to defense efforts—George Hayes, James Cobb, and George Parker—and because this was where the case was tried, in some ways they were more important than the quartet from New York who traveled southward for this case: Congressman Vito Marcantonio, Bernard Jaffe, Stanley Faulkner, and Gloria Agrin. Like good lawyers should, they engaged in extensive pretrial preparation, exhaustively examining every bit of evidence. But they also knew that this was not an ordinary trial, given the political climate and the public persona of the leading defendant.

One major hurdle to leap was the apostasy of one O. John Rogge, who had become active and well known in Du Bois's inner circle but chose to become a chief prosecution witness. Born in rural Illinois in 1903, this wunderkind had graduated from Harvard Law School at the tender age of twenty-one and then rocketed to further prominence when, in the 1940s, he was among the first to draw a link between Nazi Germany and leading conservative circles in the United States (e.g., Horne, *Color*, 2007). Then, as chief of the criminal division of the U.S. Justice Department, he launched persistent fusillades at the gathering Red Scare, lambasting the so-called loyalty program of Truman's White House, which had led to purges from numerous important governmental agencies, like the post office. It was also on Rogge's initiative and at his apartment that the PIC was founded. Eventually, he was to become a sharp critic not only of Du Bois but also of the doomed alleged atomic spies, Julius and Ethel Rosenberg, and other cherished figures of a rapidly diminishing left-wing movement. It was Rogge who was supposed to carry the weight of the prosecution's case, demonstrating that the PIC was little more than a Trojan horse on Moscow's behalf, but he proved to be a wholly ineffective witness.

A liability for many federal prosecutions brought in Washington was the demography of this capital, which featured a significant Black population that often was not in accord with the rightward drift of the nation, and this may have been even more the case in 1951, as the Jim Crow the denizens of this city had to endure put few in the mood to accept that Dr. Du Bois, a man they had been taught was a hero, was now a despised figure. Thus, the jury of twelve featured eight African Americans, over-whelmingly from the working class, which disproportionately leaned away from conservatism.

This prosecution also was something of a test case, a controlled experi-ment that would shed light on the ongoing controversy that had led to a profound rift between Du Bois and the NAACP leadership in the first place. For the former had come to believe that courtroom legerdemain—or histrionics, as the case might be—was the key to civil rights advance. The outsized role played on the staff by the admittedly brilliant Thurgood Mar-shall seemed to justify this predisposition. But Du Bois thought otherwise. First of all, as he saw it, justice was hard to find in a legal system where the deck was stacked automatically against Black American and leftist defen-dants, and consequently, something more than legal skill was required to prevail. As Du Bois saw it, legal cases were political—just as federal prose-cutors were political appointees by the party in power—and, thus, political mobilization was the critical factor in prevailing in court. It was one thing to argue this important point in a conference room at NAACP headquar-ters or in a seminar room at Atlanta University, but it was quite another to have a dramatization of this otherwise abstract debate in a courtroom with life and liberty on the line. As things turned out, Du Bois prevailed. After six days of hearing testimony about Du Bois and his comrades being agents of an unnamed foreign power, the judge directed a verdict in favor of the defendants, ruling in essence that the jury would not be allowed, as the saying goes, to "speculate on a speculation."

One reason for the acquittal was the inability of the prosecution to use the technique of "parallelism." According to Bernard Jaffe, one of the defense lawyers and a longtime friend of the Du Boises: "Somebody would be declared to be a Communist because the policies that he carried out were similar to those that were being advocated by Communists, and once you established that one became a 'follower,' a 'fellow traveler,' or whatever it was and just as guilty as a Communist himself. . . . At the time the Du Bois prosecution took place, it was not an outlandish theory, and it had never before been rejected by a court during that period" (Lewis, interview with Bernard Jaffe). Parallelism was one of the primary techniques used in anticommunist cases, and it was rejected for perhaps the first time in the PIC trial. As codefendant Elizabeth Moos averred, "Deprived of the use of parallelism, unable to confuse the issues with redbaiting, the case proved... 'as thin as the broth made from the shadow of a homeopathic pigeon that had starved to death'" (Du Bois Papers, Dec. 1951).

As things turned out, this acquittal was one of the few victories for the left as the Red Scare juggernaut gathered steam. It seemed that Du Bois's preexisting celebrity, the international renown that attached to him, his spouse's multifaceted contacts among pastors, his connections to the

African-American press, and the fact that McCarthyism was still in its infancy in 1951, all combined to save him from a prison term, though the same destiny was not enjoyed by others (e.g., Ben Davis, the Communist City Councilman from Harlem, who found himself imprisoned in the same year that Du Bois was allowed to escape this fate).

The Red Scare had a particularly detrimental effect on leftists of African descent like Du Bois, not least because their domestic agitation for civil rights and internationalist struggles against imperialism and colonialism put the United States on the defensive. The National Committee to Defend Negro Leadership, for example, was organized in the early 1950s to protest the persecution of African-American leaders including Du Bois, Paul Robeson, Claudia Jones, and Charlotta Bass. These persons were denied passports for international travel by the federal government; labeled as "subversives" by the House Un-American Activities Committee (HUAC); arrested, indicted, and convicted under the Smith Act; cited for contempt of court for refusing to "name names"; stripped of their citizenship if foreign-born; and threatened with or subjected to Ku Klux Klan violence.

Government authorities even targeted persons like Mary McLeod Bethune, the esteemed educator and advisor to Franklin Roosevelt, who belonged to more moderate organizations like the NAACP and the National Council of Negro Women, if they sympathized or associated with radicals and if they were vocal about equality for African Americans. In a document titled "An Appeal in Defense of Negro Leadership," the National Committee to Defend Negro Leadership enjoined, "Things have reached such a state in our country that almost any Negro leader who dares to fight hard for Negro rights is headed for trouble with the law, with 'public opinion,' or with hoodlum assassins. . . . They are labeled 'subversive,' or 'communistic,' or 'undesirable aliens,' or 'dangerous trouble-makers.' . . . These growing attacks against Negro leaders are really directed against Negro citizens as a whole. They are designed to frighten off our leaders and curb the mounting struggles of the masses of our people against the rising tide of 'white supremacy' during these years of war hysteria . . ." (Du Bois Papers, 1952).

Du Bois was not sufficiently chastened by this narrow escape, for instead of retreating into a cocoon of passivity or at least lowering his voice of opposition, he returned to his small but comfortable office at the CAA and resumed the activism for world peace and African liberation that had brought him to the brink of disaster quite recently. There in his office in Manhattan, just north of Greenwich Village, which was then in the throes of a cultural upsurge that was to rock the nation subsequently, he wrote lectures and articles and carried on a wide correspondence with a broad array of figures across the world. He taught classes at the currently defunct Jefferson School of Social Science, a socialist-oriented independent school that counted among its staff Howard professor turned "professional revolutionary" Doxey Wilkerson, and enrolled countless students, including the inquisitive and eager young journalist Lorraine Hansberry.

A primary task for Du Bois was raising funds for the numerous anticolonial movements in Africa, though he tended to give priority to Kenya and South Africa. Not long after Du Bois escaped imprisonment, the British authorities then ruling in Nairobi imposed a state of emergency against an insurgent movement known colloquially as Mau Mau, which led to mass incarceration of Africans and an increase in their mortality rates. In South Africa, in 1948—the year Du Bois was ousted from the NAACP— the authorities imposed a system of apartheid, or turbocharged racial segregation that bordered on slavery. As in Kenya, this crackdown only led to an escalation of the insurgency, requiring more funds to be funneled abroad by Du Bois.

In his dotage, some may have viewed Du Bois as ineffectual, isolated from the main currents of his homeland, alienated from the NAACP. Yet this perception hardly coincided with the ruckus that ensued when, in May 1952, Du Bois sought to cross the border into Canada for a peace conference. Ordinarily, this was a simple matter, with Ottawa and Washington regularly hailing the fact that this was the longest undefended border in the world. But these were not ordinary times. So, when he and Shirley Graham arrived in Toronto, they were brusquely refused entry. Ultimately, the passports of Du Bois and his spouse and comrades like Robeson were snatched so that the authorities would not have to worry about being embarrassed abroad. For the global peace movement, this was a real setback as they were deprived of some of their more intelligent voices. Not only did the United States not want the peace activist's voices to be heard abroad, but Washington also denied visas for international campaigners to enter its borders (e.g., in the case of Pablo Picasso). Nevertheless, Du Bois was not sufficiently cowed by his indictment or such harassment to steer clear of knotty matters of foreign policy, which is why, on Independence Day in 1952, he was in sweltering and sweaty Chicago providing the keynote address at the Progressive Party convention. His remarks were spare and simple: "The platform of the Progressive Party," he exclaimed, "may be reduced to these planks: Stop the Korean War; Offer Friendship to the Soviet Union and China; Restore and Rebuild the United States" (*National Guardian*, July 10, 1952).

In addition to the Progressive Party, much of Du Bois's activism concerning world peace was channeled through the American Peace Crusade (APC). As the authorities saw it, this was like the snake shedding its skin; in other words, the PIC was forced into dissolution and taking its place was the APC, pursuing a similar agenda. It was not long before the APC also began to feel the heat from Washington. In between traveling to Chicago and seeking to enter Canada, Du Bois had to take the time to respond to an incredibly detailed interrogatory from the U.S. Justice Department, which seemed as a predicate for yet another prosecution. As Washington saw it, the APC was just another "front" for the Communist Party, and, akin to an associative law of mathematics, this meant that it was also a "front" for Moscow, which made it a threat to national security. Demanded were the names and addresses of virtually anyone who could have been connected with the APC; the government's surveillance of the group was certainly a deterrent to many wanting to associate with it, because it was clear that membership could mean undergoing scrutiny under a government microscope. Not reassuring was the fact that the government seemed most interested in the activities of Robeson, Howard Fast, and Du Bois. Stiffening its spine, the APC responded stoutly that it would not respond to these inquiries and, instead, forwarded all its public statements, resolutions, and the like. The Justice Department was not assuaged, and, given that the CAA was under similar pressure, it seemed that the government decided if it could not jail Du Bois, at least it could eliminate his base of operations, rendering him less effective.

Du Bois found it hard to accept that in the United States in the 1950s championing peace was akin to championing communism. This contrasted sharply with the situation elsewhere, particularly in Europe, where memories of the ravages of war remained acute, or in Japan, the first and only victim of nuclear attack, or China, where clashes with the U.S. military on the Korean peninsula were sharp. Of course, there were internal problems in this peace movement that government harassment could not obscure: Shirley Graham was one of the few women in the top leadership, and there was only one representative west of Iowa. Indeed, the communist leader Claudia Jones had criticized the lack of women's leadership in the peace movement as early as 1948, analyzing the problem and offering a series of solutions in articles including "For New Approaches on the Woman Question" and "Women in the Struggle for Peace and Security" (Davies, 2011).

Still, when the APC and the CAA were driven into extinction in the mid-1950s, it was not simply the struggle for peace and the campaign against colonialism that fell victim, and neither was it only Du Bois who suffered as a result. Ultimately, a message was sent that dissent was dangerous, and in such an atmosphere, it became easier to hatch ill-considered schemes like the war in Vietnam—which a revivified peace movement and anticolonial movement could have forestalled, thereby saving millions of lives. Unbowed, Du Bois soldiered on as the 1950s unfolded.

12

A Life of Redemption

In the 1950s, Du Bois could look back with satisfaction on a life well spent. He had been present at the creation of the NAACP and was widely hailed as the locomotive behind the epic May 17, 1954 decision by the U.S. Supreme Court in *Brown v. Board of Education* to overturn racist segregation in public education—and, by implication, in society as a whole. This was a bittersweet moment for Du Bois, as it was the culmination of a life-long dream to which he had contributed copious amounts of sweat and tears. And yet, the ebullient NAACP leadership that held a press conference to hail this epochal decision dared not mention Du Bois's name for fear of being enveloped by the nation's latest custom, Red-baiting, or the fear of being associated with the reviled communists. The historic decision of *Brown* came in the midst of a Cold War struggle, and the high court judges were reminded repeatedly that the nation could hardly compete effectively for hearts and minds in Africa, Asia, and Latin America as long as their descendants and relatives in this nation were being treated so atrociously: Jim Crow had to go—and it did.

Du Bois was equally ecstatic when this decision was rendered. "Many will say complete freedom and equality between black and white Americans is impossible," he said. "Perhaps; but I have seen the Impossible happen. It did happen on May 17, 1954" (*National Guardian*, May 31, 1954). Du Bois may have been taken aback by this decision, for just weeks before it was handed down, he was addressing a New York conference where his theme was "Colonialism in Africa Means Color Line in USA." But with "separate but equal" legislation effectively nullified in the United States, the implication, which proved to be accurate, was that colonialism was next on the chopping block (*Freedom*, Apr. 1954).

Like a wrangler whose horse had been shot out from under him, Du Bois had to stumble along as his base of support in the CAA and APC were removed from the scene. He seemed particularly aggrieved by the liquidation of the CAA. It seemed ironic that at a time when those of African descent in the United States were celebrating a new birth of freedom, their attempt to buoy their brethren in Africa was under siege. Du Bois thought he knew why. He found it curious that the African-American press did not cover African struggles more assiduously and thought it to be part of an understanding with the rulers of the United States that if they—and other Negroes—acquiesced in the exploitation of Africa, they would be rewarded accordingly (*National Guardian*, Feb. 14, 1955). Actually, at the time Du Bois was drafting these weighty words, Washington was in the process of dispatching abroad leading Negro personalities such as the journalist Carl Rowan to ports of call in India particularly to reassure that the United States was not as bad as resistance to desegregation made it seem (Horne, 2008).

Du Bois had become a regular columnist for the now-defunct weekly, the *National Guardian*, which was tied closely to the Progressive Party; and in the wake of the profound high court decision, he may have felt that Africa, wallowing in colonial misery, merited more of his attention. Thus, readers were told regularly of the difficulties faced in Ethiopia, one of the continent's few independent states; the problems of Uganda; the difficulties in Ghana and Nigeria; the exploitation of the Congo (which has the unfortunate honor of being the nation that has probably suffered more than any other in the twentieth century); and Kenya, whose anticolonial leader, Jomo Kenyatta, Du Bois knew well (*National Guardian*, Feb. 21, 1955; Mar. 14, 1955; Mar. 21, 1955; Mar. 28, 1955; Apr. 4, 1955).

One redeeming factor was the comfortable house he now shared with his new bride, Shirley Graham. Once it had belonged to the prize-winning playwright Arthur Miller, but now this lovely Brooklyn Heights abode housed the Du Bois family. A frequent visitor was Graham's son, who took the name David Du Bois in honor of his new stepfather, and his avid interest in Africa matched that of his parents. This guaranteed that a steady stream of visitors crossed the Brooklyn Bridge from Manhattan, after campaigning at the United Nations, to seek succor at the Du Bois home. It was also at the Du Bois home that the two young children of the accused-then-executed atomic spies, Julius and Ethel Rosenberg, came to be enveloped in a warm embrace of friends and supporters before moving to their new home. The Rosenberg sons recalled later the joy of espying a large Christmas tree when entering the Du Bois's home, festooned with all

Smith Act Trials

Between 1948 and 1958, dozens of top-tier and second-tier leaders of the Communist Party of the United States of America (CPUSA) were arrested by the FBI, indicted and prosecuted by the Department of Justice, and sent to federal prison. The charge was conspiracy to violate the Smith Act, formally known as the Alien Registration Act of 1940, which made it a criminal offense to advocate the violent overthrow of the U.S. government and to belong to any group that promoted same. The first of the Smith Act prosecutions in 1941 took aim at the Socialist Workers Party. After World War II, the CPUSA became the primary target of the Smith Act. These trials rested largely on the testimony of paid informants.

Black communists including New York City Councilman Benjamin J. Davis Jr., Henry Winston, Pettis Perry, Claudia Jones, and James E. Jackson received prison sentences ranging from one to three years and fines between $2,000 and $6,000. Jones was deported in 1955. Their "overt acts" of conspiring against the government included publishing articles, mailing letters, and attending meetings that openly supported communist doctrine and ideals. Opponents of the Smith Act claimed the true offense of these leaders was protesting the war in Korea, supporting full equality for African Americans, and demanding an end to the Taft-Hartley Act that severely undermined the power of unions and labor organizing.

The constitutionality of these prosecutions was upheld in 1951 in *Dennis v. United States* but was eroded in the 1957 decision *Yates v. United States*.

manner of lights and a huge mound of presents eyed expectantly by many other children. This is where they met their adoptive parents, Abe and Ann Meeropol, as no one from their mother's or father's family would dare take them in for fear of further persecution. Robert Meeropol, the Rosenbergs' son, recalled the vases and other artifacts from places like China and the Soviet Union that caught the eye in the Du Bois home.

In Brooklyn, the loving couple quickly developed a comfortable routine. He arose every morning shortly before eight o'clock; shaved (he continued to maintain a lush mustache and pointed Van Dyke to his dying days); took a leisurely bath, allowing his thoughts to unwind; and ambled downstairs to breakfast by nine o'clock. Despite Du Bois's antisexist inclinations, Graham did almost all the cooking, and she was the one who would fix him a bourbon and ginger ale, a quite tall one with Ritz crackers and blue cheese, as the evening wound down.

It was also at their Brooklyn abode that the first issue of a quarterly magazine, *Freedomways*, which was to have enormous impact on the emerging freedom movement, was unveiled. Joining them in celebration were John Oliver Killens, Ossie Davis, Alice Childress, and other artistic luminaries.

It was not good news that Du Bois's organizational anchors—groups focusing on Africa and peace—had been driven out of business. It was even less fortuitous that this had occurred when he had reached an advanced age. Yet, there was an upside to what was otherwise a dilemma, for he now had considerable time to devote to writing; and though the venues for his writing were often limited to precincts of the left—even some Negro organs were reluctant to share a printed page with him—he still had the opportunity to avoid total censorship and quashing of his distinct voice.

A tangible result of his prodigious labor during this difficult period was *The Black Flame: A Trilogy*. Published in seriatim as *The Ordeal of Mansart*, *Mansart Builds a School*, and *Worlds of Color*, these often-insightful volumes present Du Bois's own view of what it meant to be an African-American man in the United States from 1876 to 1956. Parading across the pages are legendary figures, many of whom he knew well, appearing under their own names: from Booker T. Washington to Franklin Delano Roosevelt; from William Monroe Trotter to Harry Hopkins (FDR's top aide); from the noted reformer Florence Kelley to Kwame Nkrumah.

Actual quotations from books, newspapers, speeches, and the like make these three volumes an underutilized resource for those seeking to comprehend this tumultuous era. All of this is imbedded within the life of Manuel Mansart, who in many ways is a stand-in for Du Bois himself. In some ways, these volumes are just as revealing about Du Bois as it is about the era of which he writes; they tell what Du Bois thought about himself and the world in which he lived in a more free-flowing, revealing way than his autobiographies. The first draft of these 1,100 pages was produced in 1955, when he was eighty-seven years old, thus providing a summary of his life and thought to that point. By the mid-1950s, Du Bois was more frail than usual, and besides, though all in this nation did not desert him, by this point his organizational base in the CAA had withered, and many had absorbed the message that to be against nuclear weapons, to advocate for world peace, was to imply that one favored the despised foe in Moscow.

Though Du Bois remained far from wealthy, he would have enjoyed renewing his acquaintance with his ancestral homeland of Haiti or even the developing anticolonial movements in Africa. The problem was that the government had deprived him of a passport. Yet liberalizing forces were beginning to emerge that would lead to his passport being renewed by 1958: The burgeoning civil rights movement embodied by the youthful Alabama pastor, Dr. Martin Luther King Jr., had pointed to the incipient demise of Jim Crow and resultant liberalization. In order to accuse Moscow more effectively of human rights violations, Washington had to make sure its own hands were clean—or in the process of being cleaned, more precisely. On the international scene—and not coincidentally—the death of Soviet leader Joseph Stalin helped to contribute to a developing thaw between the two superpowers, which was also a liberalizing force.

This led directly to Du Bois regaining his passport. This atmosphere also led to a sentimental journey for Du Bois that preceded his globetrotting. For it was in 1958 that his alma mater, Fisk University, chose to honor him. But suggestive of the fact that the Red Scare had not left Fisk unaffected, it was at this same time that his alma mater—over Du Bois's stout objections—chose to dismiss a young professor of mathematics, Lee Lorch, with little pretense of due process because of his alleged ties to the CPUSA (Horne, 1986).

Thus, when Du Bois and his spouse departed by ship for Europe in 1958, it was as much an escape as a well-deserved vacation. (The following pages are based upon the account presented in Horne, *Race Woman*.) In London they encountered the impact of the Afro-Caribbean immigration on Britain when they witnessed the Nottingham Riots, an uprising against maltreatment. They stayed at the home of Paul Robeson and spent considerable time with the luminary Claudia Jones who had been deported to England in 1955 after serving time in prison in the United States because of her leadership of the CPUSA.

In Holland they were besieged by reporters and photographers eager to get a close-up view of the man heralded abroad as the father of Pan-Africanism but hounded at home for similar reasons. They arrived in Paris just in time for the pivotal 1958 elections and had a ringside seat as the bitter conflict over the colonial occupation of Algeria unfolded.

But it was in Moscow that their reception seemed boundless. They arrived in the wake of the Soviets sending Sputnik into outer space, which was a landmark for humanity but a fear-inducing event in the United States, which thought it had reason to fear a military assault from the heavens. While Du Bois had been persecuted and prosecuted by his own government, in Moscow they met for two hours with the top Soviet leader, Nikita Khrushchev. The subject of their intense discussions were the principal concerns of Du Bois—the peace movement and the movement against colonialism. The concrete result of this meeting was Moscow's decision to establish an Institute on Africa, which continues to specialize in various topics of urgent interest to the still-beleaguered continent. The royal treatment they received there, compared to what they had left behind at home, contributed to the gathering idea that, perhaps, living abroad should be considered seriously.

They stayed in a charming dacha about fifty miles from Moscow in a pine forest near a lake. On New Year's Eve in 1958, Cuban revolutionaries were preparing to seize Havana. Meanwhile in Moscow, their future patrons were feting Du Bois, his spouse, and their friend, Robeson. As the clock reached midnight, the orchestra played lustily, lights blazed, and a small army of butlers approached bearing large silver trays groaning with culinary delights. World-class dancers from the Bolshoi Ballet pranced to the tunes laid down by globally recognized musicians.

Du Bois was now approaching the age of ninety, and though he was still sprightly for such an advanced age, he was far from being in the best of health, and his condition did not improve when his spouse and earnest helpmate chose to leave him in Moscow as she departed for Ghana in December for the All-African People's Conference, at which she read her husband's address promoting Pan-African socialism. Though she was gone for less than two weeks, she returned to find that Du Bois was slightly depressed and lonely. This was something new for Du Bois, whose previous marriage had been marked by lengthy periods apart. But he had changed—evolved—and, beyond that, he was in love and alone in a strange and distant land.

From the Soviet Union they traveled together to China. Du Bois had traveled there in the 1930s, but that had hardly prepared him for what he witnessed in what remains the planet's most populous nation. It was in 1949 that the Communist Party had come to power, and it was not long before this regime clashed with U.S. forces on the Korean peninsula. But now the mood was changing in the capital that came to be known as Beijing, and, ironically, the communists there were coming into ever-sharper conflict with communists in Moscow—tensions that would be exploited adroitly by U.S. President Richard M. Nixon. Du Bois and his spouse found time to confer with the top Chinese leader, Mao Zedong, in his lakeside villa. China was undergoing wrenching change at that precise moment as a result of Chairman Mao's purges and policies that had contributed to mass famine and massive dislocation. They visited Wuhan, a center of heavy industry, and, per usual, were honored and celebrated. Du Bois was provided with a skilled nurse around the clock—just one aspect of how he was venerated.

Apparently, this veneration in China did not impress back home, for while they were gone, their Brooklyn home was burglarized, with desks pried open and papers searched and scattered—there was a thorough and exhaustive scrutiny of their humble abode. Graham Du Bois was convinced the FBI was behind the home invasion.

But back in China, even this violation seemed tolerable in light of the intoxicating treatment that they received. It seemed that Beijing, which was to compete with Moscow in various venues over the coming decades, was vying with its competitor regarding who could treat the Du Boises the best. Though the conflict between China and the Soviet Union weakened the overall struggle against imperialism, it also helped to bring race to the fore of anticolonial struggles and to make racial unrest in the United States an international issue, much to the chagrin of the U.S. government. The Sino-Soviet split began in the 1950s as a disagreement over the devaluation of Soviet leader Joseph Stalin—a position contested by China—but soon developed into a geopolitical and ideological break that was perceived as having racial overtones. The conflict intensified when China objected to and criticized the Soviet Union's detente with the United States and its subsequent policy of peaceful coexistence. China believed that the Soviet Union was abdicating its responsibility to the international communist movement by normalizing relations with North Atlantic governments. Moscow contended that peaceful coexistence only applied to differing socioeconomic systems—socialism versus capitalism, for example—and did not preclude aid to national liberation movements, such as the aid that had boosted the revolution in China in 1949 and that was to keep Cuba afloat post-1959. Thus it was that, by the early 1960s, the Sino-Soviet alliance was disintegrating and the two were ceasing to collaborate in building a world revolution.

The Du Boises returned to the United States, but it was clear at this juncture that it made little sense to reside in a nation where the political climate was frequently hostile and unforgiving when they could be comfortable and safe abroad. Thus on June 25, 1960, Du Bois and his spouse boarded a Sabena Airlines flight from New York City to Brussels, with Prague being their destination, before heading to what was the become their eventual home—Accra, Ghana.

Again, the red carpet was rolled out when Du Bois and his wife landed in Prague. They were rushed to their hotel in a comfortable automobile, and he bathed and rested for an hour before dressing, at which point he was chauffeured to a stadium filled with cheering throngs where, after being presented to Czechoslovakia's president, they witnessed an extraordinary sports festival. There were 16,000 girls in colorful attire wielding white hoops dexterously as rhythmic music blared. Their five days and nights in Prague—a city of magnificent medieval architecture, fortunately not wounded grievously by wartime bombing—were a dizzying succession of such festivities, followed by banquets, state receptions, more sports sessions, and an array of convivial gatherings.

Then it was on to Rome and then Ghana, and with every passing moment, it was evident that it no longer made sense for Du Bois to continue residing in the United States. It was not only the exquisite treatment he received, but also the issue of the kind of medical treatment he would be accorded abroad at little or no cost—no small matter for a man of his advanced age—that shaped his deepening resolve to leave the United States for good.

But for Du Bois, his departure was punctuated by a grand, dramatic gesture. For it was in 1961 that he chose to join the CPUSA, which his detractors saw as simply the validation of a continuing reality. Of course, Du Bois had long been an advocate of socialism; however, he also had long looked askance at the possibility of constructing such a system in the United States—the major aim of the CPUSA—because of his skepticism as to whether white workers could ever be won over to this cause. Yet, ironically and contradictorily, when he came under assault, culminating with his handcuffing and trial in 1951, he became progressively isolated, but standing resolutely by his side were communists like his Brooklyn neighbors, James and Esther Cooper Jackson. Esther had collaborated with Du Bois's spouse in the founding of the journal *Freedomways* while James was a CPUSA leader, who had been seeking to recruit Du Bois to his ranks for years.

Finally, in 1961 Jackson succeeded, though Du Bois then moved thousands of miles away, signaling that this new affiliation was intended as abject defiance of his political foes as much as anything else. Moreover, impending decisions by the U.S. Supreme Court made many—including Du Bois—suspect that a new era of repression was in the works: this made him want to not only move far away but also to signal that there were some who would not retreat from the ranks of those who were being demonized, that is, the communists. This was not minor, for if this suspicion of repression were to materialize in a difficult reality, Du Bois's passport could again be revoked, and, again, he could find himself bereft of the expert medical treatment he could enjoy abroad—and which, arguably, had extended his life-span.

Above all, in discussions with Nkrumah, he had agreed to embark on the crowning achievement of his lengthy life: chief editor in the production of a proposed *Encyclopedia Africana*, a definitive reference work that was designed to transform not only the world's view of Africans but, perhaps more importantly, how Africans viewed themselves.

It did not take an expert accountant to recognize that the ledger of assets and liabilities seemed to be in Accra's—and not New York's—favor. The scale was tipped even further when Du Bois heard that the court ruling he feared was in the pipeline. On June 5, 1961, the Supreme Court ruled in *Communist Party of the United States. v. Subversive Activities Control Board*, 367 U.S. 1, that, inter alia, the Subversive Activities Control Act of 1950 was constitutional because it did not target specific organizations and because Congress had the authority to define and deal with the serious threat of international communism however it deemed fit (Supreme Court, 1961). Thus, though Du Bois had planned to move to Ghana in the spring of 1962, this turn of events caused him to accelerate his timetable. Du Bois and his wife sold their comfortable Brooklyn Heights home for a handsome $69,000—receiving about $20,500 in cash—and, so armed, departed in early October 1961 for their new home in Ghana.

BROWN V. BOARD OF EDUCATION AND THE COLD WAR

On May 14, 1954, the U.S. Supreme Court ruled in *Brown v. Board of Education of Topeka Kansas* that, regarding education, "separate but equal has no place," and separate facilities were "inherently unequal." On May 31, 1955, the court ruled in what was dubbed *Brown II* for desegregation to proceed with "all deliberate speed."

Brown and *Brown II* were the culmination of several desegregation cases litigated by the NAACP Legal Defense and Education Fund spearheaded by Charles Hamilton Houston and Thurgood Marshall. One such case was *Murray v. Maryland* in which the Maryland Court of Appeals ordered the University of Maryland School of Law to admit the African American Donald Gaines Murray. Another was *Sweatt v. Painter* in which the U.S. Supreme Court ruled the University of Texas law school erected for Black students was separate but not equal and therefore Heman Marion Sweatt must be admitted to the official law school.

Cold War foreign policy concerns, especially U.S. efforts to attract allies in the decolonizing world, profoundly influenced the move to overturn *Plessy v. Ferguson* in the 1950s. Institutional racism and white supremacy impeded the ability of the United States to present itself as the arbiter of freedom and equality, especially because the Soviet Union took every opportunity to publicize its enemy's maltreatment of African Americans. U.S. policy advisors believed domestic discrimination impeded the fight against communism abroad and the ability to take the USSR to task for its own human rights violations. As such, the *Brown* decision is best understood in the context of the Cold War, anticommunism, and decolonization.

Ghana had invited Du Bois to Accra to witness this now-independent nation's accession to the Commonwealth as a republic. After they landed in Accra, an official came on board seeking, he said, "Dr. Du Bois." Acknowledging his name, the elderly U.S. national and his spouse were then escorted from the plane as if they were arriving dignitaries and, upon poking their heads beyond the plane, noticed a full military guard. Then a band began to play, officials stood waiting, and behind barricades straining as hundreds sought to get closer to the visiting couple, Du Bois was hailed as the father of Pan-Africanism and, in many ways, the architect of Ghana's long-awaited independence. Du Bois was invigorated by this "rock-star" treatment with his wife, concluding sagely that "years . . . literally dropped" from him as a result. It was clear that self-imposed exile in Africa was the luminous destiny of this elderly couple.

Du Bois attended the opening of the first session of the Ghanaian Parliament and looked on in awe as an African carried the mace of power in the presence of 104 parliamentarians, as drums pounded out an ancient call, as a paramount chief gowned and crowned in gold poured libations. Women danced in solemn rhythm—then, like the Red Sea parting, President Nkrumah entered robed and alone. The symbolic Golden Stool of power was unveiled, and the national anthem was sung lustily. (The description and much of what follows is from Horne, 1986.)

The journey featured a festive dinner in honor of Du Bois, organized by the Ghana Academy of Learning and attended by the new nation's leaders and leading academics from the Americas, including St. Clair Drake of Chicago and C. L. R. James of Trinidad and Tobago.

Du Bois did not pull punches in instructing the Ghanaians that, like himself, they should not follow Washington's Cold War policies and, instead, should accept aid from any who offered—and this should not exclude Moscow and Beijing. He may have been preaching to the converted, as stormy applause greeted every word. With every passing moment, it seemed to Du Bois that exile appeared ever more attractive.

Exile was nothing new for African Americans. The novelist Richard Wright had moved to Paris in the late 1940s, where he spent the rest of his life. He was preceded by the chanteuse Josephine Baker, whose attachment to her new homeland was affixed when she became an honored member of the anti-Nazi resistance during World War II. The novelist James Baldwin chose exile in France and Turkey. Robeson spent years in London. The ravages of Jim Crow had chased away African American too numerous to mention, and Du Bois was no exception to this trend.

There was a vibrant African-American émigré community in Ghana, especially after 1957, comprising teachers, farmers, diplomats, business professionals, intellectuals, artists, and trade unionists. There was also a significant number of political expatriates who, like Du Bois, sought to escape McCarthyist repression; these included the master labor organizer Vicki Garvin and former CAA leader W. Alphaeus Hunton, Jr. Nkrumah, who had become a powerful symbol of African liberation, Pan-African solidarity, and African diasporic connection and consciousness, strongly encouraged skilled African Americans to move to Ghana and help bring to fruition his vision of a united and prosperous Africa. The small expatriate community, which probably never numbered over 300 but consisted of prominent figures like Julian Mayfield and Ana Livia Cordero, used their sojourn in Ghana not only to support African independence but also to internationalize their objection to U.S. racism and imperialism. Indeed, most who took up Nkrumah's clarion call had become disillusioned with Cold War anticommunism, the slow pace of civil rights gains in the United States, nonviolent protest, and the continued indifference of the federal government to white supremacist terrorism (Gaines, 2006).

Certainly, the Du Boises did not seem to suffer a precipitous drop in their standard of living, thanks in no small part to Nkrumah, who treated the couple like honored guests. They were provided a beautiful seven-room residence in Accra with many windows, situated high on a hill in the center of an acre of land. The grounds were divided, like a British estate, by hedges and blooming trees. Two scarlet flamingo trees guarded the entrance. The house had a library, a living room, a dining room, two bedrooms with private baths, a study room for Graham Du Bois, and a screened porch with netting. They had a steward, a cook, a driver, and a night watchman. They had two cars, one a Soviet model and the other an English make, preferred by Du Bois's spouse, who was often seen about town chauffeuring him about. On the walls of their lovely home were richly and prettily wrought red hangings of Chinese silk and a few similarly fetching paintings. Placed strategically about their home were busts of Marx, Lenin, and Mao.

Needless to say, by Ghanaian standards, this was all quite plush. The former Gold Coast, as was typical of an African colony, had been veritably looted by the former British colonizer, and in the countryside, many Africans resided in mud huts with no electricity and no indoor plumbing.

The Du Bois home, perhaps because it offered amenities that even many in the United States did not enjoy, became a beacon attracting to West Africa numerous African-American visitors, who—in any case—felt that a trip to this Accra estate was akin to a pilgrimage. The list quickly widened to include Southern African exiles, who knew Du Bois's name from his days with the CAA and had read about him in dusty tomes about Pan-Africanism, and Chinese diplomats who knew of him because of his many publications and his visits to their homeland.

While in Ghana, Du Bois felt compelled to make another fateful decision. He had been driven to the U.S. legation in Accra in order to have his passport renewed, but he was instead subjected to a surprise decision. The authorities refused to renew his passport because under legislation then in force, it was a crime subject to ten years' imprisonment for a member of the CPUSA to have a passport. Du Bois faced the distinct possibility of statelessness, a man without a country. This was no superficial matter for a man whose ability to travel from underdeveloped Ghana to other nations for medical treatment was more than a theoretical concern. Consequently, Du Bois, the man who had done more than most to paint a more realistic picture of this diverse and multifaceted continent, chose in his last days to become a citizen of an African nation: Ghana.

Thus, becoming a national of an African nation while supervising an encyclopedia important to its future development was like a dream come true for Du Bois. He had considered the idea of developing such an encyclopedia as early as 1909, simultaneous with the formulation of the NAACP, but that commitment and a dearth of funding compelled him to drop this estimable project. Then in 1934, after departing from the

NAACP, he sought to revive this admirable initiative, but once again, it was aborted because he was unable to raise the requisite support that was needed. In 1947, back at the NAACP, he expressed further interest in launching this enterprise, but—again—failed.

Underlining the importance of liberating Africa from colonialism, it was Ghanaian independence that reanimated the idea to bring this laudable idea to fruition. Du Bois was not sufficiently spindly to be kept from drawing up an ambitious scheme to bring this project to completion. His proposed encyclopedia was focused on Africans because, at this juncture, knowledge of them and their accomplishments were either shrouded or distorted, whereas virtually all European explorers, missionaries, colonial officials, and so on were to be excluded, simply because this information could be found in abundance elsewhere. The estimated length was to be a bountiful ten million words and was to touch on arts, politics, economics, and agriculture from prehistory to the present. With his usual optimism, the ninety-three-year-old Du Bois acknowledged that he was embarking on a mission that would last at least a decade—if not longer—but, undeterred, he pushed on. The budget called for a then-hefty $43,000 to be expended in the first year, with a sharp rise to $74,600 by the fourth. Du Bois fully intended to have the first volume in hand by 1970.

Du Bois's final burst of inventiveness and ingenuity was to be done in conjunction with the University of Ghana. He reached out to scholars across the globe. Early on he contacted Eric Williams, the leading historian and founding father of modern Trinidad and Tobago; eventual Nobel laureate and favorite son of St. Lucia, W. Arthur Lewis; noted Kenyan paleontologist L. B. S. Leakey; progressive scholar-journalist Cedric Belfrage; British philosopher Bertrand Russell; and the Academy of Sciences in the major European powers, including Lisbon, Rome, and Madrid. The leading Africanist Kenneth Dike of the university at Ibadan, Nigeria, signed on, as did Jamal Mohammad Ahmed, Sudan's ambassador in Ethiopia; and various other academics from Ivory Coast, France, and Germany.

A zenith in transnational intellectual cooperation occurred in late December 1962 when over 500 participants gathered at the University of Ghana in support of the encyclopedia's aims. There were participants from China, Brazil, Australia, and, of course, Africa. Press coverage was substantial, and Du Bois's own unique role was highlighted. But the fact was that his energy was ebbing rapidly, and it is possible that the often-intense heat of Accra was notably enervating.

For even before this important meeting at the University of Ghana, medical specialists from the Soviet Union and Romania traveled to Accra to provide treatment to him. Then he was transported to University College Hospital in London because of a prostate problem and remained there and in Switzerland for a considerable period, convalescing as his doctors prescribed. It was there that he had time to confer with Charles Chaplin, the famed actor who was also in exile for reasons not unlike those that had driven Du Bois away from the United States.

Yet, Du Bois's time was up. As the heralded March on Washington for Jobs and Freedom was launched—a manifestation that was to emblazon Martin Luther King Jr.'s name into history for all time—symbolically, his predecessor as leader of Black America expired in Accra, Ghana, on August 27, 1963. Du Bois was accorded the equivalent of a state funeral, with soldiers at attention and the masses weeping. As he was lowered into his final resting place in Accra—now the site of one of his adopted nation's top tourist attractions—his widow wobbled visibly as the tears she shed seemed to weaken her composure.

W.E.B. Du Bois had lived a fruitful ninety-five years in a life that had spanned the zenith of Reconstruction to the onset of Jim Crow's demise. Throughout this time, he had pursued various paths and utilized various tools—scholarship, political activism, Pan-Africanism, Black nationalism, Black Marxism—on behalf of the liberation of Africa and African Americans. Though by the time he passed away, he was hardly hailed in the land of his birth, it is no accident that today he is recognized as one of the most prolific and protean intellectuals and skilled political activists that this nation as a whole, and Black America in particular, has produced. Yet, sadly, as happens all too often, Du Bois's redemption arrived long after he was placed in his grave.

Why W.E.B. Du Bois Matters

In 1950, at the age of eighty-two, William Edward Burghardt Du Bois accepted the American Labor Party's nomination to run for the New York seat of the U.S. Senate. Regarding this decision, his second wife, Shirley Graham, wrote: "The fact that you have done this now is conclusive proof of your own in[n]ate greatness. You accept the historic role in which events have cast you!" (Du Bois Papers, Shirley Graham Du Bois to W.E.B. Du Bois, Sept. 1, 1950). As noted by his lover and comrade, it was W.E.B. Du Bois's willingness to accept the numerous historical roles in which he was cast that makes him one of the greatest activist-scholars in modern history. Du Bois matters today because his persistent engagement with the most pressing issues during his lifetime offers a template for scholar-activism that is still instructive today; his combination of ideological acumen and liberatory striving remains relevant to contemporary freedom movements. Likewise, given his unparalleled contributions to the reigning debates, political formations, and intellectual innovations over more than eight decades, his life is a veritable entrepôt of African-American, Pan-African, and radical Black history.

Prolific in his publishing, profound in his insights, rigorous in his research, and steadfast in his commitment to the freedom and flourishing of oppressed people, Du Bois remains significant to subsequent generations more than half a century after his transition as both a model of engaged scholarship and an archive of the global Black experience between 1868 and 1963. Attention to Du Bois's sociopolitical thought helps to situate "radicalism" in its historical context and specific social relations. For example, in the late nineteenth and early twentieth centuries, Du Bois's militant liberal agitation for racial equality to combat Booker T. Washington's conciliatory politics was a source of radicalism given the endemic white supremacist racial order. In the 1930s, by contrast, his radicalism was enunciated through a Black Marxist critique of capitalist failure and its anti-Black effects, given the pervasive immiseration wrought by the Great Depression. Du Bois's articulations of radicalism reveal that the most progressive critique of any given society depends on the exigencies of the time.

Drawing on a nexus of ideologies, Du Bois expertly analyzed and examined national and international phenomena of deep significance to African descendants. His multifaceted praxis conveys that freedom struggles are best served not by dogmatism and orthodoxy, but rather by taking advantage of the best political-intellectual tools of a given epoch. Thus, what some scholars have construed as inconsistency, contradiction, and backpedaling is better understood as flexibility and experimentation, deep attunement to the problems of the time, consistent self-reflection, and an abiding dedication to liberation and equality.

Du Bois's praxis is exceptionally relevant to our current moment. Despite his different ideological approaches, he remained inexorably committed to anti-imperialism, internationalism, and peace. This was due in no small part to his affiliations—whether cordial or contentious—with paragons of letters, criticism, and organizing with who he worked tirelessly for the liberation of Black people in the United States and throughout the African Diaspora. Without this mutual comradeship, his countless accomplishments would not have been possible. Stated differently, consistent connection, collaboration, and even conflict allowed Du Bois to make his indelible mark on history as part of a community of thinkers. His interlocutors included antilynching crusader Ida B. Wells-Barnett; Niagara movement cofounder William Monroe Trotter; noted Howard University sociologist E. Franklin Frazier; radical journalist Marvel Cooke; communist educator and union leader Doxey Wilkerson; Communist Party activist Louise Thompson (Patterson); Black internationalist artist and activist Paul Robeson; and the Pan-Africanist and first president of Ghana, Kwame Nkrumah. Furthermore, Du Bois built lasting bonds through his work in a number of overlooked organizations such as the interracial left-wing Civil Rights Congress, founded in 1946; the Jefferson School of Social Sciences, a communist adult education institute in existence from 1944 to 1956; the Council on African Affairs, an African advocacy organization that folded after eighteen years due to anticommunist harassment; and the Peace Information Center, for which Du Bois served as chairman during its six-month existence in 1950.

Additionally, an essential but often-overlooked reason Du Bois still matters is his gradual move leftward—an evolution not unrelated to his early belief in socialism. Du Bois's unique approach to Black Marxism proved that race and class, culture and material conditions, structure and ideology, must be understood as mutually constitutive. For this reason, Du Bois's work serves as the epistemological and political foundation of Black Studies and its growth and development in the U.S. academy.

Militant liberalism was one framework through which Du Bois advocated political and juridical freedom for African descendants, enjoined the best and the brightest class of Black leaders to use their skills and resources to serve and uplift the race, positioned culture emanating from Africa and its diaspora as the special provenance and gift of Black people, and encouraged personal and group responsibility. The continued salience of militant liberalism is manifested in the institutionalization and professionalization of Black Studies (and related interdisciplines) in U.S. colleges and universities, especially from the 1980s onward.

During the Progressive Era, militant liberalism was the primary expression of Du Bois's politics. His writings and activism cohered around the belief that through exceptional leadership, sustained striving, race responsibility, and unified expression of policy, Black people could develop, advance, and assert influence. Perhaps the best example of Du Bois's militant liberalism was his critique of Booker T. Washington's hegemonic accommodationist and conciliatory politics. Instead of "adjustment" and "submission" that reaffirmed Black inferiority, Du Bois supported defense of rights alongside property ownership, the assertion of manhood alongside thrift and self-respect, and higher training according to ability alongside the teaching of practical skills. He did not disagree that the ignorance and "low social level" of the Black masses were a cause of prejudice and discrimination, but he insisted that the solution to these was advanced education and an adherence to the wider ideals of citizenship and civic engagement (Du Bois, *Souls*, 2007, 40–44).

Like Washington, Du Bois believed that interracial social interaction should not be the primary concern of Black people; however, unlike Washington, he believed that the essential elements of equality were civil rights and liberties, higher education, and the elimination of barriers to access and opportunity that precluded the best of the race from realizing their full potential. Following his exemplar, Alexander Crummell, Du Bois argued that adhering to the foundations of liberal democracy was a means of honoring Christian principles. One of the most important foundations was meritocracy, which included education according to ability, equality of opportunity for the leaders of the race, and political and juridical freedom, especially the vote, for those who were qualified. Likewise, Du Bois believed that the improvement of race relations would come not only through expunging the social legacies of slavery—immorality, criminality, and shiftlessness—but also through greater respect for personal liberty and worth and a more equitable integration of the "Talented Tenth" into political, economic, and intellectual life to propagate mutual understanding.

Du Bois's militant liberalism had a distinctly racial orientation not least because, at the turn of the century, he understood race as a sociological fact in world history that could not be overcome. As a group separate from whites, Black people must cultivate autonomous institutions, ideals, and identity. This was possible through individual advancement in service to race uplift, racial cooperation and unity, and the cultivation of and appreciation for Black culture. Black people also needed to develop social mores like temperance, chastity, and frugality that could gain the recognition and respect of whites and thus promote peaceful coexistence. For Du Bois, this approach would ensure a more responsible, representative, equitable, and ethical American society.

Unlike many men in the early-to-mid twentieth century, Du Bois's belief in merit, rights, suffrage, and leadership extended to women. Du Bois's militant antisexism manifested in his recognition of the unique oppression of women generally and Black women particularly, in his agitation for women's enfranchisement and full participation in politics and society, and in his belief that intimate relationships should be based on mutual support and an equal share of resources. Du Bois's emphasis on the political empowerment and social importance of women is of the utmost importance to the current sociopolitical climate in which women's reproductive rights—especially abortion—are being undermined, women increasingly bear the burden of production and reproduction, and Black women and girls are the fastest-growing population affected by AIDS and HIV.

Du Bois believed that women were just as important and capable as men. For example, when he was soliciting participants for the second Amenia Conference, Howard University professor Abram Harris responded with the following: "You will note I have not given the names of many women. I really don't know what females should be invited. You are by far the better judge" (Du Bois Papers, Abram Harris to W.E.B. Du Bois, Mar. 20, 1933). Harris's letter conveys that while women were often treated as an afterthought or an addendum, Du Bois was unique from his peers in his appreciation for and attunement to women's leadership capacity. He knew their contributions were essential to any conversation pertaining to the betterment of Black people.

His militant antisexism also manifested in his acknowledgement that women made his life, and society in general, better. In 1951, he wrote, "Women have played a great role in my life . . . [as] faithful companion[s] and help-mate[s] of my last years, sustaining and helping me in my last thoughts and efforts . . . [they have been] friends and helpers in many times and places who worked with me and whom I loved for their belief and sacrifice" (Du Bois Papers, W.E.B. Du Bois, "Greetings to Women," July 1951). Given the importance he ascribed to women, Du Bois worked tirelessly to create opportunities for them, to include them in projects and organizations, and to challenge their exclusion and oppression. To be sure, Du Bois was not exempted from Victorian sexual standards, patriarchal practices, and gendered notions of respectability; nonetheless, he displayed an uncanny commitment to the equality of the sexes throughout his lifetime.

Du Bois's writings regularly offered an analysis of sexism that revealed multilayered forms of exploitation, challenged bourgeois social values that reified capitalist hegemony, and centered the issues and concerns of the working class. Du Bois and Black women educated and supported each other. Many Black progressive women were inspired by his courage and commitment. The notable playwright and radical activist Lorraine Hansberry sums it up with her declaration that Du Bois's consistent condemnation of oppressive forces, tireless attention to the "genuine needs of humankind," outright rejection of racism in all its forms, and sincere dedication to the realization of a global socialist society made him a "fact," "bulwark," and "institution" of Black culture and society (Hansberry in Clarke, 1970, 17). As peace activist and labor organizer Thelma Dale raised money and organized meetings for Du Bois's 1951 defense, she wrote, "I never had a more pleasant and rewarding assignment. I only wish I were working full-time so that I could really see the full fruits of Labor" (Du Bois Papers, Thelma Dale to W.E.B. Du Bois, Sept. 26, 1951). When he was acquitted, Dale penned an article opining that the dismissal of the case against Du Bois represented a victory for lovers of freedom and peace throughout the world (Dale, 1952, 17).

At the same time, Du Bois was constantly learning from Black women. Bill V. Mullen argues that comrades including Shirley Graham Du Bois, Claudia Jones, and Vicki Garvin helped to "gender" Du Bois's analysis by emphasizing the importance of (Black) women to the realization of world peace, the elevation of the working class, and the forging of proletarian internationalist alliances (Mullen, 2015, 156–157). Such influence is evident in his 1949 unpublished essay entitled "The American Negro Woman," in which he argues that the Black woman's role as worker, head of household, and leader in cultural development provided the key to resolving the central problem of the "woman question"—economic dependence (Du Bois Papers, W.E.B. Du Bois, "The American Negro Woman" [unpublished], ca. 1949). The essay took its cue from the arguments of Louise Thompson Patterson in "Toward a Brighter Dawn" and Claudia Jones in "An End to the Neglect of the Problem of the Negro Woman!" that analyzed the triple oppression of Black women "as workers, as women, and as Negroes."

These pieces also emphasized the leading role of their activism in combating exploitation (Patterson, 1936; Jones, 1949). Whereas previous writings like "The Woman in Black" and "The Freedom of Womanhood" in *The Gift of Black Folk* emphasized Black women's spiritual strength and the idealism of Black womanhood, in "The American Negro Woman" Du Bois attempted to outline the importance of Black women to proletarian struggle and to the potential resolution of working class exploitation. Du Bois's transgenerational relationship with women like Hansberry, Dale, Thompson Patterson, and Jones is representative of the feedback loop of affection, protection, and struggle that constituted Du Bois's militant antisexism.

Especially later in life, Du Bois modeled militant antisexism in his personal relationships. A letter he wrote to Shirley Graham Du Bois on January 23, 1951, about their impending marriage is a case in point. He explained that ordinarily in marriages, the husband controlled the family's resources, making the wife dependent on whatever he was willing to allocate. Du Bois admitted that his first marriage had been of that sort, and he found it to be unfulfilling and immoral. What he wanted with Graham was a marriage built upon love, companionship, friendship, and common work. He expected each partner to contribute financially to the marriage and to "share and share alike." He ended the letter with the contention that "This is the marriage for men and women, but not for parasites" (Shirley Graham Du Bois Papers, W.E.B. Du Bois to Shirley Graham, Jan. 23, 1951). Here, Du Bois was eschewing the patriarchal practice of husbands financially controlling wives, the sexist practice of men subordinating women, and the inegalitarian assumption that it was the responsibility of the man to take care of the woman. Instead, he proposed a marriage in which he and Graham were partners and equals in all aspects of their life together. In the final analysis, Du Bois was not only militantly antisexist in his work with Black women and in his scholarship and journalism—he also strove to be so in every aspect of his life.

In addition to equality of the sexes, Du Bois was also sympathetic to Black nationalism throughout his life. As residential segregation becomes more pronounced, the allocation of public resources continues to recede, and the polarization of wealth entrenches along racial lines, Du Bois's promotion of Black cooperation, independent Black institutions, and the ability of Black people to be self-determining offers a means of analyzing and challenging these and other forms of racial injustice. Du Bois critiqued the failures of desegregation and integration to promote racial solidarity and responsibility, strong community-oriented Black institutions, and cooperative economic formations that addressed the needs of Black people.

Especially in the 1930s, as Black communities bore the brunt of the Great Depression and racism ran rampant in the labor movement, Du Bois increasingly espoused the need for Black people to take their destinies into their own hands as the dominant society was reticent to invest in the flourishing of their darker brothers and sisters. In writings including the "The Right to Work," "A Negro Nation within a Nation," and "Social Planning for the Negro, Past and Present," he urged Black people to plan a separate economy in the spirit of survival, self-preservation, and sustainable struggle. Likewise, in "Does the Negro Need Separate Schools?" he argued that it was up to the Black community to educate its own children to ensure care, sympathy, and equality and to ward against racism, neglect, and what historian Carter G. Woodson called "miseducation."

Du Bois's promotion of pragmatic segregation, at the intersection of socialism and nationalism, was especially pronounced at the second Amenia Conference on a New Programme for the Negro, held August 18–21, 1933. Moving away from his earlier advocacy of militant liberalism, he excoriated the extant labor movement's anti-Black and elitist methods of organizing, particularly its policy of securing employment and wage increases primarily for highly skilled whites; criticized the failure of integrationist efforts; and championed all-Black cooperatives to secure Black economic betterment. His program of nation building required Black consumer and producer cooperation, careful planning, and intense scientific economic study. Du Bois believed that if Black farmers worked together, they could produce food for large segments of the Black population; that artists and artisans could organize their services to produce clothing, shelter, and goods; and that Black workers could harness "cheap power" in the Southeast to form manufacturing cooperatives. This economic "protective separatism" discouraged exploitation, selfishness, and profiteering. For Du Bois, it was through Black nationalist efforts that Black people would be properly educated, economically sound, unified, and self-supported (Du Bois Papers, "Second Amenia Conference on a New Programme for the Negro," Jan. 9, 1933; "Notes on Amenia Conference," 1933; "Proposed Program of the Amenia Conference," 1933).

Du Bois's belief in the flourishing of African descendants extended beyond U.S. borders; he is rightly considered a father of modern Pan-Africanism. Defined as the ideas, activities, and movements preeminently concerned with the commonality of purpose among, and the social, political, and economic emancipation of, African peoples wherever they are located, Pan-Africanism is as important as ever. To an unprecedented degree, structural adjustment and "poverty reduction" programs undermine sovereignty, life chances, well-being, and progress in the Global South generally, and for African people particularly. As political parties like the South African Economic Freedom Fighters suggest, concerted African efforts are necessary to ensure prosperity on the continent and in the Diaspora. Here, much can be learned from Du Bois's Pan-African vision through which he unceasingly brought African people together in organizations, congresses, publications, and protest to collectively dismantle the global system built upon exploitation, expropriation, and exclusion.

Along with leaders like Amy Ashwood Garvey, George Padmore, and Kwame Nkrumah, Du Bois profoundly shaped Pan-African ideology with his voluminous scholarship about the history and contemporary realities of Africa, his activism on behalf of African liberation, and his ultimate repatriation to the African continent in 1961. One of his most important contributions was his instrumental role in convening the Pan-African Congresses between 1900 and 1945. Du Bois helped to lead, coordinate, publicize, and forge the philosophy of the Pan-African Conference of 1900 (London), and the Congresses of 1919 (Paris), 1923 (Paris, London, Lisbon, and Brussels), and 1927 (New York). Here, African descendants convened to build and sustain networks; to pass resolutions condemning colonialism, imperialism, white supremacy, and European domination; to air their grievances to an international audience; and to agitate for mutual progress. They supported nonviolent nonintervention, including strikes and peaceful demonstrations, on behalf of civil rights, self-determination, an end to discrimination, and the abolition of forced labor.

Perhaps the most important Pan-African Congress, though, convened in Manchester, England, just as the Second World War was coming to an end in 1945. Influenced by the World Trade Union and Subject Peoples' Conferences held earlier that year, the fifth Pan-African Congress signaled a militant phase of the African anticolonial struggle, emphasizing the right of all colonized nations to self-determine, self-govern, and control their own destinies using every tool at their disposal, including armed struggle. Participants insisted upon emancipation for the whole of the Black world, including complete and absolute independence of West Africa, the removal of armed forces from and the establishment of democratic rights in North Africa, and the practice of the principles of the Atlantic Charter and the Four Freedoms in East Africa. They passed resolutions supporting the voluntary federation of the British West Indies predicated on self-government, universal adult suffrage, and the introduction of modern social legislation afforded to citizens in the metropoles. They also supported defense against imperial machinations in Haiti and Ethiopia and made a case for the representation of colonized and oppressed people in the United Nations (Adi & Sherwood, 1995). Du Bois had taken up all of these issues—anticolonialism, West Indian Federation, Haitian independence, Ethiopian sovereignty—in numerous writings since the 1890s.

While the fifth Pan-African Congress included participation from prominent intellectuals, activists, and future heads of state like Kwame Nkrumah, Jomo Kenyatta, Ras T. Makonnen, Amy Ashwood Garvey, and

Nnamdi Azikiwe, Du Bois and the other delegates emphasized that peasants, workers, and the laboring classes were the key actors in throwing off colonialism and imperialism.

Such support indicates Du Bois's increasing embrace of Black Marxism, which provides invaluable analytical, theoretical, and practical resources to understand the current global landscape. Black Marxism can be understood as African descendants' deployment of anticapitalist principles to challenge the structural and material conditions of local, national, and global Blackness and to imagine and bring into being liberating possibilities for all oppressed people. Internationalist in scope, it links the conditions of Black people to other colonized and racialized groups through anti-imperial, anticolonial, antiracist, and socialist praxis. Additionally, Black Marxism centers critical political economy analysis, attends to intraracial class conflict, emphasizes the importance of labor and workers, theorizes Blackness as a special condition of surplus value extraction, and strives for the eventual overthrow of capitalism.

Current research, scholarship, activism, organizing, and teaching would be enriched by embracing Du Bois's example. As the late political scientist Cedric Robinson argued in his *Black Marxism: The Making of the Black Radical Tradition*, Du Bois was one of the most influential Black Marxists of the modern era (Robinson, 2000). While Du Bois had been a socialist since the first decade of the twentieth century, by the 1930s, he had begun to diligently study Marxism-Leninism and to update it with his own insights about the Black experience. *Black Reconstruction in America: An Essay toward a History of the Part Which Black Folk Played in the Attempt to Reconstruct Democracy in America, 1860–1880* was Du Bois's Black Marxist tome. To write it, he enlisted a number of Black radicals to help him research the project, including Howard "Red Top Roundtable" scholars Emmett Dorsey, E. Franklin Frazier, and Abram Harris (Du Bois Papers, W.E.B. Du Bois to E. Franklin Frazier, Oct. 16, 1933; W.E.B. Du Bois to E. Franklin Frazier, Oct. 19, 1933; W.E.B. Du Bois to Abram Harris, Dec. 4, 1933; Emmett E. Dorsey to W.E.B. Du Bois, Dec. 6, 1933; W.E.B. Du Bois to Harold O. Lewis, Dec. 7, 1933; Emmett Dorsey, "Reconstruction Bibliography," 1933, Du Bois Papers; David Levering Lewis, "Interview with Doxey Wilkerson, Tape #7"; "Interview with Esther and James Jackson, Tape #14 and #15," David Levering Lewis Papers [MS 827], Interview Transcripts, University of Massachusetts Amherst). In doing so, he was employing a critical practice of consulting and elevating the scholarship of often-ignored Black scholars who generally had the most up-to-date historical, sociological, and economic scholarship and data about Black people, past and present.

Black Reconstruction analyzed the Civil War and Reconstruction as phases of capitalist exploitation, U.S. imperialism, global white supremacy, and Black labor insurgency. Du Bois's earnest study of Marxism, long-standing dedication to Pan-Africanism, and increasing commitment to Black internationalism underwrote his assertion that, "The emancipation of man is the emancipation of labor and the emancipation of labor is the freeing of that basic majority of workers who are yellow, brown, and black" (Munro, 2017, 18–19; Du Bois, *Black Reconstruction*, 1962, 16). Du Bois's attention to class conflict signaled his growing facility with Marxism, and his argument that slavery as a system of surplus value extraction was the unequivocal cause of the Civil War dovetailed with his earlier and later critiques of imperial capitalism as the source of world war. Likewise, his analysis of Reconstruction as a global phenomenon signaled his Black internationalism that connected the condition and fate of all racialized and colonized laborers. And, his emphasis on Black folks as self-determining subjects underscored his belief that the oppressed masses possessed the capability to liberate themselves.

Importantly, Du Bois's Black Marxism is manifested in *Black Reconstruction*'s discussion of white workers that captured both his disillusionment with this group, which led him to advocate separate Black economic cooperation throughout the 1930s, and his later belief that Black and white workers must unite against the ruling class to bring about a socialist future. Eric Foner contends that for Du Bois, "the tragedy of Reconstruction was that white laborers, in the North and South, failed to see their interests were intimately tied up with the emancipated slaves. Reconstruction represented a lost opportunity, a moment when black and white labor could have united to seek common goals but failed to do so" (Foner, 2013, 412). As a Black Marxist, Du Bois simultaneously acknowledged the ability of Black workers to organize themselves *and* the potential of all laborers to unite against systems of exploitation. More comprehensively than any other work of its time, *Black Reconstruction* conveyed that any study of class conflict required a sincere consideration of race, and a deep understanding of racism could not be apprehended without attention to class conflict.

The study of Du Bois's praxis—his application of ideology, epistemology, and theory to practical action—elucidates a road map of struggle against myriad forms of exploitation to which oppressed people have been, and continue to be, subjected. Enduring features of his praxis that provide lessons for the present include anti-imperialism, peace advocacy, and mutual comradeship.

Anti-imperialism remains important as international and regional conflicts rage throughout the Middle East and West Africa, in the Crimean region, and in Latin America. These imperial antagonisms—increasingly on behalf of powerful multinational corporations—over strategic geopolitics, control of mineral and natural resources, homelands, and access to markets have an unsustainable human and environmental cost. Likewise, endless war and militarism drain vital resources from public goods like education, health care, and welfare that have been systematically defunded or privatized over the past several decades. Advocacy for peace, then, is advocacy for human security, economic sustainability, and prosperity for the many. Moreover, mutual comradeship—the practice of collaboration, reciprocal care, and learning in community—vehemently contests the neoliberal ethos of individualism, selfishness, ruthlessness, and apathy.

Since the sixteenth century, imperialism has resulted in the immiseration of the laboring classes of the world, racialization as the basis for gross inequality, sustained militarism within national borders and between states, and the diminished ability of weaker nations to pursue their own programs of political and economic development. As an anti-imperialist, Du Bois rejected and condemned this violent conscription of the entire world into the project of capitalist accumulation through processes of expropriation, dispossession, and violent obtrusion. In his scholarship over several decades, Du Bois revealed that imperialist foreign policy created relations of economic dependence between exploiter and exploited countries, not least because surplus value was transferred from the colonies to the metropole, the productive forces in the colonies were retarded, and colonies became an extension of foreign capitalist imperatives. Such dependency undermined the ability of oppressed nations not only to help themselves but also to forge bonds of solidarity with other oppressed nations through mutual aid and cooperation. Moreover, imperialism fundamentally disrupted endogenous social relations by creating "comprador," landlord, and parasitic bourgeois classes that were appendages of the international bourgeoisie (Du Bois Papers, "Lenin in Africa," Feb. 1959). In effect, Du Bois understood that imperialist relations arrested the historical, cultural, political, and economic development of countries that had been ravaged by slavery, colonialism, and expropriation.

Imperialism, Du Bois analyzed, also had catastrophic effects within U.S. borders. He argued that imperialist foreign policy was directly related to repression and inequality at home. Imperial exploits in places like the Philippines, Puerto Rico, and Cuba were directly linked to the maintenance of Jim Crow terrorism in the South, not least because both were undergirded by white supremacy and labor expropriation. Likewise, Du Bois held that full equality for Black people, workers, and other oppressed groups in the United States could only be achieved by ensuring freedom, security, and self-determination for all peoples of the world. The abdication of rights and democracy in the United States, he argued, was entangled with the continuation of colonialism in other parts of the world, including Africa, Asia, and the Middle East. If the United States continued to use its immense wealth and resources in the service of imperialism, Americans would continue to be denied quality education, health care, and other basic necessities (Du Bois Papers, "The American Negro and the Darker World," Apr. 30, 1957).

Du Bois's anti-imperialism manifests in a number of his writings. In "The African Roots of War" written in 1915, for example, he analyzed World War I as an imperialist war at the intersection of colonialism, racism, and capitalist exploitation. His guiding premise was that this deadly clash of imperialist powers was grounded in the white supremacist pact between the ruling and working classes to profit from the subjection of the "others" of the world (Du Bois, May 1915, 707–714). In 1942 he argued in "The Realities in Africa: European Profit or Negro Development" that, while Germany had been the enemy in each of the World Wars, it was African self-determination that continued to be undermined by these imperialist conflicts. Du Bois's writings in the aftermath of World War II, including "Imperialism, United Nations, and Colonial People" (1944), *Color and Democracy: Colonies and Peace* (1945), "The Rape of Africa" (1956), and "Africa and World Peace" (1960), persisted in developing the inextricability of imperialism, colonial domination, racist oppression, capitalist exploitation, and war.

In addition to using the pen to protest imperialism in Haiti, Liberia, Ethiopia, and other nations, he joined, sponsored, and organized a multitude of anti-imperialist groups, meetings, and conventions. These included the League of Oppressed Peoples, formed in 1919; the Pan-African Congresses, spanning 1919–1945; the League Against Imperialism and Colonial Oppression, organized in 1927; the Council on African Affairs, founded in 1937; the Jefferson School of Social Science, founded in 1943; and the Progressive Party Convention of 1952. It is no wonder, then, that in 1946 Marvel Cooke, the radical journalist and Assistant Managing Editor at the leftwing newspaper *The People's Voice* requested an article from Du Bois about the "golden anniversary" of his "splendid fight against imperialist forces," detailing what could be expected "for the next fifty years if we all join you in a fight against imperialism" (Du Bois Papers, Marvel Cooke to Du Bois, May 24, 1926).

Anti-imperialism and international peace activism were intimately related in Du Bois's praxis. He knew that peace was impossible without the eradication of imperialism; likewise, anti-imperialism made little sense without dedication to a durable peace. Du Bois's peace activism demanded the cessation of global conflict, disarmament, nonproliferation, international cooperation, and economic progress. Thus, the elimination of war was not merely the absence of global antagonism; it was also the historical fulfillment of equality, justice, and the end of capitalist exploitation (Morris, 2015, 158–159, 220). Especially after World War II, Du Bois's belief in peace inhered in a vision of a new world order in which the United States was displaced as the world's police, and militarism was no longer a viable mode of global interaction.

With the help of comrades like Shirley Graham, Du Bois provided a critical link between Black and white antiwar activists by helping to cultivate Black opposition to the Korean War (Horne, 1986, 130). Internationally, he and Robeson garnered support for peace, especially in Africa and the Black world, through the Council on African Affairs. For this tireless work, he received the International Peace Prize from the World Council of Peace in 1952 and the International Lenin Prize for the Strengthening of Peace among Nations from the Soviet Peace Committee in 1959. He was also nominated for a Nobel Peace Prize in 1961. Domestically, Du Bois and Graham influenced Americans "from California to Massachusetts" to join the peace cause (Du Bois Papers, "Report on W.E.B. Du Bois's Indictment and Trial," Dec. 1951). Likewise, in the spirit of using all of the opportunities at his disposal to advocate peace, Du Bois ran for the U.S. Senate in 1950. With the motto "peace and civil rights," he became the candidate of the American Labor Party because it was "the only recognized political party in New York that st[ood] unequivocally for Peace and world conference to end war" (Du Bois Papers, "The American Labor Party," Oct. 18, 1953). Though he did not expect to win, he seized the opportunity to "talk freely," without the threat of imprisonment, about peace.

Some of Du Bois's most important international peace activism came through the Peace Information Center. Members went on speaking tours to raise funds and to cultivate a network of support. They collaborated with and spoke before a host of left-wing organizations, including the American Labor Party and the Civil Rights Congress (Du Bois Papers, "Minutes of Peace," Apr. 18, 1950). They distributed a biweekly periodical called *Peacegram* to furnish facts about councils, activities, demonstrations, and petitions that were challenging the threat of war. They also published leaflets, including *The People of the World Want Peace* and *The Negro People Speak of Peace*, to provide an alternative narrative to the rampant war propaganda of the U.S. government. Most importantly, they helped to circulate the Stockholm Peace Appeal, also known as the "ban the bomb petition." The document emerged in March 1950 out of a worldwide push to outlaw atomic weapons, for international controls to enforce the measures, and to treat any country that used atomic bombs as war criminals who had committed crimes against humanity. According to the former Howard professor and communist Doxey Wilkerson, "The Peace petitions and declarations circulated by the Peace Information Center 'caught on' in a big way among the people of our country. They helped give rise here to a powerful upsurge for peace. . . . Dr. Du Bois and his associates are bright symbols of the widespread opposition of the U.S. people to the war drive of the Truman administration" (Wilkerson, 1951).

Mutual comradeship was an essential element of Du Bois's anti-imperialism and international peace activism. In "Four Theses on the

Comrade," Jodi Dean argues for comradeship as a "relation, a set of expectations for action" that articulates "the sameness of those who share a politics, a common horizon of political action." In addition to unity in political beliefs, comradeship, Dean suggests, is a commitment to common practice that works "toward a certain future" (Dean, 2017, 2). Mutual comradeship retrofits the specifications of the comrade to the racialized realities of domination, exploitation, and exclusion. Stated another way, mutual comradeship specifies a political commitment and an ethical practice particularly rooted in work on behalf of the racialized, colonized, and oppressed.

Mutual comradeship describes Du Bois's cooperative social activity, shared values, common conception of "social good," and mutual political goals with others likewise devoted to the flourishing of racialized and oppressed people. His expectations for and standards of mass-based struggle were set and maintained through consistent participation in a variety of interactions, including conversation, debate, organizing, institution building, and political struggle. His ethical practice prioritized justice and honesty to ensure equal treatment among comrades and demanded courage—the willingness to place one's self at risk for the betterment of others—to cultivate reciprocal care and concern.

Du Bois's praxis of mutual comradeship included the dedication of time and other resources to left-wing causes; mutual support for radical organizations, institutions, and periodicals; the provision of jobs and income for persons whose politics deemed them undesirable as employees; and protection from and defense against state repression. It also encompassed concern for and responsibility to all stigmatized groups—including African descendants, Jews, workers, immigrants, and communists—given their linked fates. Moreover, through his leadership, involvement, and intellectual production, Du Bois trained and inspired a generation of Black women and men to struggle against anti-Blackness, colonialism, imperialism, fascism, racist misogyny, and war. In turn, these comrades motivated, supported, and defended Du Bois, especially in his latter, more leftwing years.

* * *

In 1968, the Black Studies Movement and its push for a "more relevant education" at U.S. colleges and universities represented the latest development in the Black Liberation Movement. Over the next several years, students on campuses including San Francisco State College, the University of California, Berkeley, Howard, Cornell, Jackson State, and Northwestern demanded more students, faculty, and staff of color; a more democratic admissions process; significantly expanded financial aid; better facilities; more egalitarian relationships with surrounding communities; and the end of white control of historically Black institutions (Biondi, 2014).

One of their most insurgent demands was for the end of white supremacist and Eurocentric curricula that ignored, marginalized, or distorted the life, history, culture, and material conditions of African people in the United States, in Africa, and in the Diaspora. They demanded systematic study, research, and knowledge production by, for, and about Black people. The institutionalization of Black studies and ethnic studies represented one of the most radical changes in the history of education in the United States. It not only brought more diverse students, faculty, and administrators to campus, but also inaugurated the fundamental restructuring of curricula, the revitalization of pedagogy, the revamping of epistemology, and the rethinking of disciplinary boundaries. Even more progressive, it created an opening for new and essential relationships between scholarship and activism, education and action, "gown and town." Black studies insurgencies continued—and are alive and well—as reactionary forces strive to reinforce and preserve the power and prerogatives of the privileged few (Ferguson, 2017).

This struggle for a more relevant education, shaped by anti-imperialist, anticolonial, Pan-African, Third Worldist, Black nationalist, and Black Marxist discourse, is one of the most important legacies of W.E.B. Du Bois. Scholars such as James Stewart, Anthony Monteiro, and Nagueyalti Warren have written about Du Bois as the progenitor of Black studies (Stewart, 2004; Monteiro, 2008; Warren, 2011). This was not least because Du Bois's scholarship challenged the racist and exclusionary foundations of traditional social science methods, language, and assumptions about progress and civilization. Du Bois centered race and racism as the central problem of modernity and moved his point of departure from Europe to Africa. Likewise, Du Bois used a multitude of approaches—what is now referred to as interdisciplinarity—to answer questions about the social world. These included ethnography, data analysis, and archival research and traversed fields such as history, sociology, literature, education studies, and political economy.

Importantly, Du Bois's *Philadelphia Negro*, Atlanta University Studies, and efforts to systematize and coordinate the study of Black people across Black land-grant institutions in the South are precursors to Black studies. Du Bois and his colleagues conveyed that it was the responsibility of Black students, scholars, and researchers to study Black communities and accurately describe their conditions; to correct distortions and biases about them; and to prescribe solutions for their material, cultural, and spiritual betterment. These should not be individual pursuits, the pioneers showed, but rather should be collaborative efforts with the ultimate purpose of aiding and uplifting the communities that were the object of inquiry. Du Bois's research efforts were meant to have enduring relevance beyond the campus and the classroom—that is, to serve a practical purpose. "The information," Nagueyalti Warren argued, ". . . would educate the world about the Black experience and also serve as a tool of social uplift among black people, in addition to serving as a basis of raising the standard of living and cultural patterns of Black Americans through education, work, law and social action" (Warren, 2011, 97).

The imprint of Du Bois's ideology and praxis on Black studies is one of the most significant reasons why he still matters. Like Du Bois, Black studies as a discipline weathered multitudinous debates, attacks, contradictions, and efforts at invalidation to forge space for a more equal, democratic, and peaceful future. Like Du Bois, it uses all the intellectual and political tools at its disposal in its efforts to change higher education, Black communities, U.S. society, and global conditions for the better. Like Du Bois, it strives to mold future generations into active, engaged, and effective scholar-activists who are servants to oppressed communities. Though Black studies, not unlike Du Bois, suffers from faults, problems, and missteps, its positive impact outweighs the negative.

In the final analysis, W.E.B. Du Bois's voluminous writing, copious research, tireless activism, unparalleled institution building, communitarian ethic, and expansive archive will continue to influence and motivate for decades to come what Walter Rodney called "guerilla scholars" (Rodney, 1968).

Charisse Burden-Stelly

Timeline

1868

Born in Great Barrington, Massachusetts, on February 23.

1897

Begins substantial participation in American Negro Academy, founded on March 5. Begins work on the Atlanta University Studies; publishes thirteen over the next sixteen years.

1899

Publishes *The Philadelphia Negro*, which offers the first comprehensive sociological study of African Americans in the city.

1900

Serves as chairman of the committee on the address of the Pan-African Conference in England organized by Henry Sylvester Williams.

1905

Cofounds and serves as general secretary of the Niagara Movement. Founds and edits *The Moon Illustrated Weekly*, which exists until the summer of 1906.

1907

Founds and edits the *Horizon* monthly journal, which is in published until 1910.

1909–1910

Cofounds National Association for the Advancement of Colored People (NAACP). Serves as director of publicity and research. Founds and edits the *Crisis*, monthly magazine of the NAACP.

1910

Joins Socialist Party but leaves in 1912 to support presidential candidacy of Woodrow Wilson.

1917–1918
Agrees to an intelligence post in the U.S. Army bureau and publishes controversial "Close Ranks" editorial in the *Crisis*, which invites heavy criticism from Black leaders and represents a deviation from his previous and subsequent antiwar, antiracist, and social justice activism.

1919
Organizes Pan-African Congress in Paris, France.

1920
Uses NAACP and the *Crisis* as venues to protest continued U.S. occupation in Haiti; continues to exert pressure on and criticize the Woodrow Wilson, Warren G. Harding, and Herbert Hoover administrations for their policy in Haiti.

1921–1923
Organizes and convenes second and third Pan-African Congresses in London, Brussels, and Paris and Lisbon, respectively.

1926
Makes first visit to the Soviet Union, after which he declares his support for Bolshevism.

1927
Aids in the organization of the third Pan-African Congress in New York.

1932
Offers course on "Karl Marx and the Negro," one the first of its kind at a U.S. college or university.

1933
Organizes the second Amenia Conference, August 18–21. Brings together thirty-three Black thought leaders to make a critical appraisal of the Negro's social and material conditions; they advocate cooperation on Black economic welfare across classes, interracial labor movement organizing, agitation for social legislation such as old age pension and unemployment insurance, and emphasize the importance of Black workers.

1934
Resigns from the NAACP and the editorship of the *Crisis*. Becomes chair of the Sociology Department at Atlanta University.

1935
Black Reconstruction published, which offers a groundbreaking challenge to dominant U.S. historiography on Reconstruction.

1940
Founds and edits *Phylon* quarterly journal to promote the perspective of Black people throughout the world through a combination of literary and scientific articles.

1941

Starts movement to unite Negro land-grant colleges of the South, along with Fisk, Howard, and Atlanta University, in a cooperative one-hundred-year social scientific study of Negro social problems.

1944

Returns to the NAACP in New York as the director of special research.

1945

Attends United Nations Conference on International Organizations founding convention in San Francisco on April 25, where he critiques the organization for not protecting colonial subjects from discrimination, for not offering a plan for the end of the colonial system, and for excluding Native representation in the governing council. Begins weekly column "The Winds of Time" for the *Chicago Defender.*

1947

Edits *An Appeal to the World* a condemnation of Jim Crow and racial violence in the United States, and presents it to the United Nations.

1948

Becomes vice chairman of the Council on African Affairs after being ousted from the NAACP over his support for Progressive Party presidential candidate Henry Wallace and his critique of the Association's support of Harry S. Truman.

1950

Becomes chair of the Peace Information Center. Runs for U.S. Senate as New York State candidate for the American Labor Party on a platform of "peace and civil rights."

1950–1951

Indicted, tried, and acquitted on charges brought by the Justice Department against him and four Peace Information Center leaders of being an unregistered foreign agent in connection with his peace activism and circulation of the Stockholm Peace Petition. Marries Shirley Graham following the death of first wife Nina Gomer.

1952

Passport revoked based on accusations of working on behalf of a "foreign agent," the Soviet Union. Publishes *In Battle for Peace* detailing his indictment and trial.

1958

Passport returned after landmark ruling by the Supreme Court.

1959

Awarded the Lenin International Peace Prize.

1961

Applies for membership in the Communist Party USA. Relocates to Accra, Ghana.

1963

Becomes a citizen of Ghana on February 15. Dies on August 27 and is buried in Accra, Ghana, with state funeral.

PRIMARY DOCUMENTS

"The Conservation of Races" (1897)

"The Conservation of Races," presented by W.E.B. Du Bois at the inaugural meeting of the American Negro Academy in 1897, emphasized the importance of race unity, race solidarity, and moral correction to the settlement of the "Negro problem." He argued that because race was a sociological fact of world history, racial coexistence was necessary so that each group could contribute its unique message and spirit of civilization to human brotherhood. "Conservation" further contended that Negroes must work doggedly and collectively for their own uplift, and cultivate autonomous institutions, ideals, and identity. Only through a "general expression of policy," sustained striving, and race responsibility, Du Bois argued, could the Black race develop, advance, and assert influence.

[. . .]

For this reason, the advance guard of the Negro people—the 8,000,000 people of Negro blood in the United States of America—must soon come to realize that if they are to take their just place in the van of Pan-Negroism, then their destiny is *not* absorption by the white Americans. That if in America it is to be proven for the first time in the modern world that not only Negroes are capable of evolving individual men like Toussaint, the Saviour, but are a nation stored with wonderful possibilities of culture, then their destiny is not a servile imitation of Anglo-Saxon culture, but a stalwart originality which shall unswervingly follow Negro ideals.

It may, however, be objected here that the situation of our race in America renders this attitude impossible; that our sole hope of salvation lies in our being able to lose our race identity in the commingled blood of the nation; and that any other course would merely increase the friction of races which we call race prejudice, and against which we have so long and so earnestly fought.

Here, then, is the dilemma, and it is a puzzling one, I admit. No Negro who has given earnest thought to the situation of his people in America has failed, at some time in life, to find himself at these cross-roads; has failed to ask himself at some time: What, after all, am I? Am I an American or am I a Negro? Can I be both? Or is it my duty to cease to be a Negro as soon as possible and be an American? If I strive as a Negro, am I not perpetuating the very cleft that threatens and separates Black and White America? Is not my only possible practical aim the subduction of all that is Negro in me to the American? Does my black blood place upon me any more obligation to assert my nationality than German, or Irish or Italian blood would?

It is such incessant self-questioning and the hesitation that arises from it, that is making the present period a time of vacillation and contradiction for the American Negro; combined race action is stifled, race responsibility is shirked, race enterprises languish, and the best blood, the best talent, the best energy of the Negro people cannot be marshalled to do the bidding of the race. They stand back to make room for every rascal and demagogue who chooses to cloak his selfish deviltry under the veil of race pride.

[. . .]

If we carefully consider what race prejudice really is, we find it, historically, to be nothing but the friction between different groups of people; it is the difference in aim, in feeling, in ideals of two different races; if, now, this difference exists touching territory, laws, language, or even religion, it is manifest that these people cannot live in the same territory without fatal collision; but if, on the other hand, there is substantial agreement in laws, language and religion; if there is a satisfactory adjustment of economic life, then there is no reason why, in the same country and on the same street, two or three great national ideals might not thrive and develop, that men of different races might not strive together for their race ideals as well, perhaps even better, than in isolation. Here, it seems to me, is the reading of the riddle that puzzles so many of us. We are Americans, not only by birth and by citizenship, but by our political ideals, our language, our religion. Farther than that, our Americanism does not go. At that point, we are Negroes, members of a vast historic race that from the very dawn of creation has slept, but half awakening in the dark forests of its African fatherland. We are the first fruits of this new nation, the harbinger of that black to-morrow which is yet destined to soften the whiteness of the Teutonic to-day. We are that people whose subtle sense of song has given America its only American music, its only American fairy tales, its only touch of pathos and humor amid its mad money-getting plutocracy. As such, it is our duty to conserve our physical powers, our intellectual endowments, our spiritual ideals; as a race we must strive by race organization, by race solidarity, by race unity to the realization of that broader humanity which freely recognizes differences in men, but sternly deprecates inequality in their opportunities of development.

For the accomplishment of these ends we need race organizations: Negro colleges, Negro newspapers, Negro business organizations, a Negro school of literature and art, and an intellectual clearing house, for all these products of the Negro mind, which we may call a Negro Academy. Not only is all this necessary for positive advance, it is absolutely imperative for negative defense. Let us not deceive ourselves at our situation in this country. Weighted with a heritage of moral iniquity from our past history, hard pressed in the economic world by foreign immigrants and native prejudice, hated here, despised there and pitied everywhere; our one haven of refuge is ourselves, and but one means of advance, our own belief in our great destiny, our own implicit trust in our ability and worth. There is no power under God's high heaven that can stop the advance of eight thousand thousand honest, earnest, inspired and united people. But—and here is the rub—they *must* be honest, fearlessly criticising their own faults, zealously correcting them; they must be *earnest.* No people that laughs at itself, and ridicules itself, and wishes to God it was anything but itself ever wrote its name in history; it *must* be inspired with the Divine faith of our black mothers, that out of the blood and dust of battle will march a victorious host, a mighty nation, a peculiar people, to speak to the nations of earth a Divine truth that shall make them free. . . .

Source: W.E.B. Du Bois. "The Conservation of Races." Washington, DC: The American Negro Academy, 1897.

The Souls of Black Folk (1903)

Around 1900, the Browne family of A. C. McClurg and Company was looking for young, unknown writers to contribute to their fledgling enterprise. They approached W.E.B. Du Bois, who had recently produced his first two books, Suppression of the African Slave Trade to America *and* Philadelphia Negro. *They were interested in an assemblage of his published, unpublished, and new essays that ultimately became* The Souls of Black Folk. *The text was equal parts history, biography, descriptive prose, criticism, statistical data, and storytelling, which, according to Du Bois, gave it a sense of "incompleteness" and "sketchiness." Nonetheless, the fourteen essays culminated in a "unity of purpose": vivid self-revelation and reflection upon the racial world in which he—and the race—dwelled.*

The problem of the twentieth century is the problem of the color-line,—the relation of the darker to the lighter races of men in Asia and Africa, in America and the islands of the sea. It was a phase of this problem that caused the Civil War; and however much they who marched South and North in 1861 may have fixed on the technical points of union and local autonomy as a shibboleth, all nevertheless knew, as we know, that the question of Negro slavery was the real cause of the conflict. Curious it was, too, how this deeper question ever forced itself to the surface despite effort and disclaimer. No sooner had Northern armies touched Southern soil than this old question, newly guised, sprang from the earth,—What shall be done with Negroes? Peremptory military commands, this way and that, could not answer the query; the Emancipation Proclamation seemed but to broaden and intensify the difficulties; and the War Amendments made the Negro problems of to-day.

[. . .]

Then amid all crouched the freed slave, bewildered between friend and foe. He had emerged from slavery,—not the worst slavery in the world, not a slavery that made all life unbearable, rather a slavery that had here and there something of kindliness, fidelity, and happiness,—but withal slavery, which, so far as human aspiration and desert were concerned, classed the black man and the ox together. And the Negro knew full well that, whatever their deeper convictions may have been, Southern men had fought with desperate energy to perpetuate this slavery under which the black masses, with half-articulate thought, had writhed and shivered. They welcomed freedom with a cry. They shrank from the master who still strove for their chains; they fled to the friends that had freed them, even though those friends stood ready to use them as a club for driving the recalcitrant South back into loyalty. So the cleft between the white and black South grew. Idle to say it never should have been; it was as inevitable as its results were pitiable. Curiously incongruous elements were left arrayed against each other,—the North, the government, the carpet-bagger, and the slave, here; and there, all the South that was white, whether gentleman or vagabond, honest man or rascal, lawless murderer or martyr to duty.

Thus it is doubly difficult to write of this period calmly, so intense was the feeling, so mighty the human passions that swayed and blinded men. Amid it all, two figures ever stand to typify that day to coming ages,—the one, a gray-haired gentleman, whose fathers had quit themselves like men, whose sons lay in nameless graves; who bowed to the evil of slavery because its abolition threatened untold ill to all; who stood at last, in the evening of life, a blighted, ruined form, with hate in his eyes;—and the other, a form hovering dark and mother-like, her awful face black with the mists of centuries, had aforetime quailed at that white master's command, had bent in love over the cradles of his sons and daughters, and closed in death the sunken eyes of his wife,—aye, too, at his behest had laid herself low to his lust, and borne a tawny man-child to the world, only to see her dark boy's limbs scattered to the winds by midnight marauders riding after "cursed N******." These were the saddest sights of that woeful day; and no man clasped the hands of these two passing figures of the present-past; but, hating, they went to their long home, and, hating, their children's children live to-day.

[. . .]

The alternative thus offered the nation was not between full and restricted Negro suffrage; else every sensible man, black and white, would easily have chosen the latter. It was rather a choice between suffrage and slavery, after endless blood and gold had flowed to sweep human bondage away. Not a single Southern legislature stood ready to admit a Negro, under any conditions, to the polls; not a single Southern legislature believed free Negro labor was possible without a system of restrictions that took all its freedom away; there was scarcely a white man in the South who did not honestly regard Emancipation as a crime, and its practical nullification as a duty. In such a situation, the granting of the ballot to the black man was a necessity, the very least a guilty nation could grant a wronged race, and the only method of compelling the South to accept the results of the war. Thus Negro suffrage ended a civil war by beginning a race feud. And some felt gratitude toward the race thus sacrificed in its swaddling clothes on the altar of national integrity; and some felt and feel only indifference and contempt.

Had political exigencies been less pressing, the opposition to government guardianship of Negroes less bitter, and the attachment to the slave system less strong, the social seer can well imagine a far better policy,—a permanent Freedmen's Bureau, with a national system of Negro schools; a carefully supervised employment and labor office; a system of impartial protection before the regular courts; and such institutions for social betterment as savings-banks, land and building associations, and social settlements. All this vast expenditure of money and brains might have formed a great school of prospective citizenship, and solved in a way we have not yet solved the most perplexing and persistent of the Negro problems.

That such an institution was unthinkable in 1870 was due in part to certain acts of the Freedmen's Bureau itself. It came to regard its work as merely temporary, and Negro suffrage as a final answer to all present perplexities. The political ambition of many of its agents and *protégés* led it far afield into questionable activities, until the South, nursing its own deep prejudices, came easily to ignore all the good deeds of the Bureau and hate its very name with perfect hatred. So the Freedmen's Bureau died, and its child was the Fifteenth Amendment. . . .

Source: W.E.B. Du Bois. *The Souls of Black Folk.* Chicago: A. C. McClurg, 1903.

"Address of the Niagara Movement, to the Country" (1906)

At the turn of the century, W.E.B. Du Bois, William Monroe Trotter, and other race leaders helped found the Niagara Movement to usher in a new era in Black history. According to Du Bois, the driving forces of the movement were courage, desire to tell the truth, unselfish efforts to establish institutions, an ethical commitment to the race, "rebuke of such race leaders as strive for the applause of the mob—especially the white mob," and the need to challenge the hegemony of Booker T. Washington's accommodationist approach to race relations. The Niagara Movement's principles included freedom of speech and press, full suffrage, the abolition of race and color caste, the recognition and practice of human brotherhood, the highest training for all persons irrespective of class or race, and the dignity of labor. This speech outlines its program and objectives.

The men of the Niagara Movement coming from the toil of the year's hard work and pausing a moment from the earning of their daily bread turn toward the nation and again ask in the name of ten million the privilege of a hearing. In the past year the work of the Negro hater has flourished in the land. Step by step the defenders of the rights of American citizens have retreated. The work of stealing the black man's ballot has progressed and the fifty and more representatives of stolen votes still sit in the nation's capital. Discrimination in travel and public accommodation has so spread that some of our weaker brethren are actually afraid to thunder against color discrimination as such and are simply whispering for ordinary decencies.

Against this the Niagara Movement eternally protests. We will not be satisfied to take one jot or tittle less than our full manhood rights. We claim for ourselves every single right that belongs to a freeborn American, political, civil and social; and until we get these rights we will never cease to protest and assail the ears of America. The battle we wage is not for ourselves alone but for all true Americans. It is a fight for ideals, lest this, our common fatherland, false to its founding, become in truth the land of the thief and the home of the Slave—a by-word and a hissing among the nations for its sounding pretensions and pitiful accomplishment. Never before in the modern age has a great and civilized folk threatened to adopt so cowardly a creed in the treatment of its fellow-citizens born and bred on its soil. Stripped of verbiage and subterfuge and in its naked nastiness the new American creed says: Fear to let black men even try to rise lest they become the equals of the white. And this is the land that professes to follow Jesus Christ. The blasphemy of such a course is only matched by its cowardice.

In detail our demands are clear and unequivocal. First, we would vote; with the right to vote goes everything: Freedom, manhood, the honor of your wives, the chastity of your daughters, the right to work, and the chance to rise, and let no man listen to those who deny this.

We want full manhood suffrage, and we want it now, henceforth and forever.

Second. We want discrimination in public accommodation to cease. Separation in railway and street cars, based simply on race and color, is un-American, un-democratic, and silly. We protest against all such discrimination.

Third. We claim the right of freemen to walk, talk, and be with them that wish to be with us. No man has a right to choose another man's friends, and to attempt to do so is an impudent interference with the most fundamental human privilege.

Fourth. We want the laws enforced against rich as well as poor; against Capitalist as well as Laborer; against white as well as black. We are not more lawless than the white race, we are more often arrested, convicted, and mobbed. We want justice even for criminals and outlaws. We want the Constitution of the country enforced. We want Congress to take charge of Congressional elections. We want the Fourteenth amendment carried out to the letter and every State disfranchised in Congress which attempts to disfranchise its rightful voters. We want the Fifteenth amendment enforced and No State allowed to base its franchise simply on color.

The failure of the Republican Party in Congress at the session just closed to redeem its pledge of 1904 with reference to suffrage conditions at the South seems a plain, deliberate, and premeditated breach of promise, and stamps that party as guilty of obtaining votes under false pretense.

Fifth. We want our children educated. The school system in the country districts of the South is a disgrace and in few towns and cities are Negro schools what they ought to be. We want the national government to step in and wipe out illiteracy in the South. Either the United States will destroy ignorance or ignorance will destroy the United States.

And when we call for education we mean real education. We believe in work. We ourselves are workers, but work is not necessarily education. Education is the development of power and ideal. We want our children trained as intelligent human beings should be, and we will fight for all time against any proposal to educate black boys and girls simply as servants and underlings, or simply for the use of other people. They have a right to know, to think, to aspire.

These are some of the chief things which we want. How shall we get them? By voting where we may vote, by persistent, unceasing agitation; by hammering at the truth, by sacrifice and work.

We do not believe in violence, neither in the despised violence of the raid nor the lauded violence of the soldier, nor the barbarous violence of the mob, but we do believe in John Brown, in that incarnate spirit of justice, that hatred of a lie, that willingness to sacrifice money, reputation, and life itself on the altar of right. And here on the scene of John Brown's martyrdom we reconsecrate ourselves, our honor, our property to the final emancipation of the race which John Brown died to make free.

Our enemies, triumphant for the present, are fighting the stars in their courses. Justice and humanity must prevail. We live to tell these dark brothers of ours—scattered in counsel, wavering and weak—that no bribe of money or notoriety, no promise of wealth or fame, is worth the surrender of a people's manhood or the loss of a man's self-respect. We refuse to surrender the leadership of this race to cowards and trucklers. We are men; we will be treated as men. On this rock we have planted our banners. We will never give up, though the trump of doom finds us still fighting.

And we shall win. The past promised it, the present foretells it. Thank God for John Brown! Thank God for Garrison and Douglass! Sumner and Phillips, Nat Turner and Robert Gould Shaw, and all the hallowed dead who died for freedom! Thank God for all those to-day, few though their voices be, who have not forgotten the divine brotherhood of all men white and black, rich and poor, fortunate and unfortunate.

We appeal to the young men and women of this nation, to those whose nostrils are not yet befouled by greed and snobbery and racial narrowness: Stand up for the right, prove yourselves worthy of your heritage and whether born north or south dare to treat men as men. Cannot the nation that has absorbed ten million foreigners into its political life without catastrophe absorb ten million Negro Americans into that same political life at less cost than their unjust and illegal exclusion will involve?

Courage brothers! The battle for humanity is not lost or losing. All across the skies sit signs of promise. The Slav is raising in his might, the yellow millions are tasting liberty, the black Africans are writhing toward the light, and everywhere the laborer, with ballot in his hand, is voting open the gates of Opportunity and Peace. The morning breaks over blood-stained hills. We must not falter, we may not shrink. Above are the everlasting stars.

Source: W.E.B. Du Bois. "Address of the Niagara Movement, to the Country." *The Public* 9, no. 418 (April 7, 1906).

John Brown (1909)

In 1904, W.E.B. Du Bois initially set out to write a biography of Frederick Douglass for the George W. Jacobs & Company "American Crisis" series. However, the contract was given to Booker T. Washington. Du Bois thus offered to write a biography of John Brown in the context of the underground railroad, abolitionism, the movements of free Negroes in the North, crucial changes in the plantation economy across the United States, and the general subjective Negro point of view on the system of slavery. Du Bois found John Brown's life worthy of commemoration because, even though the raid at Harper's Ferry failed, the act itself was a triumph insofar as "First, it produced a man; secondly, it laid before the world the supreme technical of an unselfish sacrifice, and thirdly it brought freedom to four million human beings."

[. . .]

Thus from the day John Brown was captured to the day he died, and after, it was the South and slavery that was on trial—not John Brown. Indeed, the dilemma into which John Brown's raid threw the state of Virginia was perfect. If his foray was the work of a handful of fanatics, led by a lunatic and repudiated by the slaves to a man, then the proper procedure would have been to ignore the incident, quietly punish the worst offenders and either pardon the misguided leader, or send him to an asylum. If, on the other hand, Virginia faced a conspiracy that threatened her social existence, aroused dangerous unrest in her slave population, and was full of portent for the future, then extraordinary precaution, swift and extreme punishment, and bitter complaint were only natural. But both these situations could not be true—both horns of the dilemma could not be logically seized. Yet this was precisely what the South and Virginia sought. While insisting that the raid was too hopelessly and ridiculously small to accomplish anything, and saying, with Andrew Hunter, that "not a single one of the slaves" joined John Brown "except by coercion," the state nevertheless spent $250,000 to punish the invaders, stationed from one to three thousand soldiers in the vicinity and threw the nation into turmoil. When the inconsistency of this action struck various minds, the attempt was made to exaggerate the danger of the invading white men. The presiding judge at the trial wrote, as late as 1889, that the number in Brown's party was proven by witnesses to have been seventy-five to one hundred and he "expected large reinforcements"; while Andrew Hunter, the state's attorney, saw nation-wide conspiracies.

What, then, was the truth about the matter? It was as Frederick Douglass said twenty-two years later on the very spot: "If John Brown did not end the war that ended slavery, he did, at least, begin the war that ended slavery. If we look over the dates, places, and men for which this honor is claimed, we shall find that not Carolina, but Virginia, not Fort Sumter, but Harper's Ferry and the arsenal, not Major Anderson, but John Brown began the war that ended American slavery, and made this a free republic. Until this blow was struck, the prospect for freedom was dim, shadowy, and uncertain. The irrepressible conflict was one of words, votes, and compromises. When John Brown stretched forth his arm the sky was cleared,—the armed hosts of freedom stood face to face over the chasm of a broken Union, and the clash of arms was at hand."

The paths by which John Brown's raid precipitated civil war were these: In the first place, he aroused the Negroes of Virginia. How far the knowledge of his plan had penetrated is of course only to be conjectured. Evidently few knew that the foray would take place on October 17th. But when the movement had once made a successful start, there is no doubt that Osborne Anderson knew whereof he spoke, when he said that slaves were ready to cooperate. His words were proven by the 200,000 black soldiers in the Civil War. That something was wrong was shown, too, by five incendiary fires in a single week after the raid. Hunter sought to attribute these to "Northern emissaries," but this charge was unproven and extremely improbable. The only other possible perpetrators were slaves and free Negroes. That Virginians believed this is shown by Hinton's declaration that the loss in 1859 by the sale of Virginia slaves alone was $10,000,000. A lady who visited John Brown said, "It was hard for me to forget the presence of the jailer (I had that morning seen his advertisement of 'fifty Negroes for sale')." It is impossible to prove the extent of this clearing-out of suspected slaves but the census reports indicate something of it. The Negro population of Maryland and Virginia increased a little over four per cent, between 1850 and 1860. But in the three counties bordering on Harper's Ferry—Loudoun and Jefferson in Virginia and Washington in Maryland, the 17,647 slaves of 1850 had shrunk to 15,996 in 1860, a decrease of nearly ten per cent. This means a disappearance of 2,400 slaves and is very significant.

Secondly, long before John Brown appeared at Harper's Ferry, Southern leaders like Mason, the author of the Fugitive Slave Bill, and chairman of the Harper's Ferry investigating committee; Jefferson Davis, who was a member of this committee; Wise, Hunter and other Virginians, had set their faces toward secession as the only method of protecting slavery. Into the mouths of these men John Brown put a tremendous argument and a fearful warning. The argument they used, the warning they suppressed and hushed. The argument was: This is Abolitionism; this is the North. This is the kind of treatment which the South and its cherished institution can expect unless it resorts to extreme measures. Proceeding along these lines, they emphasized and enlarged the raid so far as its white participants and Northern sympathizers were concerned. Governor Wise, on November 25th, issued a burning manifesto for the ears of the South and the eyes of President Buchanan, and the majority report of the Senate Committee closed with ominous words. On the other hand, the warning of John Brown's raid—the danger of Negro insurrection, was but whispered.

Third, and this was the path that led to Civil War and far beyond: The raid aroused and directed the conscience of the nation. Strange it was to watch its work. Some, impulsive, eager to justify themselves, rushed into print. To Garrison, the non-resistant, the sword of Gideon was abhorrent; Beecher thundered against John Brown and Seward bitterly traduced him. Then came an ominous silence in the land while his voice, in his own defense, was heard over the whole country. A great surging throb of sympathy arose and swept the world. . . . (352–356)

Source: W.E.B. Du Bois. *John Brown.* Philadelphia: George W. Jacobs & Company, 1909.

"The African Roots of War" (1915)

In "The African Roots of War," W.E.B. Du Bois analyzed World War I as the culmination of imperialist rivalry for the booty on offer from Africa, as Germany sought its place alongside other European empires, most notably Great Britain. He argued that colonialism and imperialism had become key tools in the quest for all Europeans to share in the exploitation of Africa. Further, "democratic despotism"—activated by the shared vision of capital and labor for racialized domination—demanded the expropriation of wealth from all of the world's "darker nations," in Africa and Asia, Central and South America, the West Indies, and the South Sea islands.

[. . .]

Thus the white European mind has worked, and worked the more fever-ishly because Africa is the Land of the Twentieth Century. . . . There can be no doubt of the economic possibilities of Africa in the near future. There are not only the well-known and traditional products, but boundless chances in a hundred different directions, and above all, there is a throng of human beings who, could they once be reduced to the docility and steadiness of Chinese coolies or of seventeenth and eighteenth century European laborers, would furnish to their masters a spoil exceeding the gold-haunted dreams of the most modern of Imperialists.

This, then, is the real secret of that desperate struggle for Africa which began in 1877 and is now culminating. Economic dominion outside Africa has, of course, played its part, and we were on the verge of the partition of Asia when Asiatic shrewdness warded it off. America was saved from direct political dominion by the Monroe Doctrine. Thus, more and more, the Imperialists have concentrated on Africa.

[. . .]

The present war is, then the result of jealousies engendered by the recent rise of armed national associations of labor and capital whose aim is the exploitation of the wealth of the world mainly outside the European circle of nations. These associations, grown jealous and suspicious at the division of the spoils of trade-empire, are fighting to enlarge their respective shares; they look for expansion, not in Europe but in Asia, and particularly in Africa. "We want no inch of French territory," said Germany to England, but Germany was "unable to give" similar assurances as to France in Africa.

The difficulties of this imperial movement are internal as well as exter-nal. Successful aggression in economic expansion calls for a close union between capital and labor at home. Now the rising demands of the white laborer, not simply for wages but for conditions of work and a voice in the conduct of industry, make industrial peace difficult. The workingmen have been appeased by all sorts of essays in state socialism, on the one hand, and on the other hand by public threats of competition by colored labor. By threatening to send English capital to China and Mexico, by threatening to hire Negro laborers in America, as well as by old-age pensions and acci-dent insurance, we gain industrial peace at home at the mightier cost of war abroad.

In addition to these national war-engendering jealousies there is a more subtle movement arising from the attempt to unite labor and capital in world-wide freebooting. Democracy in economic organization, while an acknowledged ideal, is to-day working itself out by admitting to a share in the spoils of capital only the aristocracy of labor—the more intelligent and shrewder and cannier workingmen. The ignorant, unskilled, and restless still form a large, threatening, and, to a growing extent, revolutionary group in advanced countries.

The resultant jealousies and bitter hatreds tend continually to fester along the color line. We must fight the Chinese, the laborer argues, or the Chinese will take our bread and butter. We must keep Negroes in their places, or Negroes will take our jobs. All over the world there leaps to articulate speech and ready action that singular assumption that if white men do not throttle colored men, then China, India, and Africa will do to Europe what Europe has done and seeks to do to them.

On the other hand, in the minds of yellow, brown, and black men the brutal truth is clearing: a white man is privileged to go to any land where advantage beckons and behave as he pleases; the black or colored man is being more and more confined to those parts of the world where life for climatic, historical, economic, and political reasons is most difficult to live and most easily dominated by Europe for Europe's gain.

What, then, are we to do, who desire peace and the civilization of all men? Hitherto the peace movement has confined itself chiefly to figures about the cost of war and platitudes on humanity. What do nations care about the cost of war, if by spending a few hundred millions in steel and gunpowder they can gain a thousand millions in diamonds and cocoa? How can love of humanity appeal as a motive to nations whose love of luxury is built on the inhuman exploitation of human beings, and who, especially in recent years, have been taught to regard these human beings as inhuman? I appealed to the last meeting of peace societies in St. Louis, saying, "Should you not discuss racial prejudice as a prime cause of war?" The secretary was sorry but was unwilling to introduce controversial matters!

We, then, who want peace, must remove the real causes of war. We have extended gradually our conception of democracy beyond our social class to all social classes in our nation; we have gone further and extended our democratic ideals not simply to all classes of our own nation, but to those of other nations of our blood and lineage—to what we call "European" civilization. If we want real peace and lasting culture, however, we must go further. We must extend the democratic ideal to the yellow, brown, and black peoples.

To say this, is to evoke on the faces of modern men a look of blank hopelessness. Impossible! we are told, and for so many reasons,—scientific, social, and what not,—that argument is useless. But let us not conclude too quickly. Suppose we have to choose between this unspeakably inhuman outrage on decency and intelligence and religion which we call the World War and the attempt to treat black men as human, sentient, responsible beings? We have sold them as cattle. We are working them as beasts of burden. We shall not drive war from this world until we treat them as free and equal citizens in a world-democracy of all races and nations. Impossible? Democracy is a method of doing the impossible. It is the only method yet discovered of making the education and development of all men a matter of all men's desperate desire. It is putting firearms in the hands of a child with the object of compelling the child's neighbors to teach him, not only the real and legitimate uses of a dangerous tool but the uses of himself in all things. Are there other and less costly ways of accomplishing this? There may be in some better world. But for a world just emerging from the rough chains of an almost universal poverty, and faced by the temptation of luxury and indulgence through the enslaving of defenseless men, there is but one adequate method of salvation—the giving of democratic weapons of self-defense to the defenseless. . . .

Source: W.E.B. Du Bois. "The African Roots of War." *Atlantic Monthly* (May 1915).

Bibliography

Abbott Simon Papers, TAM 346, Tamiment Library and Robert F. Wagner Labor Archive, Elmer Holmes Bobst Library, New York University, New York, NY. Contains correspondence, Peace Information Center minutes, internal documents and circulars, 1964 Carnegie Hall memorial documents, and commemoration documents pertinent to W.E.B. Du Bois.

Adi, Hakim, and Marika Sherwood. *Pan-African History: Political Figures from Africa and the Diaspora since 1787.* London: Routledge, 2003.

Adler, Alan. *Theses, Resolutions, and Manifestos of the First Four Congresses of the Third International.* London: Pluto Press, 1983.

Africana Age: African & African Diasporan Transformation in the 20th Century (website). Contains essays, images, multimedia project, and maps pertaining to W.E.B. Du Bois. http://exhibitions.nypl .org/africanaage/index2.html. Accessed May 20, 2019.

Aiello, Thomas. *The Battle for the Souls of Black Folk: W.E.B. Du Bois, Booker T. Washington, and the Debate That Shaped the Course of Civil Rights.* Santa Barbara: Praeger, 2016.

Akassi, Monique Leslie, ed. *W.E.B. Du Bois and the Africana Rhetoric of Dealienation.* Newcastle upon Tyne: Cambridge Scholars Publishing, 2018.

Alexander, Shawn Leigh. *W.E.B. Du Bois: An American Intellectual and Activist.* Lanham: Rowman & Littlefield, 2015.

Ali, Omar H. *In the Lion's Mouth: Black Populism in the New South, 1868–1900.* Jackson: University Press of Mississippi, 2013.

Allen, James S. *Negro Liberation.* New York: International Publishers, 1938.

Andrews, Gregg. *Thyra Edwards: Black Activist in the Global Freedom Struggle.* Columbia: University of Missouri Press, 2011.

Appiah, Kwame Anthony. *Lines of Descent: W.E.B. Du Bois and the Emergence of Identity.* Cambridge: Harvard University Press, 2014.

Aptheker, Herbert. *The Correspondence of W.E.B. Du Bois, Volume I.* Amherst: University of Massachusetts Press, 1973.

Arthur B. Spingarn papers, 1850–1968, MSS40949, Manuscript Division, Library of Congress, Washington, DC. Contains correspondence, NAACP files, miscellany, and printed materials pertinent to W.E.B. Du Bois.

Baker, Ella, and Marvel Cooke. "The Bronx Slave Market." *The Crisis* 42 (November 1935).

Balfour, Katharine Lawrence. *Democracy's Reconstruction: Thinking Politically with W.E.B. Du Bois.* New York: Oxford University Press, 2011.

Bass, Amy. *Those About Him Remained Silent: The Battle over W.E.B. Du Bois.* Minneapolis: University of Minnesota Press, 2009.

Battle-Baptiste, Whitney, and Russert, Britt, eds. *W.E.B. Du Bois's Data Portraits: Visualizing Black America.* Hudson: Princeton Architectural Press, 2018.

Bauerlein, Mark. *Negrophobia: A Race Riot in Atlanta, 1906.* San Francisco: Encounter Books, 2001.

Bernard Jaffe Papers, MS 906, Special Collections and University Archives, University of Massachusetts Amherst Libraries, Amherst, MA. Contains correspondence, legal documents, financial records, and copyright materials pertinent to W.E.B. Du Bois.

Biondi, Martha. *The Black Revolution on Campus.* Berkeley: University of California Press, 2014.

Blaine, Keisha. *Set the World on Fire: Black Nationalist Women and the Global Struggle for Freedom.* Philadelphia: University of Pennsylvania Press, 2018.

Booker T. Washington Papers, 1853–1946, MSS44669, Manuscript Division, Library of Congress, Washington, DC. Contains correspondence pertinent to W.E.B. Du Bois.

Broderick, Francis L. *W.E.B. Du Bois: Negro Leader in a Time of Crisis.* Palo Alto: Stanford University Press, 1959.

Bromell, Nick, ed. *A Political Companion to W.E.B. Du Bois.* Lexington: University of Kentucky Press, 2018.

Burden-Stelly, Charisse. 2018. "W.E.B. Du Bois and the Tradition of Radical Blackness: Radicalism, Repression, and Mutual Comradeship, 1930-1960." *Socialism and Democracy* 32, no. 3: 181–206.

Byerman, Keith. *Seizing the Word: History, Art, and Self in the Work of W.E.B. Du Bois.* Athens: University of Georgia Press, 2010.

Chandler, Nahum Dimitri. *X—The Problem of the Negro as a Problem for Thought.* New York: Fordham University Press, 2014.

Chandler, Nahum Dimitri, ed. *The Problem of the Color Line at the Turn of the Twentieth Century: The Essential Early Essays.* New York: Fordham University Press, 2014.

Clarke, John Henrik, ed. *Black Titan, W.E.B. Du Bois: An Anthology by the Editors of Freedomways.* Boston: Beacon Press, 1970.

Communist International. *The 1928 and 1930 Comintern Resolutions on the Black National Question in the United States.* Washington, DC: Revolutionary Review Press, 1985.

Crummell, Alexander. *The Race-Problem in America.* Washington, DC: William R. Morrison, 1889.

Dale, Thelma. "Dr. Du Bois Victory: A Victory for All." *New Aspects* 1 (1952): 17–18.

David Levering Lewis Papers, MS 827, Special Collections and University Archives, University of Massachusetts Amherst Libraries, Amherst, Massachusetts. Contains research materials and interviews for W.E.B. Du Bois biographies (1993, 2000), each of which was awarded a Pulitzer Prize.

Dean, Jodi. "Four Theses on the Comrade." *E-flux Journal* 86 (November 2017): 2.

Digital Collection of the W.E.B. Du Bois Papers at the University of Massachusetts, Amherst. http://credo.library.umass.edu/view/collection/mums312.

Doku, Samuel O. *Cosmopolitanism in the Fictive Imagination of W.E.B. Du Bois: Toward the Humanization of a Revolutionary Art.* Lanham: Lexington Books, 2015.

Dorrien, Gary J. *The New Abolition: W.E.B. Du Bois and the Black Social Gospel.* New Haven: Yale University Press, 2018.

Du Bois, Shirley Graham. *Du Bois: A Pictorial Biography.* Chicago: Johnson Publishing Company, 1979.

Du Bois, W.E.B. "The Address to the Country." *W.E.B. Du Bois Papers— University of Massachusetts-Amherst,* 1906.

Du Bois, W.E.B. "Africa." *World Tomorrow* 11 (October 1928): 420–421.

Du Bois, W.E.B. "The African Roots of War." *Atlantic Monthly* 115 (May 1915): 707–714.

Du Bois, W.E.B. *The Autobiography of W.E.B. Du Bois: A Soliloquy on Viewing My Life from the Last Decade of Its First Century.* New York: Oxford University Press, 2007.

Du Bois, W.E.B. "Back to Africa." *Century* 105 (February 1923): 539–548.

Du Bois, W.E.B. "Bayen." *New York Amsterdam News* (June 1, 1940).

Du Bois, W.E.B. *The Black Flame: A Trilogy.* New York: Mainstream, 1957–1961.

Du Bois, W.E.B. *Black Reconstruction: An Essay toward a History of the Part Which Black Folk Played in the Attempt to Reconstruct*

Democracy in America, 1860–1880. New York: Atheneum Books, 1962.

Du Bois, W.E.B. "Colonialism in Africa Means Color Line in U.S.A." *Freedom* (April 1954).

Du Bois, W.E.B. *Color and Democracy: Colonies and Peace.* New York: Harcourt, Brace, 1945.

Du Bois, W.E.B. "Color-Line." *Pittsburgh Courier* (Sept. 5, 1936).

Du Bois, W.E.B. "The Color Line Belts the World." *Collier's* 28 (October 20, 1906): 20.

Du Bois, W.E.B. *Dark Princess: A Romance.* New York: Harcourt, Brace, & Co., 1928.

Du Bois, W.E.B. *Darkwater: Voices from within the Veil.* New York: Oxford University Press, 2007.

Du Bois, W.E.B. "Does the Negro Need Separate Schools?" *Journal of Negro Education* 4 (July 1935): 328–335.

Du Bois, W.E.B. "Douglass as a Statesman." *Journal of Negro History* 49 (October 1964): 264–268.

Du Bois, W.E.B. *Dusk of Dawn: An Essay toward an Autobiography of a Race Concept.* New York: Oxford University Press, 2007.

Du Bois, W.E.B. "The Economic Aspects of Race Prejudice." *Editorial Review (New York)* 2 (May 1910): 488–493.

Du Bois, W.E.B. "The Enforcement of the Slave Trade Laws." In *Annual Report of the American Historical Association for the Year 1891.* Washington, DC: Senate Misc. Doc. 173, 52nd Congress, 1st Sess., 1892.

Du Bois, W.E.B. "The Evolution of Negro Leadership." *Dial* 31 (July 1, 1901): 53–55.

Du Bois, W.E.B. *The Gift of Black Folk: Negroes in the Making of America.* Boston: Stratford, 1924.

Du Bois, W.E.B. "The Hampton Strike." *The Nation* 135 (November 2, 1927): 471–472.

Du Bois, W.E.B. "The Home of the Country Freedmen." *Southern Workman* 30 (October 1901): 535–542.

Du Bois, W.E.B. "Hopeful Signs for the Negro." *Advance* 54 (October 2, 1902): 327–328.

Du Bois, W.E.B. "I Am Resolved." *Crisis* 3 (January 1912).

Du Bois, W.E.B. *In Battle for Peace: The Story of My 83rd Birthday, with Comment by Shirley Graham.* New York: Masses and Mainstream, 1952.

Du Bois, W.E.B. "Insanity." *Chicago Globe* (October 28, 1950).

Du Bois, W.E.B. "Inter-Racial Implications of the Ethiopian Crisis: A Negro View." *Foreign Affairs* 14 (October 1935): 82–92.

Du Bois, W.E.B. "Liberia and Rubber." *New Republic* 44 (November 18, 1925): 326–329.

Du Bois, W.E.B. "The National Committee on the Negro." *Survey (New York)* 22 (June 12, 1909): 407–409.

Du Bois, W.E.B. *The Negro.* New York: Henry Holt, 1915.

Du Bois, W.E.B. "The Negro as He Really Is." *World's Work* 2 (June 1901): 848–866.

Du Bois, W.E.B. "Negro Literature." In *The Encyclopedia Britannica, 13th edition, Volume 29.* New York: Encyclopedia Britannica, 1926, 110–111.

Du Bois, W.E.B. "A Negro Nation within the Nation." *Current History* 42 (June 1935): 265–270.

Du Bois, W.E.B. "Negroes in College." *The Nation* 122 (March 3, 1926): 228–230.

Du Bois, W.E.B. "On the U.S.S.R." *Labor Defender* (November 1928): 248.

Du Bois, W.E.B. "The Opening of the Library." *Independent* 54 (April 3, 1902): 809–810.

Du Bois, W.E.B. *The Philadelphia Negro.* Millwood: Kraus-Thomson, 1973.

Du Bois, W.E.B. "The President and the Soldiers." *Voice of the Negro* 3 (December 1906): 552–553.

Du Bois, W.E.B. "The Primitive Black Man." *The Nation* 119 (December 17, 1924): 675–676.

Du Bois, W.E.B. "The Problem of Problems." *Intercollegiate Socialist* 6 (December 1917–January 1918): 5–9.

Du Bois, W.E.B. "The Problem of Tillman, Vardaman, et al." *Central Christian Advocate* 49 (October 18, 1905): 1324–1325.

Du Bois, W.E.B. *The Quest of the Silver Fleece: A Novel.* Chicago: A. C. McClurg & Co., 1911.

Du Bois, W.E.B. "Race and the Laboring Classes." *Pittsburgh Courier* (November 14, 1936).

Du Bois, W.E.B. "Results of the Ten Tuskegee Conferences." *Harper's Weekly* 45 (June 22, 1901): 641.

Du Bois, W.E.B. "The Right to Work." *Crisis* 40, no. 4 (April 1933): 93–94.

Du Bois, W.E.B. "The Savings of Black Georgia." *Outlook* 69 (September 14, 1901): 128–130.

Du Bois, W.E.B. "The School Desegregation Decision." *National Guardian* (May 31, 1954).

Du Bois, W.E.B. "Socialism and the Negro Problem." *New Review* (February 1, 1913).

Du Bois, W.E.B. "Socialism Is Too Narrow for Negroes." *Socialist Call* (January 21, 1912).

Du Bois, W.E.B. *The Souls of Black Folk.* New York: Oxford University Press, 2007.

Du Bois, W.E.B. *The Souls of Black Folk: Essays and Sketches.* Chicago: McClurg, 1903.

Du Bois, W.E.B. "The Souls of White Folk." *Independent* 69 (August 18, 1910): 339–342.

Du Bois, W.E.B. "The Spawn of Slavery, the Convict Lease System in the South." *Missionary Review of the World* 14 (October 1901): 737–745.

Du Bois, W.E.B. "Strivings of the Negro People." *Atlantic Monthly* 80 (August 1897): 194–198.

Du Bois, W.E.B. "The Study of the Negro Problem." *Annals of the American Academy of Political and Social Science* 11 (January 1898): 1–23.

Du Bois, W.E.B. *The Suppression of the African Slave Trade to the United States of America, 1638–1870* [Harvard Historical Series Number 1]. New York: Longmans, Green, 1896.

Du Bois, W.E.B. "Talented Tenth." In *The Negro Problem: A Series of Articles by Representative American Negroes of Today*, edited by Booker T. Washington. New York: Pott, 1903, 33–75.

Du Bois, W.E.B. "Violations of Property Rights." *Crisis* 2, no. 1 (May 1911): 28–32.

Du Bois, W.E.B. "The Woman in Black." Du Bois Papers, 1913.

Du Bois, W.E.B. "Woman Suffrage." *Crisis* 11 (November 1915).

Du Bois, W.E.B. "Worlds of Color." In *The New Negro*, edited by Alain Locke. New York: Boni, 1925, 385–414.

Ellis, Mark. *Negro Subversion: The Investigation of Black Unrest and Radicalism by Agencies of the United States Government, 1917–1920.* Ph.D. Dissertation. University of Aberdeen, 1984.

Engels, Fredrich. "Socialism in Germany." Marxist Internet Archive, 1892. https://www.marxists.org/archive/marx/works/1892/01/socialism -germany.htm. Accessed May 20, 2019.

Essien-Udom, E. U. "Introduction." In *Philosophy and Opinions of Marcus Garvey*, edited by Amy Jacques Garvey. London: Cass, 1967.

Ethel Ray Nance Papers, 1895–1979, Manuscript Collection, Minnesota Historical Society, Saint Paul, Minnesota. Contains correspondence and newspaper clippings pertinent to W.E.B. Du Bois.

Ferguson, Roderick. *We Demand: The University and Student Protest.* Berkeley: University of California Press, 2017.

Foner, Eric. "Black Reconstruction: An Introduction." *The South Atlantic Quarterly* 112 (Summer 2013): 412.

Foner, Phillip, ed. *W.E.B. Du Bois Speaks: Speeches and Addresses, 1890–1919.* New York: Pathfinder Press, 1970.

Frazier, E. Franklin, and C. Eric Lincoln. *The Negro Church in America/The Black Church since Frazier.* New York: Schocken Books, 1974.

Gaines, Kevin. *American Africans in Ghana: Black Expatriates and the Civil Rights Era.* Chapel Hill: The University of North Carolina Press, 2006.

Gerald Horne Papers, 1953–2016, Sc MG 559, Schomburg Center for Research in Black Culture, New York Public Library, New York, NY. Contains research files pertinent to W.E.B. and Shirley Graham Du Bois.

Graves, John Temple, and W.E.B. Du Bois. "The Tragedy of Atlanta." *The World Today* (November 1906).

Harlan, Louis R. *Booker T. Washington: The Making of a Black Leader, 1856–1901.* New York: Oxford University Press, 1972.

Haywood, Harry. *Negro Liberation.* Chicago: Liberator Press, 1976.

Haywood, Harry. *The Road to Negro Liberation: Report to the Eighth Convention of the Communist Party of the U.S.A.* New York: Workers Library Publisher, 1934.

Herbert Aptheker Papers, 1842–1999, M1032, Department of Special Collections and University Archives, Stanford University Libraries Stanford, California. Contains correspondence, manuscript drafts, published articles, and research files pertinent to W.E.B. Du Bois.

Hicks, James H. "Main Speakers Snub DuBois Party." *Baltimore Afro-American*, March 3, 1951.

Hill, Robert, ed. *The FBI's RACON: Racial Conditions in the United States during World War II.* Boston: Northeastern University Press, 1995.

Hooker, Juliet. *Theorizing Race in the Americas: Douglass, Sarmiento, Du Bois, and Vasconcelos.* New York: Oxford University Press, 2017.

Horne, Gerald. *The Apocalypse of Settler Colonialism: The Roots of Slavery, White Supremacy, and Capitalism in Seventeenth Century North American and the Caribbean.* New York: Monthly Review Press, 2017.

Horne, Gerald. *Black and Brown: African-Americans and the Mexican Revolution, 1910–1920.* New York: New York University Press, 2005.

Horne, Gerald. *Black Liberation/Red Scare: Ben Davis and the Communist Party.* Newark: University of Delaware Press, 1994.

Horne, Gerald. *The Color of Fascism: Lawrence Dennis, Racial Passing and the Rise of Right-Wing Extremism in the United States.* New York: New York University Press, 2007.

Horne, Gerald. *The Counter-Revolution of 1776: Slave Resistance and the Origins of the United States of America.* New York: New York University Press, 2014.

Horne, Gerald. *The Deepest South: The United States, Brazil and the African Slave Trade.* New York: New York University Press, 2007.

Horne, Gerald. *The End of Empires: African-Americans and India.* Philadelphia: Temple University Press, 2008.

Horne, Gerald. *Facing the Rising Sun: African Americans, Japan, and the Rise of Afro-Asian Solidarity.* New York: New York University Press, 2018.

Horne, Gerald. *The Final Victim of the Blacklist: John Howard Lawson, Dean of the Hollywood Ten*. Berkeley: University of California Press, 2005.

Horne, Gerald. *Race War! White Supremacy and the Japanese Attack on the British Empire*. New York: New York University Press, 2004.

Horne, Gerald. *Race Woman: The Lives of Shirley Graham Du Bois*. New York: New York University Press, 2000.

Horne, Gerald. *W.E.B. Du Bois: A Biography*. Santa Barbara: Greenwood Press, 2010.

Horne, Gerald. *The White Pacific: U.S. Imperialism and Black Slavery in the South Seas after the Civil War*. Honolulu: University of Hawaii Press, 2007.

Horne, Gerald, and Mary Young, eds. *W.E.B. Du Bois: An Encyclopedia*. Westport: Greenwood, 2001.

Hugh H. Smyth Papers, 1942–1963, Sc Micro R-966, Schomburg Center for Research in Black Culture, New York Public Library, New York, NY. Contains articles, speeches, and correspondence pertinent to W.E.B. Du Bois.

Intondi, Joseph. *African Americans Against the Bomb: Nuclear Weapons, Colonialism, and the Black Freedom Movement*. Palo Alto: Stanford University Press, 2015.

James, C. L. R. *The Black Jacobins: Toussaint L'Ouverture and the San Domingo Revolution*. New York: Vintage Books, 1989.

James, Joy. *Transcending the Talented Tenth: Black Leaders and American Intellectuals*. New York: Routledge, 1997.

James Aronson Collection of W.E.B. Du Bois, MS 292, Special Collections and University Archives, University of Massachusetts Amherst Libraries, Amherst, MA. Contains correspondence, speeches, news clippings, and articles pertinent to W.E.B. Du Bois.

Joel E. Spingarn Collection, 1910–1947, JWJ MSS 11, Joel E. Spingarn Collection. James Weldon Johnson Collection in the American Literature Collection, Beinecke Rare Book and Manuscript Library, Yale University, New Haven, CT. Contains correspondence and memoranda pertinent to W.E.B. Du Bois.

Joel E. Spingarn Papers, MS 62-4281, Howard University, Moorland-Spingarn Research Center, Washington, DC. Contains correspondence, memoranda, Amenia Conference materials, and Niagara Movement printed materials pertinent to W.E.B. Du Bois.

Johnson, Karen A. *Uplifting the Women and the Race: The Educational Philosophies of Anna Julia Cooper and Nannie Helen Burroughs*. New York: Routledge, 2000.

Jones, Claudia. *An End to the Neglect of the Problems of the Negro Woman!* New York: National Women's Commission CPUSA, 1949.

Jones, Jacqueline. *Goddess of Anarchy: The Life and Times of Lucy Parsons, American Radical.* New York: Basic Books, 2017.

Kahn, Jonathon Samuel. *Divine Discontent: The Religious Imagination of W.E.B. Du Bois.* New York: Oxford University Press, 2011.

Katz, Michael B., and Thomas J. Sugrue, eds. *W.E.B. Du Bois, Race, and the City: The Philadelphia Negro and Its Legacy.* Philadelphia: University of Pennsylvania Press, 1998.

Kellogg, Charles F. *NAACP.* Baltimore: Johns Hopkins University Press, 1967.

Lemons, Gary L. *Womanist Foremothers: Frederick Douglass and W.E.B. Du Bois.* Albany: SUNY Press, 2009.

Lenin, Vladimir I. *Selected Works,* vol. 3. Moscow: Progress Publishers, 1971.

Lenin, Vladimir I., and Joseph Stalin. *Selections from V. I. Lenin and J. V. Stalin on National Colonial Question.* Calcutta: Calcutta Book House, 1970.

Lester, Julius. *The Seventh Son: The Thoughts and Writings of W.E.B. Du Bois.* New York: Random House, 1971.

Lewis, David Levering. *W.E.B. Du Bois: Biography of a Race.* New York: Henry Holt, 1993.

Lewis, David Levering. *W.E.B. Du Bois: The Fight for Equality and the American Century, 1919–1963.* New York: Holt, 2000.

Lewis, David Levering. *W.E.B. Du Bois: A Biography.* New York: Henry Holt and Company, 2009.

Lincoln, C. Eric. *The Black Church Since Frazier.* New York: Schocken Books, 1974.

Lloyd, Vincent W. *Black Natural Law.* New York: Oxford University Press, 2016.

Locke, Alain, ed. *The New Negro: Voices of the Harlem Renaissance.* New York: Touchstone, 1925.

Makalani, Minkah. *In the Cause of Freedom: Radical Black Internationalism from Harlem to London, 1917–1939.* Raleigh: University of North Carolina Press, 2011.

Marable, Manning. *W.E.B. Du Bois: Black Radical Democrat.* Boulder: Paradigm Publishers, 2005.

McDuffie, Erik. *Sojourning for Freedom: Black Women, American Communism, and the Making of Black Left Feminism.* Durham: Duke University Press, 2011.

McKay, Claude. *Home to Harlem.* New York: Harper and Bros., 1928.

Meier, August. "Booker T. Washington and the Negro Press." *Journal of Negro History* 38 (January 1953): 67–90.

Mixon, Gregory. *The Atlanta Riot: Race, Class and Violence in a New South City.* Gainesville: University Press of Florida, 2005.

Monteiro, Anthony. "W.E.B. Du Bois and the Study of Black Humanity: A Rediscovery." *Journal of Black Studies* 38 (March 2008): 600–621.

Morris, Aldon D. *The Scholar Denied: W.E.B. Du Bois and the Birth of Modern Sociology*. Oakland: University of California Press, 2015.

Muhammad, Khalil Gibran. *The Condemnation of Blackness: Race, Crime, and the Making of Urban America*. Cambridge: Harvard University Press, 2010, 1–14.

Mullen, Bill V. *Un-American: W.E.B. Du Bois and the Century of World Revolution*. Philadelphia: Temple University Press, 2015.

Mullen, Bill V. *W.E.B. Du Bois: Revolutionary Across the Color Line*. London: Pluto Press, 2016.

Munford, Clarence. *Production Relation, Class and Black Liberation: A Marxist Perspective in Afro-American Studies*. Amsterdam: B. R. Grüner, 1978.

Munro, John. *The Anticolonial Front: The African American Freedom Struggle and Global Decolonisation, 1945-1960*. Cambridge: Cambridge University Press, 2017.

National Association for the Advancement of Colored People Records, 1842-1899, MSS34140, Manuscript Division, Library of Congress, Washington, DC. Contains meeting minutes, reports, annual conference files, correspondence, memoranda, speeches and writings pertinent to W.E.B. Du Bois.

New York Courier. "Mordecai Johnson, Charlotte Brown Fail to Attend DuBois Testimonial." March 3, 1951.

Patterson, Louise Thompson. "Toward a Brighter Dawn." *Woman Today* (April 1936).

Paul Robeson Collection, Sc MG 170, Schomburg Center for Research in Black Culture, The New York Public Library, New York, NY. Contains correspondence, speeches, clippings, and articles, pertinent to W.E.B. Du Bois.

Perry, Jeffrey B. *Hubert Harrison: The Voice of Harlem Radicalism, 1883–1918*. New York: Columbia University Press, 2010.

Phelps-Stokes Fund Records, 1893–1970, Sc MG 162, Schomburg Center for Research in Black Culture, New York Public Library, New York, NY. Contains study commissions, reports, project grants, and correspondence pertinent to W.E.B. Du Bois. Of particular note is correspondence about the *Encyclopedia of the Negro* and Du Bois's opposition to the Fund in the 1930s and 1940s.

Porter, Eric. *The Problem of the Future of the World: W.E.B. Du Bois and the Race Concept at Midcentury*. Durham: Duke University Press, 2010.

Provenzo, Eugene F. *W.E.B. Du Bois' Exhibit of American Negroes: African Americans at the Beginning of the Twentieth Century*. Lanham: Rowman & Littlefield, 2013.

Provenzo, Eugene F., and Edmund Kobena Abaka, eds. *W.E.B. Du Bois on Africa.* Walnut Creek: Left Coast Press, 2012.

Rabaka, Reiland. *Against Epistemic Apartheid: W.E.B. Du Bois and the Disciplinary Decadence of Sociology.* Lanham: Lexington Books, 2010.

Rabaka, Reiland. *Du Bois's Dialectics: Black Radical Politics and the Reconstruction of Critical Social Theory.* Lanham: Lexington Books, 2008.

Rabaka, Reiland, ed. *W.E.B. Du Bois.* Farnham: Ashgate, 2010.

Rasberry, Vaughn. *Race and the Totalitarian Century: Geopolitics in the Black Literary Imagination.* Cambridge: Harvard University Press, 2016.

Reed, Adolph L. *W.E.B. Du Bois and American Political Thought: Fabianism and the Color Line.* New York: Oxford University Press, 1997.

Reed, John. The Negro Question in America: Speech at the 2nd World Congress of the Communist International. July 25, 1920. Moscow: Publishing House of the Communist International, 1921.

Resources on W.E.B. Du Bois compiled by the Angela McMillan, Digital Reference Specialist for the Library of Congress. https://www.loc.gov/rr/program/bib/dubois/. Accessed May 20, 2019.

Robinson, Cedric. *Black Marxism: The Making of the Black Radical Tradition.* Chapel Hill: University of North Carolina Press, 2000.

Rodney, Walter. "African History in the Service of Black Liberation." October 12, 1968. Historyisaweapon.com. https://www.historyisaweapon.com/defcon1/rodneylib.html. Accessed May 20, 2019.

Schama, Simon. *Rough Crossings: Britain, the Slaves, and the American Revolution.* New York: Ecco, 2006.

Schneider, Ryan. *The Public Intellectualism of Ralph Waldo Emerson and W.E.B. Du Bois: Emotional Dimensions of Race and Reform.* New York: Palgrave Macmillan, 2010.

"Sees Nation's Gain in Negro Welfare." *New York Times* (May 13, 1933): 25.

Shaw, Stephanie J. *W.E.B. Du Bois and the Souls of Black Folk.* Chapel Hill: The University of North Carolina Press, 2013.

Shirley Graham Du Bois Papers, 1865–1998, MC 476, Schlesinger Library on the History of Women in America, Radcliffe Institute for Advanced Study, Cambridge, MA. Contains correspondence, research materials, manuscript drafts, and financial records pertinent to W.E.B. Du Bois.

Sinitiere, Phillip Luke, and Kirschke, Amy Helene, eds. *Protest and Propaganda: W.E.B. Du Bois, the* Crisis, *and American History.* Columbia: University of Missouri Press, 2013.

Staton-Taiwo, Sandra. *Broad Sympathies in a Narrow World: The Legacy of W.E.B. Du Bois.* Detroit: Broadside Lotus Press, 2018.

Stewart, Carole Lynn. *Strange Jeremiahs: Civil Religion and the Literary Imaginations of Jonathan Edwards, Herman Melville, and W.E.B. Du Bois.* Albuquerque: University of New Mexico Press, 2010.

Stewart, James. *Flight in Search of Vision.* Trenton: African World Press, 2004.

Stewart, Ruth Ann. *The Life of Portia Washington Pittman, the Daughter of Booker T. Washington.* Garden City: Doubleday, 1977.

Stormquist, Shelton. *Reinventing "The People": The Progressive Movement, the Class Problem, and the Origins of Modern Liberalism.* Urbana: University of Illinois Press, 2006.

Supreme Court. Communist Party v. SACB, 367 U.S. 1 (1961). https://supreme.justia.com/cases/federal/us/367/1/. Accessed May 20, 2019.

"A Symposium on Garvey." *Messenger* 4 (Dec. 1922): 551.

"To the Nations of the World." In *Report of the Pan-African Conference,* 23–25 July 1900, London. W.E.B. Du Bois Papers, University of Massachusetts-Amherst.

"U.S. Will Come to Communism, Du Bois Tells Conference." *Baltimore Afro-American* (May 20, 1933).

USC Annenberg Digital Archives, compiled by Dr. Ernest James Wilson III. http://digitaldubois.net/index-cat=4.html. Accessed May 20, 2019.

Van Wienen, Mark W. *American Socialist Triptych: The Literary-Political Work of Charlotte Perkins Gilman, Upton Sinclair, and W.E.B. Du Bois.* Ann Arbor: University of Michigan Press, 2012.

Warren, Nagueyalti. *Grandfather of Black Studies: W.E.B. Du Bois.* Trenton: African World Press, 2011.

Warren, Nagueyalti. *W.E.B. Du Bois: Grandfather of Black Studies.* Trenton: Africa World Press, 2011.

Washington, Booker T. *Up from Slavery.* New York: Penguin, 1986.

W.E.B. Du Bois Collection, 1867–1963, Fisk University Archives, Franklin Library, Nashville, TN. Personal papers of W.E.B. Du Bois.

W.E.B. Du Bois Collection, JWJ MSS 8, Beinecke Rare Book and Manuscript Library, Yale University Library, Yale University, New Haven, CT. Contains correspondence, writings, chapter drafts, and subject files pertinent to W.E.B. Du Bois.

W.E.B. Du Bois National Historic Site in Great Barrington, Massachusetts. http://www.duboisnhs.org/index.html. Accessed May 20, 2019.

W.E.B. Du Bois Papers. "The Storm and Stress in the Black World." *Dial (Chicago)* 3 (April 16, 1901): 262–264.

W.E.B. Du Bois Papers, 1803–1999, MS 312, Special Collections and University Archives, University of Massachusetts Amherst Libraries, Amherst, MA. Personal papers of W.E.B. Du Bois.

W.E.B. Du Bois Papers, Sc MG 109, Schomburg Center for Research in Black Culture, The New York Public Library, New York, NY.

Contains a small body of speeches, articles, correspondence, and related material primarily authored by W.E.B. Du Bois.

W.E.B. Du Bois Research Materials, Sc MG 197, Schomburg Center for Research in Black Culture, New York Public Library, New York, NY. Contains research materials for the 1959 biography *W.E.B. Du Bois: Negro Leader in a Time of Crisis*, donated by the author Francis L. Broderick.

WEBDuBois.org, maintained by Dr. Robert W. Williams. http://www.webdubois.org/wdb-rw.html. Accessed May 20, 2019.

Weinberg, Meyer. *The World of W.E.B. Du Bois: A Quotation Sourcebook.* Amherst: University of Massachusetts Press, 2012.

Wells, Ida B. *Southern Horrors: Lynch Law in All Its Phases.* New York: The New York Age Print, 1892.

Westbrook, Randall. *Education and Empowerment: The Essential Writings of W.E.B. Du Bois.* East Brunswick: Hansen Publishing Group, 2013.

White, Walter. *A Man Called White.* New York: Viking, 1948.

Wilkerson, Doxey. "They Are Trying to Sentence Dr. Du Bois to Death." *New York Times*, October 19, 1951.

Williams, Eric. *Capitalism and Slavery.* Chapel Hill: University of North Carolina Press, 1994.

Wolgemuth, Kathleen. "Wilson and Federal Segregation." *Journal of Negro History* 44 (April 1959): 158–173.

Wortham, Robert. *The Sociological Souls of Black Folk: Essays by W.E.B. Du Bois.* Lanham: Lexington Books, 2011.

Wortham, Robert. *W.E.B. Du Bois and the Sociology of the Black Church and Religion, 1897–1914,* Lanham: Lexington Books, 2017.

Wortham, Robert, ed. *W.E.B. Du Bois and the Sociological Imagination: A Reader.* Waco: Baylor University Press, 2019.

Wright, Earl. *The First American School of Sociology: W.E.B. Du Bois and the Atlanta Sociological Laboratory.* New York: Routledge, 2017.

Zhang, Juguo. *W.E.B. Du Bois: The Quest for the Abolition of the Color Line.* London: Routledge, 2014.

Index

Abolitionism, 4, 6, 8, 12, 16, 47, 55
Abraham Lincoln Brigade, 139
Abyssinia, 133
Act Prohibiting Importation of Slaves, 16
"Address of the Niagara Movement, to the Country" (Du Bois, W.E.B.), 219–222
Afghanistan, 167
AFL. *See* American Federation of Labor
Africa, 10–11, 146; African Americans and, 34; "Back-to-Africa" movements, 85; colonialism, Africans struggling against, 169, 202; imperialism and, 84. *See also* Colonialism
African-American press, 175, 177
African Americans, 4, 22, 102; Africa and, 34; African-American banks, 9; antiwar sentiment among, 167; colleges designated for, 19; empowerment of, 7; exile and, 190; Great Migration from South to North, 68, 73, 78; Harvard and, 12; literature and arts, flowering among, 71; mass arrests of African-American men, 38; military and, 67; music made by, 10; racial uplift of, 24; racist treatment of Black troops, 68; scholarly neglect of, 29; struggle of, 61; voting rolls, African

Americans eliminated from, 11; youth, 3
African Blood Brotherhood, 40
African Communities League, 85
African Diaspora, 1, 168, 196, 201
African Methodist Episcopal Zion Church, 6, 45
"The African Plymouth Rock" (Du Bois, W.E.B.), 84
"The African Roots of War" (Du Bois, W.E.B.), 76, 86, 224–227
African slave trade. *See* Slavery
Agrin, Gloria, 175
Ahmed, Jamal Mohammad, 192
All-African People's Conference, 186
Amenia Conference on a New Programme for the Negro, 198, 201, 212
American Bar Association, 64
American Colonization Society, 84, 85
American Federation of Labor (AFL), 104, 134
American Historical Association, 10, 13
American Labor Party, 168, 207, 213
American Missionary Association, 8
American Negro Academy, 28, 211
American Negro Exhibit, 33
American Negro Labor Congress (ANLC), 104, 123, 126

The American Negro: What He Was, What He Is, and What He Might Become: A Critical and Practical Discussion (Thomas, W.), 56
"The American Negro Woman" (Du Bois, W.E.B.), 199
American Peace Crusade (APC), 178–179, 182
Amherst, 13
Anarchism, 43
ANLC. *See* American Negro Labor Congress
Anti-Catholicism, 103
Anticolonialism, 162, 178, 202
Anticommunism, 122, 155, 156, 160, 176, 189, 197
Antifascism, 139; antifascist alliance, 143–144; antifascist war, 136, 146, 155
Anti-imperialism, 154, 196, 204–206, 207
Anti-Imperialist League, 64
Anti-Lynching Crusaders, 129
Antioch College, 20
Antiracism, 57, 81, 96
Anti-Semitism, 103, 141
Antisexism, 198–200
Anti-Socialist Law, 17
Antiwar sentiment, 167
Apartheid, 159, 166, 168
APC. *See* American Peace Crusade
"An Appeal to the World" (Du Bois, W.E.B.), 213
Aptheker, Herbert, 27
Armstrong, Louis, 108
Atlanta, Georgia, 30, 52; Jim Crow and, 149; return to, 144–145, 149
"Atlanta Compromise" (Washington, B.), 24, 28, 29, 46
Atlanta Race Riot, 53, 58
Atlanta University, 30, 35, 48, 131, 135, 144; fracases with leadership at, 154; leaving, 62
Atlantic Charter, 202
Atlantic Monthly (journal), 28
Atomic bombs, 154, 165
Azikiwe, Nnamdi, 203

"Back-to-Africa" movements, 85
Baker, Ella, 116, 117, 151
Baker, Josephine, 88, 190
Baker, T. Nelson, 55, 56
Baldwin, James, 88, 190
Baldwin, William, Jr., 36
Baltimore Afro-American (newspaper), 127
Bancroft, Frederic, 145
Baptist church, 37
Barber, Jesse Max, 64
Bass, Charlotta, 161, 177
Bates, Ruby, 119
Bayen, Malaku, 136
Bechet, Sidney, 108
Belfrage, Cedric, 192
Benson, Elmer, 174
Berlin Conference, 84
Berlin Olympics, 138
Bermuda, 111
Bernstein, Leonard, 162
Bethune, Mary McLeod, 169, 177
The Birth of a Nation (1915), 41, 79, 105, 145
Black America, 2, 6, 10, 21, 33, 37, 41, 47, 48; analytical studies of, 38; Brownsville, Texas, and, 65; building businesses in, 95; *Crisis* (journal) and, 63; Democratic Party and, 160; growing militancy in, 46; Hoover and, 128; Jews and, 15; NAACP and, 75; rural Europe and, 16; Talented Tenth and, 124; Washington, B., primary gatekeeper of, 28
Black Belt Thesis, 118
Black bourgeoisie, 24, 94, 174
Black businesses, 64
Black churches, 6
Black communists, 104, 112
The Black Flame: A Trilogy (Du Bois, W.E.B.), 184
Black Folk Then and Now: An Essay in the History and Sociology of the Negro Race (Du Bois, W.E.B.), 146
Black Independence Day, 4
Black Jacobins, 16

Black laborers, 13–14
Black liberation, 87
Black Liberation Movement, 208
Black Marxism, 193, 196, 197, 203–204
Black Marxism: The Making of the Black Radical Tradition (Robinson), 203
Black middle class, 9
Black nationalism, 40, 42, 85, 200
Blackness, 105
Black Panther Party, 74
Black petit-bourgeoisie, 9
Black Reconstruction in America: An Essay toward a History of the Part Which Black Folk Played in the Attempt to Reconstruct Democracy in America, 1860–1880 (Du Bois, W.E.B.), 145, 203–204, 212
Black Star Line, 93, 98
Black Studies, 30, 208, 209, 210
The Black Worker (Harris, A., and Spero), 145
Black worker militancy, 151
Blease, Cole, 122
Blyden, Edward, 23
Boers, 33
Boissevain, Inez Milholland, 64
Bolden, Buddy, 108
Bolshevik Revolution, 109, 127
Bolsheviks, 89, 92, 110, 111, 113
Bond, Horace Mann, 160
Bontemps, Arna, 120
Booker, Cory, 129
Borroughs, Nannie Helen, 24
Brando, Marlon, 162
Brawley, Benjamin, 107
Brazil, 21
Briggs, Cyril V., 91
British Preparatory Academy, 120
British rule, 2
British West Indies, 91
Brooklyn, New York, 182–183, 188
Brotherhood of Sleeping Car Porters, 102, 104, 137
Brown, Charlotte Hawkins, 173
Brown, John, 51, 55, 61, 222–224

Brown II, 189
Brownsville, Texas, 53, 55, 65, 69
Brown v. Board of Education, 22, 44, 181, 189
Buffalo, New York, 52
Bunche, Ralph, 124, 161, 173
Bureau of Labor Statistics, 31

CAA. *See* Council on African Affairs
Cambridge, Massachusetts, 10, 13
Campbell, Grace, 40, 112
Canada, 49, 51
Cane (Toomer), 106
Cape of Good Hope, 33
Capitalism, 27; capitalist class, 11; capitalist exploitation, 203; communism suppression of, 109; exploitation of, 206; Japan and, 143; rise of, 75; white supremacy and, 112
The Caribbean, 76, 93, 94
Carl Schurz Memorial, 137
Carnegie Hall, 46–47
Casement, Roger, 71
Central America, 86
Channing, Edward, 10
Chaplin, Charles, 162, 193
Chesnutt, Charles Waddell, 40
Chicago, 132
Chicago Defender (journal), 213
China, 76, 142, 172, 179, 186–187
Christie, Agatha, 153
CIO. *See* Congress of Industrial Organizations
Citizenship rights, 3
Citron, Alice, 174
City of Brotherly Love, 26
Civil libertarians, 79
Civil rights, 197
Civil Rights Congress, 207
Civil Rights Division of the Justice Department, 159
Civil Rights Movement, 40
Civil War, 6, 12, 19, 30, 55, 121, 203
The Clansman (Dixon), 79
Clark, Tom, 158
Clarke, John Henrik, 171

Clarke, Septima, 40
Class conflict, 26
Class oppression, 43
Clef Club Orchestra, 63
Clement, Rufus, 150
Cleveland, Grover, 70
"Close Ranks" (*Crisis*), 85–86, 212
Cobb, James, 175
Cold War, 110, 143, 155, 167, 173, 189
Colonialism, 6, 23, 71, 74, 89, 118, 141–142, 146, 153, 161, 173; anticolonial movements, 169, 178, 202; battle again, 155; color line and, 28; continuation of, 205; internationalism and, 177; Irish anticolonialists, 92; liberation from, importance of, 192; Moscow interest in destabilizing, 101; neocolonialism, 155; racism and, 154; segregation and, 137; settler colonialism, 55; slavery and, 11; throwing off, 203
Color and Democracy: Colonies and Peace (Du Bois, W.E.B.), 153, 206
Colored Agricultural Wheels, 11
Colored Farmers' Alliance, 11
Color line, 22, 27–28, 155, 181
Comintern. *See* Communist International
Communism, 152, 179; anticommunism, 122, 155, 156, 160, 189, 197; Black communists, 104, 112; capitalism, suppression by, 109; China and, 172; NAACP, purge of communists from, 158. *See also* Socialism
Communist International (Comintern), 104, 109, 112, 118
Communist Labor Party, 109
Communist Manifesto (Marx and Engels), 17, 144
Communist Party, U.S. (CPUSA), 89, 112, 123, 128–129, 156, 158, 183, 214; aim of, 188; embrace of, 135; Graham and, 172
Communist Party of the United States v. Subversive Activities Control Board, 188

Confederate States of America, 8, 12, 30, 79
The Congo, 71, 182
Congress of Industrial Organizations (CIO), 134
Congress of Racial Equality, 40
"The Conservation of Races" (Du Bois, W.E.B.), 215–217
Constigan-Wagner Anti-Lynching Bill, 129
Constitution, U.S., 9
Convict lease system, 38
Cook, Will Marion, 63
Cooke, Marvel, 116, 117, 206
Coolidge, Calvin, 94, 100, 102
Cooper, Anna Julia, 33
Cooperative Workers of America, 11
Corvée, 77
Cosmopolitanism, 123
Cotton States International Exposition, 24
Council on African Affairs (CAA), 154, 161, 165, 179, 182, 190–191, 207, 213
CPUSA. *See* Communist Party, U.S.
The Crisis: A Record of the Darker Races (journal), 49, 62, 64, 69, 80, 125, 211; Black America and, 63; "Close Ranks," 85–86, 212; Debs and, 70; growth of, 89; lynchings reported by, 74
Crummell, Alexander, 22, 23, 24, 42, 197
Cuba, 21, 31, 185, 187, 205
Cuffe, Paul, 85
Cullen, Countee, 119–120, 130
Cultural and Scientific Conference for World Peace, 162
Cultural development, 24
Cuney, Maud, 13, 14
Cuney, Norris Wright, 13
Czarist Russia, 52, 92

Dale, Thelma, 199, 200
"The Damnation of Women" (Du Bois, W.E.B.), 90, 117
Dark Princess: A Romance (Du Bois, W.E.B.), 108, 120

Darkwater (Du Bois, W.E.B.), 90, 146
Davis, Benjamin J., Jr., 183
Davis, Jefferson, 12
Dean, Jodi, 208
Debs, Eugene Victor, 70, 110
Debt peonage, 14, 60
Debt slavery, 13
"Declaration of Principles" (Niagara Movement), 52
Decolonization, 33, 189
Deep South, 12, 60, 78, 89, 124
Delaney, Martin, 23
Delany, Hubert, 161
Delany, Martin, 43
Democratic Party, 11, 26, 157; Black America and, 160; KKK and, 81; working class and, 70
Dennis v. United States, 183
Department of Justice, 65, 93, 159, 167
Department of Labor, 71
"The Descent of Dr. Du Bois" (Harrison), 86
Desegregation, 117, 130, 200
Des Moines, Iowa, 83–84, 130
Dictatorship of the proletariat, 92, 109
Dike, Kenneth, 192
Diphtheria, 32
Disenfranchisement, 38, 45, 69
Disfranchisement, 19
Dixiecrats, 69, 144
Dixon, Thomas, 79
Domingo, Wilfred A., 93
Double-consciousness, 28
Douglas, Aaron, 96
Douglass, Frederick, 5, 6, 21–22, 25, 51, 63, 102, 121
Du Bois, Alexander, 2, 6, 13
Du Bois, Alfred, 1–2
Du Bois, Graham, 186, 191
Du Bois, James, 2
Du Bois, Mary. *See* Silvina, Mary
Du Bois, Nina Gomer, 170
Du Bois, Nina Yolande, 37, 130
Du Bois, W.E.B. *See specific topics*
Dunbar, Paul Laurence, 20, 25

Dusk of Dawn: Essay toward an Autobiography of a Race Concept (Du Bois, W.E.B.), 79, 146
Dusseldorf, 14
Dyer, Leonidas C., 121
Dyer Anti-Lynching Bill, 129

Eaton, Isabel, 64
Economic and Social Council, UN, 159
Economic growth, 26–27
Economic independence, 74–75
Education, 12, 209; graduate study, 14; proponents of white-only education, 9; right to, 47; Talented Tenth and, 123, 131; United States, apartheid-like educational system in, 19
Edwards, Thyra, 139
Egypt, 76
Einstein, Albert, 162
Electoral College, 70
Emancipation Act, 4
Emancipation Day, 4
Encyclopedia Africana, 188
Engels, Friedrich, 17, 27, 144
England, 33, 137
Espionage Act, 152
The Essentials of Marx (Lee), 145
Ethiopia, 33, 34, 133, 136, 202, 206
Ethiopian Pacific League, 152
Ethnic studies, 209
Ethnology, 23
Eurocentric curricula, 209
European imperial powers, 10
Exile, 190, 193

Fairmount Park, 26
Farmer, James, 40
Fascism, 128, 166. *See also* Antifascism
Faulkner, Stanley, 175
Fauset, Jesse, 96, 106
Federal Bureau of Investigation (FBI), 152, 183, 186
Ferguson, John Howard, 44
Fifteenth Amendment, 47, 78
Fifth Amendment, 4
Firestone, Harvey, 110
Firestone Rubber, 101

First Amendment, 4
First Universal Race Congress, 71
Fisk Herald (newspaper), 48
Fisk Jubilee Singers, 42
Fisk University, 8, 9, 10, 120, 185
Foner, Eric, 204
Forced labor, 77
Ford, Henry, 133
Ford, James, 112, 123–124
Forrest, Nathan Bedford, 41
Fortune, Timothy Thomas, 10
Fort-Whiteman, Lovett, 104
Four Freedoms, 202
Fourteenth Amendment, 4, 44
France, 33, 76, 87–88
Frank, Leo, 103
Frazier, E. Franklin, 160, 203
Freedmen, 7
Freedom's Journal (magazine), 48, 63
Freedomways (magazine), 183, 188
Free speech, 79
Freud, Sigmund, 21

Gandhi, Mohandas K., 108
Garnet, Henry Highland, 43, 121
Garvey, Amy Ashwood, 202
Garvey, Amy Jacques, 40, 154
Garvey, Marcus, 42, 76, 85, 90–95,
    115; on Liberia, 100; movement
    led by, 117; self-determination,
    119
Garvin, Vicki, 190, 199
Gender egalitarianism, 6
General Education Board, 123
General Electric, 61
Georgia, 30
German Romanticism, 15
Germany, 11, 12, 14, 60, 81, 138
Ghadr conspiracy trial, 108
Ghana, 42, 154, 182, 186, 187, 188–191,
    214
Gide, Charles, 145
*The Gift of Black Folk: Negroes in the
    Making of America* (Du Bois,
    W.E.B.), 102–103, 200
The Globe (newspaper), 5

Gomer, Nina, 25, 32, 213
Gordon, Mittie Maude Lena, 85
Graduate study, 14
Graham, Shirley, 25, 44, 151, 167, 170–
    172, 174, 179, 207
Grassroots activism, 157
Great Barrington, 1, 3, 5, 7, 211
Great Britain, 76
Great Depression, 116, 133, 134, 135,
    196, 200
Great Migration, 68, 73, 78
Great Mississippi Flood of 1927,
    115–116
Great War, 67
Griffith, D. W., 41, 79, 105
Group Areas Act (South Africa), 168
Guillen, Nicolas, 96

Haiti, 2, 83, 184, 202, 206, 212; U.S.
    invasion of, 76–77, 78, 86, 126
Haitian Revolution, 2, 16, 21
Hallam, Mabel, 60
Hammond, John, 161
Hampton Institute, 5, 30, 122
Handy, W. C., 108
Hansberry, Lorraine, 174, 178, 199, 200
Harding, Warren G., 212
Harlem, 116, 119, 120, 170
Harlem Renaissance, 63, 71, 95,
    104–107
Harpers Ferry, Virginia, 51, 55
Harper's Weekly (magazine), 36
Harrington, Ollie, 88
Harris, Abram Lincoln, 145, 198, 203
Harris, Joel Chandler, 31
Harris, Kamala, 129
Harrison, Hubert, 86
Hart, Albert Bushnell, 10
Harvard College, 8, 10, 12, 119–120
Harvard Historical Studies, 20
Hayes, George, 175
Hayes, Rutherford B., 14
Hayford, Joseph Ephraim Casely, 23
Haymarket, 11
Haywood, Harry, 4, 112
Hearst, William Randolph, 45

Hegel, Georg, 15
Hellman, Lillian, 162
Herero peoples, 60
Hiroshima, 154
Hispaniola, 16
History of Economic Doctrines
    (Gide and Rist), 145
Hitler, Adolf, 138, 140
Hollywood, 79–80, 150
Home to Harlem (McKay), 106
Homosexuality, 120
Hong Kong, 143
Hoover, Herbert, 127–128, 212
Hoover, J. Edgar, 151
Hope, John, 38, 40, 135, 149
Hopkins, Harry, 143, 184
*The Horizon: A Journal of the
    Color Line* (journal), 49, 53, 63,
    211
Hose, Sam, 31
Hosmer, Frank, 3, 5, 8
House Un-American Activities
    Committee (HUAC), 177
Houston, Charles Hamilton, 189
Houston, Texas, 89
Howard University, 124
Howell, Clark, 58
HUAC. *See* House Un-American
    Activities Committee
Hughes, Evans, 97, 120
Hughes, Langston, 96, 106, 111
Huiswoud, Otto, 104
Human rights, 166
Hunton, W. Alphaeus, Jr., 120, 190

ILD. *See* International Labor Defense
Imperialism, 23, 31, 112, 155; Africa
    and, 84; anti-imperialism, 154, 196,
    204–206, 207; color line and, 28;
    European imperial powers, 10;
    laboring classes, immiseration of,
    205; rise of, 75; struggle against, 186;
    throwing off, 203
"Imperialism, United Nations, and
    Colonial People" (Du Bois, W.E.B.),
    206

In Battle for Peace (Du Bois, W.E.B.),
    174, 213
India, 76, 182
Industrial capitalists, 4
Industrialization, 73
Industrial revolution, 84
Industrial Workers of the World, 44
Infant mortality, 32
Integration, 40, 84, 132, 200
Intercollegiate Socialist Society, 81
International Bureau of Labor, 97
International Congress of the
    Oppressed Nations, 112
International Institute for the Study of
    the Negro Problems and for the
    Evolution and Protection of the
    Negro Race, 97
Internationalism, 96, 177, 196, 203
International Labor Defense (ILD), 119
International Lenin Prize for the
    Strengthening of Peace among
    Nations from the Soviet Peace
    Committee, 207
International Longshore and
    Warehouse Union, 174
International Peace Prize from the
    World Council of Peace, 207
International Workers of the World, 11
Interracial social interaction, 197
Irish anticolonialists, 92
Israel, 111
Italy, 33, 133, 136

Jackson, Esther Cooper, 188
Jackson, James E., 44, 183, 188
Jaffe, Bernard, 175, 176
Jamaica, 76, 77
James, C. L. R., 21
Japan, 33, 52, 141–142, 151; atomic
    bombing of, 154, 165; capitalism
    and, 143; rise in power, 111
Jefferson, Thomas, 16, 117
Jefferson School of Social Science, 177,
    206
Jews, 16; Black America and, 15; Jewish
    Americans, 103, 138

Jim Crow, 9, 11, 22, 32, 36, 55, 68, 101, 122, 159; antifascist war and, 146; Atlanta, Georgia and, 149; "Atlanta Compromise" and, 24; curbing, 47; debilitating effects of, 25; demise of, 193; denouncing, 45; destruction of, 71; eroding, 138; growing disaffection with, 158; Houston, Texas and, 89; KKK and, 40; mass transit and, 59; Moscow on, 166; national security and, 65; ossifying of, 35; poisonous nature of, 72; terrorism of, 111, 205; Washington, B., acceptance of, 39
Joblessness, 28
John Brown (Du Bois, W.E.B.), 222–224
Johnson, Jack, 60
Johnson, James Weldon, 77, 96, 98, 120
Johnson, J. Rosamond, 107
Johnson, Mordecai, 124
Jones, Claudia, 91, 112, 177, 179, 183, 185, 199
Jones, Tillman, 116
Joplin, Scott, 108
Jordan, Robert, 152
Journal of Negro Education (journal), 135
Journal of Negro History (journal), 135
Jubilee Singers, 10

Das Kapital (Marx), 17, 144
Kee, Salaria, 139
Kelley, Florence, 184
Kenya, 155
Kenyatta, Jomo, 155, 202
Kerensky, Alexander, 92
Khrushchev, Nikita, 185
Killens, John Oliver, 174
King, C. D. B., 100
King, Martin Luther, Jr., 26, 157, 160, 184, 193
KKK. *See* Ku Klux Klan
Knights of Columbus, 102
Knights of Labor, 11

Korean peninsula, 163, 167, 172, 179, 186
Korean War, 207
Ku Klux Klan (KKK), 7, 40, 41, 54, 57, 128; Democratic Party and, 81; electoral victories by, 102; Garvey, M., and, 92; nativism spread by, 103; second iteration of, 96

Labor activists, 26
Labor exploitation, 33
Labor militancy, 43
Labor organizations, 102
Labor unions, 8
Labour Party, 110
La Follette, Robert, 101, 121
League Against Imperialism and Colonial Oppression, 206
League of Nations, 113
League of Oppressed Peoples, 206
Leakey, L. B. S., 192
Lee, Algernon, 145
Legal Defense and Education Fund, NAACP, 189
Lehman, Herbert, 168, 169
Lenin, Vladimir I., 92, 109, 128, 191; premature death of, 110; on revolutionary movements of dispossessed nations, 118
Lewis, W. Arthur, 192
Liberal antiracists, 57
Liberalism, 197, 198
Liberia, 22, 83, 84, 95, 100, 206
Liberia Exodus Arkansas Colony, 85
Library of Congress, 33
Lincoln, Abraham, 5
Lindbergh, Charles, 142
Literacy testing, 11
Livingstone, David, 9
Locke, Alain LeRoy, 105, 160
Logan, Rayford, 124
London, 71–72, 143
Lorch, Lee, 185
Louisiana Purchase, 2, 21
Loving, Walter Howard, 86
Lunceford, Jimmy, 120

Luther, Martin, 16
Lynch, John R., 145
Lynching, 4, 19, 35, 69, 98, 103;
    Constigan-Wagner Anti-Lynching
    Bill, 129; *Crisis* (journal) reporting
    on, 74; Dyer Anti-Lynching Bill, 129;
    of Hose, 31; increase in, 121;
    international movement against,
    157; protesting, 67; waves of, 39

MacDonald, J. Ramsay, 71
Mack, Julian, 94
Madison, James, 16
Madison Square Garden, 137
Makonnen, Ras T., 202
Malan, Daniel François, 168
Malcolm X, 3, 40, 74
Manchester, 27, 154, 155, 202
Manchuria, 141
Mandela, Nelson, 119
Mansart, Manuel, 184
Mansart Builds a School (Du Bois,
    W.E.B.), 184
Mao Zedong, 186, 191
Marcantonio, Vito, 175
March on Washington for Jobs and
    Freedom, 193
Marine Cooks and Stewards, 174
Marshall, Thurgood, 156–157, 176,
    189
Marx, Karl, 17, 21, 27, 132, 144,
    191
Marxism, 144–145; Black Marxism,
    193, 196, 197, 203–204
Marxism-Leninism, 203
Masses & Mainstream (journal),
    171
Mass incarceration, 178
Mass transit, 59
Materialism, 23
Mau Mau, 178
May, Samuel, Jr., 56
McCarthyism, 177
McKay, Claude, 91, 106, 109, 111
Meeropol, Abe, 183
Meeropol, Ann, 183

Meeropol, Robert, 183
Mexican Revolution, 67
Mexico, 64–65, 69, 78, 83
Milholland, John, 71
Militant self-defense, 74
Military, 67; militarism, 205–206;
    military intelligence, 85–87, 89, 90,
    92, 100; racist treatment of Black
    troops, 68
Miller, Arthur, 162, 182
Miller, Kelly, 80, 94, 102
Mixed Marriages Act (South Africa),
    168
Monteiro, Anthony, 209
Moon: Illustrated Weekly (journal), 48,
    63, 211
Moore, Audley, 41
Moore, Richard B., 2, 91, 104
Moos, Elizabeth, 176
Morgan, Lewis Henry, 23
Moscow, 90, 111, 143–144, 147;
    colonialism, interest in
    destabilizing, 101; Du Bois, W.E.B.,
    and, 115, 127, 158; on Jim Crow, 166;
    Talented Tenth and, 113
Mullen, Bill V., 199
Multinational corporations, 204
Murray, Donald Gaines, 189
Murray v. Maryland, 189
Music, 10, 63, 107–108
Mussolini, Benito, 128, 136
Mutual aid, 24, 27
Mutual comradeship, 196, 204–205,
    207, 208

NAACP. *See* National Association
    for the Advancement of Colored
    People
Nagasaki, 154
Nairobi, 178
Nama peoples, 60
Namibia, 11, 14, 60
Nance, Ethel Ray, 171
Narragansett Bay, 6
Nashville, 8–9, 123
The Nation (journal), 61

National Association for the
Advancement of Colored People
(NAACP), 42, 47, 84, 150, 212;
ambitiousness of, 64; beginnings of,
63; Black America and, 75; at critical
juncture, 72–73; Du Bois, W.E.B.,
parting ways with, 115, 126, 159,
191–192; formulation of, 191;
founding of, 211; Graham and, 171;
Hollywood and, 80; joining, 62;
launch of, 59; leadership of, 67; Legal
Defense and Education Fund, 189;
purge of communists from, 158;
recruiting got, 99; return to, 151,
157; structure, 157; Tuskegee
Machine and, 78; Washington, B.,
and, 67
National Bar Association, 156
National Black Baptist Convention, 6
National Business League, 35
National Committee to Defend Dr. Du
Bois and Associates in the Peace
Information Center, 174
National Committee to Defend Negro
Leadership, 177
National Council of Negro Women,
156
National Guardian (newspaper), 182
National Liberty Congress, 86
National Medical Association, 158
National Negro Baptist Convention,
134
National Negro Business League, 45
National Negro Conference, 59
National Party (South Africa), 168
National Recovery Act, 143
National security, 65
National Veterans Hospital, 125
Nation of Islam, 40, 117
Native Americans, 5, 8
Nativism, 103
Nazis, 138, 143
The Negro (Du Bois, W.E.B.), 75, 146
Negro Champion (newspaper), 104
Negroes, 9
Negro Problem, 29

Negro Sanhedrin, 102
Negro World (newspaper), 95
Neocolonialism, 155
Neruda, Pablo, 162
New Deal, 143
New England Conservatory of Music,
13
New Haven, Connecticut, 2
New Negro, 96, 105
New Review (journal), 54
Newspaper publishing, 5
New York City, 63, 68, 91, 93, 131
New York Globe (newspaper), 5
New York Post (newspaper), 61, 87
New York Times (newspaper), 112, 127,
167
Niagara Movement, 42, 47, 52; Atlanta
Race Riot and, 53; Harpers Ferry,
Virginia, and, 55; meeting in Boston,
58
Nigeria, 182
Nixon, Richard M., 186
Nkrumah, Kwame, 154, 184, 188, 190,
196, 202
Norris, Frank, 70
Nottingham Riots, 185
Nuclear weapons, 154, 165, 169, 184

Oberlaender Trust, 137
Oberlin, 58
Oberlin College, 171
Ogden, Robert C., 36
Oklahoma, 117
The Ordeal of Mansart (Du Bois,
W.E.B.), 184
Organized labor, 54
Ovington, Mary White, 59, 63, 69, 120
Owen, Chandler, 93–94
Owens, Jesse, 138

Padmore, George, 154, 202
Palestinians, 111
Pan-African Association, 34
Pan-African Conference, 33, 202, 211
Pan-African Congresses, 23, 28, 87,
96–97, 126, 206, 212; Fifth

Pan-African Congress, 154, 158, 202; opening of, 155

Pan-Africanism, 2, 15, 22, 76, 92, 136, 173, 185, 189; dedication to, 203; ideology of, 202; importance of, 201

Parallelism, 176

Parker, Charlie, 167

Parker, George, 175

Parsons, Albert, 11

Parsons, Lucy, 11

Paton, Alan, 162

Patterson, Haywood, 119

Patterson, William, 2

Peabody, George Foster, 36

Peacegram (periodical), 207

Peace Information Center (PIC), 167, 170, 172, 175, 176, 196, 207, 213

Peace Movement of Ethiopia, 85

Perry, Pettis, 183

Phi Beta Kappa, 119

Philadelphia, 25–26, 27

The Philadelphia Negro (Du Bois, W.E.B.), 27, 28, 29, 209, 211

Philippines, 205

Phillips, Wendell, 10, 12

Phylon: A Quarterly Review of Race and Culture (journal), 135, 150, 212

PIC. *See* Peace Information Center

Pickens, William, 112

Plessy, Homer, 44

Plessy v. Ferguson, 22, 35, 44, 189

Police brutality, 73–74

Poll tax, 11

Population Registration Act (South Africa), 168

Populist movement, 11, 26, 35, 44

Powell v. Alabama, 119

Praxis, 108, 196, 203, 204, 206, 208, 210

Price, Victoria, 119

Primus, Pearl, 167

Private enterprise, 166

Progressive Era, 197

Progressive movement, 26, 27, 35

Progressive Party, 157, 159, 168, 178, 182, 206

Proletarian revolutionary struggle, 109

Propaganda, 107

Property relations, 26

Protective separatism, 201

Protestant Reformation, 16

Public Opinion Committee, 52

Public persona, 90

Public school, 3

Puerto Rico, 205

The Quest of the Silver Fleece (Du Bois, W.E.B.), 70, 108

Race-baiting, 52

Race relations, 198

Racial progress, 38

Racism, 11, 74, 135, 141, 199; antiracism, 57, 81, 96; battle again, 155; colonialism and, 154; criminality, racist myths around, 73; in England, 137; escalation of postwar racism, 96; institutional, 189; pestilence of, 26; salience of, 3; SP and, 69; white working class and, 109, 132

RACON. *See Survey of Racial Conditions in the United States*

Radicalism, 196

Rai, Lajpat L., 81, 108

Railroad strikes, 11

Randolph, A. Philip, 102

"The Rape of Africa" (Du Bois, W.E.B.), 206

Read, Florence, 149

"The Realities in Africa: European Profit or Negro Development" (Du Bois, W.E.B.), 206

Reconstruction, 3, 7, 11, 79, 151, 193; capitalist exploitation and, 203; end of, 9; post-Reconstruction years, 41; promise of, 8

Red Cross, 86

Red Scare, 175, 176–177, 185

Red Summer, 89

Reed, John, 112

Rent tenancy, 14

Repatriation, 23
Republican government (Spain), 139
Republican Party, 26, 160
Revolutionary movements of
    dispossessed nations, 118
Revolutionary vanguard, 110–111
Rist, Charles, 145
Rivera, Diego, 162
Robeson, Eslanda Goode, 161
Robeson, Paul, 2, 137, 154, 157, 167,
    174; exile and, 190; persecution of,
    177; USSR and, 163
Robinson, Cedric, 203
Rodney, Walter, 210
Rogge, O. John, 175
Roosevelt, Eleanor, 159
Roosevelt, Franklin, 54, 76, 143, 150,
    177, 184
Roosevelt, Theodore, 37, 47, 53, 54, 69
Rosenberg, Ethel, 175, 182
Rosenberg, Julius, 175, 182
Rosenwald Fund, 127
Rowan, Carl, 182
Russell, Bertrand, 192
Russia, 33, 52, 71, 89, 109–110, 150

Saint Domingue, 16
Schiff, Jacob, 36
Scott, Tim, 129
Scottsboro Boys, 119, 128
Second Amendment, 4
Segregation, 9, 22, 129, 133, 181;
    colonialism and, 137; residential,
    200; vulgarity of, 39; in Washington,
    DC, 32
Selassie, Haile, 136
Self-determination, 118–119, 202, 205
Self-government, 23
Senate Foreign Relations Committee,
    156
Senegal, 96
Settler colonialism, 55
Sexton, S. M., 44
Shanghai, 141
Sharecropping, 14, 70, 90
Shiloh Baptist Church, 58

Sierra Leone, 85
Silvina, Mary, 1–2, 3, 8
Sinclair, Upton, 70
Sino-Soviet split, 186–187
Siqueiros, David, 162
Slater Fund, 17
Slaveholders, 7, 21
Slave revolts, 2
Slavery, 4, 56, 178; American
    Historical Association and, 10;
    colonialism and, 11; debt slavery, 13;
    Douglass escape from, 6; social
    legacies of, 198; United States
    promiscuous participation in
    African slave trade, 21
Slave trade, 2
Smith, Al, 127
Smith, Ferdinand, 161
Smith, Hoke, 58
Smith Act, 183
Social good, 26, 208
Socialism, 16–17, 36, 37, 43, 69, 92, 139,
    152, 162; pessimism about, 110
Socialist Party (SP), 54, 68–69, 70,
    80–81, 211; Communist Labor Party
    and, 109
Son, death of, 32
The Souls of Black Folk (Du Bois,
    W.E.B.), 14, 24, 32, 146, 153, 217–
    219; double-consciousness and, 28;
    influence of, 42–43; publishing of,
    41; translations of, 142
"The Souls of White Folk" (Du Bois,
    W.E.B.), 61, 62
South Africa, 166, 168, 178
South African Economic Freedom
    Fighters, 201
Southern white landowners, 13
SP. *See* Socialist Party
Spanish Civil War, 139
Spanish Empire, 31
Spanish Roman Catholic Church, 139
Spelman College, 149
Spencer, Herbert, 23
Spero, Sterling D., 145
Spingarn, Arthur, 173

Spingarn, Joel, 73, 85
Springfield, Illinois, 59–60
Springfield Republican (newspaper), 7
Sputnik, 185
Stalin, Joseph, 110, 118, 144, 185, 187
Stewart, James, 209
Stockholm Peace Appeal, 172, 207
Stockholm Peace Petition, 167
Stock market collapse, 116
Storey, Moorfield, 64
Sumner, Charles, 64
"The Suppression of the African Slave Trade to the United States of America, 1638–1870" (Du Bois, W.E.B.), 20
Supreme Court, 44, 78, 181
Survey of Racial Conditions in the United States (RACON), 151
Sweatt v. Painter, 189
Sylvain, Benito, 33

Taft, William Howard, 37, 54
Taft-Hartley Act, 183
Talented Tenth, 29, 43, 47, 104, 110, 173, 198; augmenting, 121; Black America and, 124; creation of, 174; education and, 123, 131; Moscow and, 113; revolutionary vanguard and, 110; Tuskegee Machine and, 40
Taylor, Zachary, 70
Terrell, Mary Church, 64
There Is Confusion (Fauset), 106
Third Force Act, 41
Third International, 109
Third World, 155
Thirteenth Amendment, 44
Thomas, Dylan, 152
Thomas, William Hannibal, 56
Thompson Patterson, Louise, 122, 139, 174, 196
Tillman, Ben, 45
Tobias, Channing, 169
Toomer, Jean, 106
Tourgée, Albion Winegar, 44
Trade unions, 24, 138
Trinidad, 111

Trotsky, Leon, 110
Trotter, William Monroe, 45, 46, 47, 58, 86, 184
Truman, Harry, 157, 159, 213
Truth, Sojourner, 121
Turner, Henry McNeal, 85
Tuskegee, 25, 33
Tuskegee Machine, 37, 39, 45, 47, 67, 71; challenge to, 62; clashing with, 49; on economic independence, 75; NAACP and, 78; newspapers and, 48; Talented Tenth and, 40
Tuskegee Syphilis Experiment, 125
Twentieth Century Club, 43

Uganda, 182
UMW. *See* United Mine Workers
UN. *See* United Nations
UN Charter, 156
Unemployment, 116, 143
Unfree labor, 38
UNIA. *See* Universal Negro Improvement Association
Union of Socialist Soviet Republics (USSR), 89, 92, 127, 130, 150, 163, 185; International Lenin Prize for the Strengthening of Peace among Nations from the Soviet Peace Committee, 207; revolutionary vanguard of, 110–111; Sino-Soviet split, 186–187
Unions, 166, 174; labor, 8; trade, 24, 138; upsurge in, 134
United Autoworkers, 174
United Hebrew Trades, 138
United Mine Workers (UMW), 44
United Nations (UN), 155, 156, 169
United Nations Conference on International Organizations, 213
United States (U.S.): apartheid-like educational system in, 19; capitalism and imperialism, rise of, 75; creation of, 2; Haiti, U.S. invasion of, 76–77, 78, 86, 126; National Archives, 33; private enterprise and, 166; promiscuous participation in

United States (U.S.)(*Cont.*)
  African slave trade, 21; white
  supremacy and, 55
Universal Negro Improvement
  Association (UNIA), 85, 91, 92
University of Berlin, 15, 17, 19
University of Pennsylvania, 25
Urbanization, 73
U.S. *See* United States
USSR. *See* Union of Socialist Soviet
  Republics

Vagrancy, 38
Vanderbilt University, 8
Vardaman, James, 45
Versailles, 87
Vietnam, 179
"The Vigilance Committee: A Call to
  Arms" (Du Bois, W.E.B.), 74
Villa, Pancho, 78
Villard, Fanny Garrison, 64
Villard, Henry, 61
Villard, Oswald Garrison, 59, 61–62,
  72; clashes with, 115; Spingarn and,
  73
Voice of the Negro (journal), 64
Von Bismarck, Otto, 10, 12, 17
Von Ranke, Leopold, 15
Voting rights, 11, 47, 56, 151
Voting rolls, 11

Waldron, J. M., 58
Wallace, David, 56–57, 213
Wallace, Henry, 159
Walling, William English, 59, 63, 69
Wall Street, 128
War of 1812, 51
Warren, Nagueyalti, 209, 210
Washington, Booker T., 5, 23, 32, 36,
  43, 133, 173; acceptance of Jim
  Crow, 39; "Atlanta Compromise," 24,
  28, 29, 46; death of, 78; donations to,
  61; Du Bois, W.E.B., conflict with,
  25, 33, 34, 39, 45, 121; experiences in
  bondage of, 36–37; liberalism and,
  197; NAACP and, 67; newspapers
  and, 48; *Souls of Black Folk* and, 41;

status quo, acceptance of, 79; on
  Thomas, 56
Washington, DC, 2, 13, 32
Waters, Maxine, 41
Watson, Tom, 52
Weber, Max, 15
Welfare programs, 74
Wells, H. G., 71
Wells, Ida B., 4, 46, 64, 196
Wells-Barnett, Ida B., 40
West Africa, 99
West Indian colonies, 34
West Indian Federation, 202
West Indian immigrants, 93–94
White, Walter Francis, 98, 115, 147,
  156–157
White businessmen, 36
White philanthropy, 122
White racial chauvinism, 61
White South, 4
White supremacy, 11, 23, 33, 52, 99,
  205; capitalism and, 112; color line
  and, 28; global struggle against, 71;
  KKK and, 41; lynching and, 4;
  ugliness of, 74; U.S., and, 55
White women, 52, 58
White working class, 37, 109, 132
Wilberforce University, 19–20, 21–22,
  25
Wilkerson, Doxey, 44, 161, 178
Wilkins, Roy, 156
Williams, Bert, 63
Williams, Eric, 21
Williams, George Washington, 10
Williams, Henry Sylvester, 33, 211
Williams College, 8
Wilson, Woodrow, 69–70, 76, 77, 78,
  80, 87, 212
"The Winds of Time" (column), 213
Winston, Henry, 183
Women, 80, 90; dedicated to socialism
  and antifascism, 139; Niagara
  Movement and, 52; white women,
  52, 58; women's rights, 11
Woodson, Carter G., 107, 135, 145, 201
Work, Monroe, 70
Workers Party (WP), 104

Working class, 26, 70, 108, 166
World Federation of Trade Unions, 174
Worlds of Color (Du Bois, W.E.B.), 184
World Trade Union and Subject Peoples' Conferences, 202
World War I, 75, 77, 108
World War II, 77, 90, 141, 171, 183
WP. *See* Workers Party
Wright, Frank Lloyd, 162
Wright, Richard R., 71, 88, 190

Xenophobia, 140

Yale School of Drama, 171
Yates v. United States, 183
Yellow Springs, Ohio, 20
Yergan, Max, 154, 161
YMCA. *See* Young Men's Christian Association
Young, Charles, 25, 83–84
Young Men's Christian Association (YMCA), 103
Young Women's Christian Association, 173

"Zimmerman Telegram," 65

About the Authors

Charisse Burden-Stelly, PhD, is assistant professor of Africana studies and political science at Carleton College in Northfield, Minnesota. She is currently working on a manuscript titled *The Radical Horizon of Black Betrayal: Antiradicalism, Antiblackness, and the U.S. Capitalist State*, and she has several published articles and works forthcoming on themes spanning Black studies, political theory, political economy, and intellectual history.

Gerald Horne, PhD, is Moores Professor of History and African-American studies at the University of Houston in Houston, Texas, and author of dozens of books including *Race Woman: The Lives of Shirley Graham Du Bois*.